"This is a book I've been longing to read! *Joyfully Just* soulfully intertwines the sacred threads of Buddhism and Black Wisdom traditions. At its core, this book is a gift that touches the very essence of humanity, holding us close to the pulse of the sacred and our collective potential. Dr. Majied not only embodies and celebrates this powerful interface through her wise and integrative teachings, but also uplifts and enlightens, offering liberative practices for personal healing, resilience, and social transformation. She is a mirror to our magnificence. This book is a rhythmic testament to the richness and strength of Blackness and Buddhism coming together for the greater good. Be ready to be joyfully moved into self-awareness and social harmony, all with a warm smile on your face.

In *Joyfully Just*, Dr. Majied offers a creative and liberative masterpiece, a pulsing testament to the richness and strength of Black wisdom and Buddhism, dancing together for the greater good. A book to savor, celebrate, and share broadly."

**RUTH KING**
author of *Mindful of Race*

"In a world so marked by social hierarchies, oppression, and violence, *Joyfully Just* stands as a beacon of hope and a call to action. Dr. Majied's approach to social justice is a refreshing and powerful reminder that when we start within, we can create a more equitable and compassionate world for ourselves and others. This book is a must-read for anyone seeking a path to personal and collective liberation."

**TARA BRACH**
author of *Radical Acceptance* and *Trusting the Gold*

"I highly recommend this beloved book. A bold and beautiful song of liberation awaits the reader. The reader is uplifted to a fresh view of justice. Kamilah Majied celebrates a dialogue between spiritual practices and cultural roots opening windows of justice. Here the reader finds inspiration and many ways to infuse justice into everything we think and do. In highlighting joy, Majied reminds us we can realize the power of joy's energy that heals and nourishes a deep resonance of justice: a justice embodied in the fabric of our individual and collective lives."

**LARRY WARD, PhD**
author of *America's Racial Karma*

"Dr. Majied is someone whom you are fortunate to be with, whether in person or in a book. Like all of Dr. Majied's work, *Joyfully Just* brings us to the deep joy that comes from engaging in contemplative practices that turn us toward inhumanity and injustice with courage, compassion, and a beginner's mind."

STEPHEN MURPHY-SHIGEMATSU
author of *From Mindfulness to Heartfulness*

"Brimming with creative and illustrative insights and connections, Kamilah Majied's *Joyfully Just* shows us what I have long thought to be true: that combining Black wisdom with Buddhist insights presents us with a rich tapestry of what is actually possible, namely, that there can be deep joy in the midst of suffering even as we strive toward liberation. *Joyfully Just* is a soulful and heartful guidebook for coming to know, and hence for bringing forth, our innate joy and for expanding that joy out into our world. Read this book with pride and with pleasure!"

JAN WILLIS
author of *Dreaming Me: Black, Baptist, and Buddhist*

"There is profound meaning that *Joyfully Just* offers in describing all the practices that allow 'the joy of facing injustice' to emerge. Dr. Majied teaches us deeply about possibilities of connecting personal change with the liberation of social transformation."

LARRY YANG
author of *Awakening Together*

"Reading this book, I threw my arms in the air and said, Yes! Kamilah Majied offers us a powerful gift: a reminder that in order to bend the arc we need fierce compassion, love, and, yes, joy to move us to action, sustain our commitment, and stay strong. Her refreshing understanding of justice includes everyone, even that often overlooked one—ourself. She holds up a wide range of contemplative practices from Buddhist and Black traditions that help us get there: dance, music, poetry, and story as well as meditation and prayer. Just reading this book will move you to joyful action."

MIRABAI BUSH
founder of The Center for Contemplative Mind in Society, author of *Walking Each Other Home* (with Ram Dass) and *Contemplative Practices in Higher Education* (with Daniel Barbezat)

"*Joyfully Just* reveals the transformative power of joy and its role in liberation from oppression. Combining wisdom from Buddhist and Black cultural traditions, Dr. Majied provides a wealth of accessible contemplative practices to help navigate a world full of suffering. By encouraging us to embrace our natural, playful curiosity and see the joy inherent in fighting injustice, she offers a vision of a world with more compassion, greater resilience, and better tools to face hardship and embrace our interconnectedness."

THOMAS HÜBL, PhD
author of *Attuned* and *Healing Collective Trauma*

"Dr. Majied's book is a lighthouse dispelling the darkness that too often shrouds Black life. *Joyfully Just* helps us navigate the waves of our collective experiences, beckoning us home to the joy that is our true nature."

OFOSU JONES-QUARTEY
meditation teacher and musician

"This book is a deep-wisdom treasure. Kamilah intimately brings the reader into the heart of white supremacy, clearly pointing out its blinders and harms, while introducing practices to awaken and liberate us all. Simultaneously, she rekindles the joy at the heart of this freedom, bringing a wholeness that animates the heart and moves the body. Leading us to look personally into our losses, she reminds us that gratitude and enjoyment of life are essential elements of grieving well, returning us to love."

JUDITH SIMMER-BROWN
Naropa University

"*Joyfully Just* is a transformative exploration of meditation and social justice, encouraging readers to start within themselves to address privilege, oppression, and equity. Majied's book intertwines contemplative practices and playful curiosity, guiding readers toward liberating self-awareness and compassionate engagement with the world."

ANGEL ACOSTA, EdD
founder of the Acosta Institute

"Kamilah Majied is our teacher in the Black wisdom of music, dance, and prayer that she relates directly to Buddhist meditation. In this revolutionary new book, she teaches us how to be joyful and just at the same time, and she shows us that this is precisely the secret of the great social activists, of the Black spiritual traditions, of a genuine and fierce historical consciousness, and of the Buddhist teachings themselves. It would be difficult to overestimate the importance of this message or the compassion with which it is performed on the page."

JEFFREY J. KRIPAL
author of *How to Think Impossibly: About Souls, UFOs, Time, Belief, and Everything Else*

"Powerful teachings in a powerful voice on every page. This book arrives just in time to reboot and expand our collective understanding of what an inclusively human, multicultural, multiracial dharma, in all its universals and in all its beautifully differentiated ancestral and cultural particulars, might look like. I will be living inside this book for a long, long time."

JON KABAT-ZINN
author of *Full Catastrophe Living*

# Joyfully Just

# Joyfully Just

### Black Wisdom
### and Buddhist Insights
### for Liberated Living

Kamilah Majied, PhD

sounds true
BOULDER, COLORADO

Sounds True

Boulder, CO

Published 2024

Cover and book design by Charli Barnes

Cover image design and collaboration by Carrie Bergman

Printed in the United States of America

BK06733

Cataloging-in-Publication data for this book is available from the Library of Congress.
Library of Congress Cataloging in Publication Control Number:
    2023044031
ISBN 9781649631398 (trade paperback)
ISBN 9781649631404 (ebook)

This book is both transmitted from and dedicated to:

My ancestors, teachers, and leaders, particularly the Black people
who have inspired me through their ways of being, their creative works,
their love for me, and their joyful resistance;

Lailah Majied, my mother, whose wisdom echoes throughout this book
and who imbues my life with timeless joy and courage;

James Haynes, my grandfather, a joyful musician whose mellifluous voice
resounds forever in my heart and throughout this book;

and Dr. Gerard DeVastey, physician-scientist, historical scholar,
and friend, who personally defeated generations of health disparities for
many families and extended my mother's life and the lives of many others
through his deep scientific inquiry and mastery of natural medicine.
His culturally engaged, humorous approach to healing infuses the
ethos of this book.

# Contents

# Introduction

Welcome! I am so excited to have you with me on the journey of being joyfully just. The goal of this book is simple—to reclaim joy by using meditative practices to be just toward ourselves and the world around us. And yet as the great Jazz artist Thelonius Monk said, "Simple ain't easy."[1]

This book illustrates how we can be joyful in our efforts for personal, familial, social, organizational, communal, and environmental justice. There is a sublime exhilaration that comes from the capacity to really know, to discern—to appreciate reality with all its beauty juxtaposed with rampant injustice. The joy of facing injustice comes when we can finally allow ourselves to *know* what we can already viscerally *feel*. In *Joyfully Just*, I offer meditative practices that allow insight to arise. As we begin to see and face—clearly and deeply, and perhaps for the first time—all that we could not see and face before, we become more free and thus more joyful. In Buddhism, emancipation from delusion is itself enlightenment. As the renowned Buddhist educator, poet, and philosopher Daisaku Ikeda states, "The joy of life is to be found not by evading life's sufferings but by grappling with them to the finish. Escapism cannot produce true happiness. Happiness based on delusion does not last. Enlightenment comes from seeing the truth, no matter how unpleasant it may be."[2]

There is joyousness in turning toward injustice with a commitment to transforming it. It's like the elated charge of resolve you get when you hear rousing African American freedom songs like "Ain't Gonna Let

Nobody Turn Me Around." That's what it feels like to be joyful in our resolve for justice. There is delight to be found in meditative practices themselves, whether we are engaging in music meditations or singing; whether practicing yoga, stillness, or dancing in the ocean; whether gardening or deep breathing. Countless practices can bring us to a deeply thoughtful, contemplative state of being. I define meditative, mindful, or contemplative practices as the activities we engage in to bring ourselves to the present moment in a way that reflects an embodied and integrated experience of our own minds, hearts, and bodies. True mindful or contemplative practice strengthens our compassion for all other beings as we deepen awareness of how our lives are interdependent with all life. *Justice is embodied wisdom and compassion toward ourselves and all that surrounds us.*

As surprising as it may sound in a book about addressing injustice, I invite you to *relax* and be at ease, to let it be enjoyable! Allow a playful curiosity to guide you to and through learning about embodying a just, joyful existence.

> Well minds nurture justice
> and just minds nurture wellness.

Because we often hear of *striving* for human and civil rights as a "struggle," it is easy for us to forget that there is joy in the journey toward justice. Sometimes there may not seem to be an evident connection between justice and joy. The joy I speak of in this book is not superficial pleasure. *Joyfully Just* is about the joy that arises when we use our meditative practices to pause and look at the suffering that injustice has caused in our own lives and in the lives of others. In that pause we can experience the joy of clarity, which is a precursor to the joy of healing. We come to know and delight in the wisdom that can arise when we see the injustices we perpetrate against ourselves and others. Whether spoken, embodied, or reflected in nature, wisdom is simply truth that enriches our insight. We experience still more joy in taking action based on wisdom as our interior lives and relationships begin to expand. This helps us become more psychologically and relationally well. Well minds nurture justice and just minds nurture wellness.

Many, if not most, iconic social justice leaders exuded indefatigable joy spawned from their deep contemplative practice. People often forget what an expansive sense of humor Rev. Dr. Martin Luther King Jr. had. I believe his humor was part of (and arose from) his embodied enactment of his faith and Christian contemplative practice. When Dr. King said "The arc of the moral universe is long, but it bends toward justice," he was not simply encouraging us to stay hopeful because things would get better.[3] Rather, he was encouraging us to lean in and *bend* the arc with the might of our minds, bodies, and spirits. This book draws from the wisdom of many Black liberation leaders and thinkers, including those who make their liberatory contributions through prayer, protest, language, and music.

The goal of *Joyfully Just* is to support people from all spiritual traditions and cultural backgrounds in using meditative practices to reclaim joy. Our spirits, bodies, and minds need to be buoyant to navigate the unceasing waves of prejudice, devaluation, and degradation that we encounter internally, interpersonally, and communally. This book is about actualizing that buoyancy, that levity, as we enact justice using diverse meditative practices. In particular, the *Joyfully Just* journey focuses on practices, teachings, and insights from Buddhism and Black wisdom traditions.

The Black wisdom traditions I explore in this book include those shared through language and dialect; musical practices such as Gospel, Blues, Jazz, R & B, and Hip-Hop; dance practices; and communicative kinesic (movement and gesture) practices. These practices are often misunderstood—especially when they are appropriated. Often they are underestimated as simply entertainment. In this book, you will come to see how much insight and guidance for wise, courageous living we receive from Black cultural traditions. I explore Buddhism and Black wisdom together in this book because although the spiritual and religious traditions of Black people are diverse, as are Buddhist lineages, many secular Black wisdom traditions and overarching Buddhist principles share common insights. For example, Black musical traditions illustrate the unity of suffering and joy and the possibility for self-transcendence and enlightenment in any circumstance. The creative, lively resilience of Black life shows us, in so many ways, what enlightenment looks like in daily living. Black wisdom traditions are the script, score, and choreography of Black love and resistance. As such, they have universal relevance to all who feel love and resist oppression. They can be and are enriching to everyone.

How do you avoid cultural appropriation with regard to Black wisdom practices? It's simple, but not easy. When you engage in Black dialect, music, or other Black cultural traditions, reiteratively reflect on how you demonstrate or could begin to demonstrate love for and solidarity with Black people. Likewise, we can avoid appropriating Buddhism by reiteratively reflecting on whether Westernized notions of mindfulness and other Buddhist principles honor and center the peoples from whom Buddhism originates and the principles that Buddhism expounds.

Buddhism, mindfulness, and meditation practices are often conflated with solemnity, with pretentiousness about being "deep." Meditation instructors may exhibit a lack of enthusiasm or joie de vivre while leading practices. For example, recordings of guided meditations on apps and YouTube are often spoken in hushed, monotone voices. But Buddhism and mindfulness are inherently infused with joy. *Mudita* is a Sanskrit and Pali word used in Buddhism to describe sympathetic joy, joy in our connected interbeing and in one another's thriving. This is the type of joy that far surpasses fleeting pleasure, and it can only be experienced as we develop insight and engage justly with everyone and everything around us.

We often think about justice as something to be sought externally and, of course, we know that we must take action in the world to ensure justice. To support that effort, I invite you to *play* with ways of being just toward *yourself*. From there, you can learn to extend that play to engage justly with family, friends, frenemies, colleagues, and nature itself. I use the word *play* intentionally because another goal of this book is to highlight and help you access the playful aspects of meditation in the context of enacting justice. I invite you to experience the freedom that comes with tearing off the restrictive garments of privilege and internalized oppression. I invite you to allow your heart and soul to be regularly cleared of oppressing thoughts and experiences and thereby feel more liberated in the world.

An essential part of this process is welcoming our hearts, our emotionality and feelings. There is a concise African American expression that describes being "in your feelings." Usually this refers to when the emotions we are having are so strong, it is like *we are in them*, rather than the feelings being *in* us. We all know what that's like. When you feel something so intensely, it's like being in a soup bowl of chunky, slimy rage or sorrow where you cannot get out. Often acts of injustice make us feel sunk in despair or rage or shame—sunk in our feelings!

This is where meditative practices help us, especially if we can engage them with playful curiosity. Cultivating a *playful* inner observer, we can learn to watch our own mind and heart and be delighted with the ways they move from one thought and feeling to another. As the poet Kahlil Gibran writes,

And could you keep your heart in wonder at the daily miracles of your life your pain would not seem less wondrous than your joy;
And you would accept the seasons of your heart, even as you have always accepted the seasons that pass over your fields.
And you would watch with serenity through the winters of your grief.[4]

We can surface an intention to regularly manifest delight with ourselves. We can manifest intentional levity to levitate us *out* of suffocating emotions and toward insightful being and acting. However, we must notice and feel our feelings first, applying our practice to the exploration of the feelings rather than trying to use the meditative practice to ignore feelings or escape. We can cultivate a playful observer mind to poke fun at (and poke holes *in*) the grip that painful thoughts and feelings have on us so that we can wriggle ourselves free.

## Practices and Exercises

The combination of Buddhist wisdom and cultural wisdom in *Joyfully Just* is intentional. It is important that we do justice to ourselves by honoring the wisdom traditions of our various lineages. This is a good thing to do even if we also practice Buddhism. The rich universality of Buddhist teachings only finds its truest expression when Buddhists of every ethnic, cultural, and spiritual background are able to express their Buddha nature, their enlightenment, in ways that are informed by their cultural traditions and lineages. As Indigenous Buddhists, Jewish Buddhists, African Buddhists, and other Dharma practitioners emerge and embody Buddhahood in their own unique way, we see the true power and relevance of the Dharma, which itself affirms the diversity of its own expression. Daisaku Ikeda references a writing of Nichiren Daishonin, a thirteenth-century Japanese priest and the founder of Nichiren Buddhism:

> Buddhism expounds the principle of cherry, plum, peach, and damson, each having their own unique characteristics, and the related principle of "illuminating and manifesting one's true nature."
>
> Cherry blossoms are cherry blossoms, and peach blossoms are peach blossoms. A cherry blossom can never become a peach blossom. Nor is there any need for it to try to do so. It would be perfectly miserable if it did. Similarly, you are none other than yourself. You can never be someone else, however much you might wish it. What matters is that you become the kind of person who can cherish, praise, and feel content with your own precious, irreplaceable life.[5]

This guidance from Ikeda encourages each of us to let the unique expression of Buddhahood that only we can manifest with our singular intersections of experience contribute to the endlessly diverse personifications of enlightened living. As such, we become gorgeous and singular flowers in an ever-expanding landscape of human flourishing.

Black wisdom traditions include practices that bring forth insight and joy. You may have heard the expression "Black joy" and wondered,

*What is that, exactly?* Black joy is self-transcendence. Black joy is a type of pleasure activism. It is embodied resistance to the life of unremitting sorrow assigned to Black people by racism. It is the insistence on and expression of internal freedom despite external restrictions. Black joy is resilient creativity that creatively grows more resilience. We can all learn and benefit from Black joy. In fact, through Black language and dialect, Black music, Black art, Black literature, Black protest, and countless other aspects of Black life, we already learn and benefit from Black people's leadership and labors for justice and joy.

To support you in reclaiming your authentic joy, I will share examples from my own experience and my work with students and clients as an educator and mental health therapist. There will be short reflective summaries and practices that invite you to explore how your efforts to experience justice in your interior life and interpersonal relationships can bring forth joy.

We'll do exercises that help you develop insight from your reflections and connect the examples given to your own experience. Meditative practice prompts will include movement practices to embody justice and joy viscerally, as well as writing practices, affirmations, and meditations where you are encouraged to play with art. You will also find nature-engaging practices to move you toward a just relationship with the natural world.

As you read this book and try the practices, I invite you to give yourself the gift of an inspiring setting whenever possible. Give your joy journey some support by putting on some music and reading with soothing surroundings and scents to accompany you. However, you can also use this book in difficult times and spaces. If you have to be at the hospital for yourself or you're waiting for a loved one to get medical treatment, if you are sitting in a waiting room at the DMV, or you're on hold forever with the IRS, this book can also help you drop into joy in those moments, too—so keep it handy!

As we let the joy of insight settle within us, we can arouse more joy through engaging with suffering and using our minds and bodies to heal it. What we can experience through an intentionally joyful approach toward justice is not the glib relative happiness that escapist activities might bring. Rather, it is the deeper joy that evolves from having the spiritual rigor to turn toward inhumanity with courageous, undefeatable curiosity—like the curiosity we had when we were children. *Joyfully Just* guides you in turning toward injustice with courageous compassion and the commitment to know, to see it all, so that we can recognize the aspects of our own delusion and defilement that are reflected in the historical and present world. Great joy comes from knowing that we are bigger than we thought; that we have the capacity to face all the world's pain, take it seriously, *and* laugh at our foibles, learning from them as we try again and again to be just toward ourselves and create justice around us.

## Your Joyfully Just Squad

As you read this book and engage in the practices, you will be building a deeper relationship with your greater self. If possible, I also encourage you to invite one or two people to read this book with you and to do the practices together. Community is one of our biggest resources! Reading and practicing with an accountability partner, team, or squad can be a wonderful source of support and connection. Even if you don't read the whole book with anyone else, share the joy you experience from any of the ideas or exercises, because when we share joy, it multiplies infinitely.

## Creating Your Joybox and Joy Journal

As you engage with these exercises and encounter ideas throughout the book, you will develop strategies and resources to inspire your journey to joyful and just ways of living. These inspirations, ideas, and insights will fill your Joybox—your ever-growing *Joyfully Just* toolbox. It's important to have a way to collect these strategies and refer to them in the future, so I recommend dedicating a journal or notebook to record your responses to the exercises. Or you can dictate your thoughts into a voice-recorder app and create an audio journal. Whatever form it takes, allow your journal to be a place to chronicle and reference your expanding, joyous inner capacities. You can call it your Joy Journal! I will invite you to note things in your Joy Journal and add things to your Joybox throughout the book. Get ready! Your first invitation to use your Joy Journal is just a few pages away.

## Oppression and Joy:
## Developing Your Own Emergent Strategies

All suffering, including the suffering of oppression, has a relationship to joy. *Joyfully Just* is about using contemplative practice to turn every situation into an opportunity to enact justice and thereby experience joy. If you resonate with the concept of emergent strategy as described by activist and writer adrienne maree brown, you may find the joyfully just practices described in this book to be emergent strategies.

> All joyfully just action is an emergent strategy because it is a positive response to what is arising in a given moment.

brown describes emergent strategy as responding to and generating change with compassionate intentions based on the interdependence of all things. She talks about learning how to be "fractal," meaning making small changes that have the ripple effect of wider impact. What it means to become joyfully just is to make small changes by being more just toward ourselves and one another out of our heightened awareness of our connection to all life. brown also talks about emergent strategy as nonlinear and iterative, which means we have to go back sometimes and do the practice we did before, again—and again—to reassert justice.[6] We need this reiteration in our habits of self-development as much as we do in our sociopolitical and environmental movements for justice. Cultivating resilience—and what is described in *Joyfully Just* as "discomfort resilience"— is also an emergent strategy that turns every difficulty into a source of possibility for generating more positive responses to injustice and the challenges of living.

All joyfully just action is an emergent strategy because it is a positive response to what is arising in a given moment. This is why contemplative practice is important, because it allows us to be present in the moment and from that heightened awareness, assess what is emerging for us as the appropriate, most just strategy.

One of my favorite Buddhist writings is entitled "The Strategy of the Lotus Sutra." In it, Nichiren Daishonin states, "Spur yourself to muster the power of faith. Regard your survival as wondrous. Employ the strategy of the Lotus Sutra before any other."[7] The faith he is referring to is faith in the limitless power of our own enlightened life force. The strategy of the Lotus Sutra Nichiren refers to is the practice of chanting the mantra Nam Myoho Renge Kyo as a means to cultivate enlightened wisdom and the courage to act on that enlightened wisdom. Employing the strategy of the Lotus Sutra is a Buddhist principle of emergent strategy. It is an enlightened strategy, a joyfully just strategy, a present-moment strategy. It is a re-emergent strategy based on the re-evaluation that we experience through contemplative practice.

How do you create a cache of emergent strategies to help you respond positively to ever-changing challenges and opportunities? This book will offer you practical steps to doing so. As you practice various types of meditation throughout the book, I encourage you to release emotions rather than repressing them or trying to bypass them. As you practice with me throughout this book, building your own Joybox full of your songs, affirmations, and embodied practices that help you transcend the matrices of oppression that have ensnared you, you will also reflect on your personal stories. A crucial role that story creation can play is to create new narratives: reflections that align with and move you toward the values you want to live by so that you are not stuck in your old, unexamined stories. For example, you may have a particular memory or experience that is defining for you. If you play the recording of that memory, that story, in a way that triggers only shame and inertia, you might lose the opportunity to grow from that experience. However, it's possible to experience power and joy from that story if you tell it from the standpoint of compassion and resilience.

I will guide you through exploring what books, art, physical activities, and other things bring *you* back to joy and toward a sense of interior and exterior justice. No cookie-cutter approach could work for everyone. So, in addition to offering examples of what inspires me, I offer guidelines to help you embed your own good practices into your life. In becoming joyfully just, we welcome grief. I show you how to use your sad songs and other grief-releasing practices to weep your way through injustice to the joy of honoring all that has been lost and all that remains.

## Songs, Songs, Songs!

One of the ways that we can see the global influence of Black wisdom is in the transmutation of suffering into music. Many genres of Black music express a present-moment state of awareness and experience while simultaneously aiming the heart, mind, body, and soul toward an intention. Black music practices from throughout the African Diaspora—including drumming and vocalizing as well as formal genres founded by Black Americans such as Blues, Jazz, R & B, Hip-Hop, and Gospel music—are so universally embraced because they are transmissions from the souls of Black people that illuminate universal truths and experiences. Drawing from these embodied wisdom traditions and recognizing Black artists as spiritual teachers who model creative resilience, I invite you to develop the score to your happy place, filled with your fight songs, your grief-releasing tear-jerker songs, your love songs, and your joy songs! This soundtrack will help you build your own safety net to catch yourself when you feel the weight of injustice pulling you down. Music is a reminder that joy is with us always, in every moment and in every experience. These songs and playlists will be part of your Joybox. It is important to create collections of encouragement because when we are feeling down, we won't necessarily remember the things that encourage us, so compiling them and having them on hand helps. This is why you want to have a dedicated Joy Journal to track your insights as we sail along.

## Introducing . . . Me! My Own Joyfully Just Journey

Let me tell you a bit about who I am. My favorite moniker is Lailah Majied's daughter. When I walk through Buddhist centers in New Jersey, the local elders rarely remember my name and always say, "Oh, you're Lailah's daughter, right?" I love that! I am also the granddaughter of Catherine and James Haynes who migrated from Savannah, Georgia, to New York City with my Grandaunt Essie Haynes in the 1940s as part of the great migration of Black people seeking more liberated living. My family's love of learning and art inspired me at an early age to enjoy brilliant artists and teachers who would become my lifelong familiars. These eternal mentors and guides include Louis Armstrong, James Baldwin, Stevie Wonder, Lou Rawls, Kahlil Gibran, Wayne Shorter, Toni Morrison, Gwendolyn Brooks, Herbie Hancock, Alice Walker, Daisaku Ikeda, Octavia Butler, Maya Angelou, bell hooks, Billie Holiday, and many others. To bolster and deepen wisdom and joy in our lives, my mother introduced us to Islam first and then to Buddhism. I have been practicing in the Mahayana Nichiren Buddhism tradition with the Soka Gakkai International for over four decades.

I was drawn to Buddhism because it illuminates the inherent connection between enlightenment, justice, and joy. My Buddhist practice launched my curiosity about the causes of unhappiness, particularly the unhappiness created by social oppression. This led me to pursue a master's degree and then a PhD in clinical social work. As a practicing clinical social work therapist and consultant for over twenty years, I have had the opportunity to support individuals, families, organizations, and communities in using Buddhist and other meditative practices in healing from racism, sexism, homophobia, and other types of oppression as we reclaim joy.

Drawing from over forty years of contemplative practice and social justice activism, I love engaging people in experiencing wonder, humor, and insight as we release oppressive patterns and deepen relationships with one another and with the natural world.

Now I invite you to introduce yourself to yourself in your Joy Journal. When we describe ourselves, it is an opportunity to see who we are and who we want to be—that's why it feels so awkward sometimes!

This book offers many of my personal insights into how contemplative practices can aid us in joyfully just living. It is my great plan that this book helps you cultivate meditative practices to enhance joy and justice in your life. May *Joyfully Just* guide you toward freedom from the limitations imposed by oppression and privilege, and also toward the wonder-filled world of compassionate, inclusive thinking and acting.

In Joy!

# Chapter One

## Contemplative Practice, Joy, Justice, and Inner Transformation

The word *contemplative* essentially means profoundly thoughtful, with an understanding that the profundity of the thought is resourced by meditation, prayer, or spiritual engagement. What counts as meditation or contemplative practice? Any activity we do with deep awareness of our physical, spiritual, emotional, and cognitive being, and with compassionate intentions to manifest our interdependent wisdom in relationships, is contemplative practice. So, in this book, when I say *contemplative* or *meditative* practices, I'm referring to this potentially vast array of activities for developing awareness and insight, not just sitting silently on a cushion.

### Contemplative Practices

Contemplative practices offer us various ways of bringing insight into our lives, and insight is vital for joyfully just living. In our modern context, people often use the word *mindfulness* interchangeably with *contemplative practice* simply because most types of contemplative practices can arouse mindfulness. Being mindful means being deeply aware or conscious of your inner and interdependent reality in every moment. For many, the word *mindfulness* has come to refer solely to the workings of the mind or the brain. However, as originally articulated in Buddhism, one of the sources of mindfulness practices, the qualities of the mind are also qualities of the heart. The Chinese symbol for mindfulness, 念, depicts the interconnection between the mind and heart. The bottom part of the symbol means "heart" and the top part, resembling a hat, means "present" or "now." Psychologist and contemplative leader Dr. Stephen Murphy-Shigematsu calls this type of awareness that includes emotional and psychological presence *heartfulness*. He writes, "Heartfulness is a way of living with mindfulness, compassion, and responsibility that enhances well-being and transformation. Practiced in groups, it creates a learning and healing community where people cross borders, finding genuine connection with self, others, and spirit."[1]

The *joy* of meditation and other contemplative practices—its liberating delight in all things—is often overlooked. Somehow enlightenment has gotten mixed up with being serious all the time. The truth is that the roots of mindfulness practices contain both joy and justice. This book will highlight some specific ways to further ground your meditative practices, whatever they may be, in the delight of being present in our multicultural world and liberated from the trappings of privilege and oppression.

Meditative practices help us move through the shame and sorrow of injustice toward the joy of justice realized. Guided by our contemplative practices, we can have difficult conversations with ourselves first and then with others as we engage in anti-racism and other anti-oppression endeavors with the awareness that any pains of doing so are *our own growing pains*. Basic mindfulness practices, such as centering ourselves with deep diaphragmatic breaths, can support us as we wade through the murky waters of oppression, buoying ourselves with the breath. Gratitude is another essential meditative contemplation that helps us to be more just. Additionally, we'll be using some mindful movement, drawing, observing, and dancing practices. These can help us be jubilant as we learn to embody justice!

At lunch one day, a friend who also happens to be a leading researcher in the world of contemplative neuroscience mentioned how the notion of mindfulness practice has become so very "precious." I laughed in agreement. The solemnity and rigidity we often see in meditation settings can seem so contrived and contradictory to the inner freedom that all spiritual traditions aspire to. In fact, that rigidity is often a residual of colonialism and the suppression of emotion and physical expressiveness, so we do justice to our bodies and minds when we release it. We'll discuss and practice this releasing throughout the book.

You know the famous aphorism that we should be the change we want to see? Buddhist practice provides one pathway to that embodied transformation. As I'll discuss in detail later, this is what *human revolution* means. It means applying our enlightened minds, what Nichiren Buddhism refers to as the ninth consciousness, to the active purification of all other levels of consciousness. This purification leads to wise, courageous thinking, speaking, and behaving in the world, which in turn causes others' enlightened minds to thrive.

## Practicing to End Oppression

The ideas and practices in this book aim to help us pause to surface a more expansive state of mind and heart from which we are able to stop thinking, speaking, and acting in ways that are oppressive to ourselves and others. The types of intersecting oppressions we'll discuss in the coming pages include adultism, ageism, sexism, racism, anti-immigrant oppression, religious oppression, homophobia, heterosexism, and ableism. Oppression operates in three intersecting dimensions: internalized, interpersonal, and institutional. The exercises in this book will guide you through examining which types of oppression have impacted you and in which intersecting dimensions. This will help you recognize and release oppressive patterns you may have developed.

Oppression can be likened to toxic rain. It pours down on us throughout our lives, and we are all soaked with it! We did not create it ourselves, and yet we wear it. Unwittingly, we spread it—pouring it on each subsequent generation. It is not our fault that we are wet and stinking from these oppressive thoughts, feelings, and actions, and yet it is our responsibility to get clean of it—to stop transmitting it. Liberation always begins with the inner work we do as individuals. As law professor and mindfulness teacher Rhonda Magee writes,

> We don't always realize that we must work continuously to make real the promise of liberating human interrelationship. Even less often do we have the skills to do this work together. Indeed, we have lacked the consciousness necessary to see our potential together and to lift ourselves up to a new plane for being in relationship with one another in ways that do not depend on power-over, but rejoice in power-with.[2]

No individual or group can manifest all of its potential without awareness of (and connection to) the diverse systems and people with which it is interdependent. For this reason, eliminating racism and other types of oppression from our view of self, others, and the world—along with an expansion of our capacity to feel, think, and behave inclusively—is central to our thriving as humans. Our meditative practices can help us experience freedom from the limitations in our minds and hearts. Much of that freedom is found when we pause. Contemplative practices help us pause, creating space between our biased thoughts and the biased speech or action we might consciously or unconsciously take because of bias.

Researchers on unconscious bias such as Dr. Jennifer Eberhardt confirm that the only way to stop acting on bias is to develop a consistent practice of examining our intuition, because our intuition is often laden with bias.[3] So, to actualize our growth—especially regarding emotionally and cognitively difficult areas such as racism, ableism, transphobia, and other forms of bias—we need to become expert practitioners of pause. We can use the pause to become aware of and extricate biases we may not know are there.

Contemplative practices help us pause, creating space between our biased thoughts and the biased speech or action we might unconsciously take because of bias.

Let's Practice!

## Making Music of this Moment

Just to get us started, try this practice for thirty seconds (set a timer so that you know when to stop). Simply drum your fingers to whatever beat they move naturally. Don't try to direct them—just let your life strum its current rhythm.

Drum the beat of your mind and heart with your fingers. This allows for grounding in the body and connects your heart and mind to your body through this simple heart-to-hand embodied practice.

Now, take sixty seconds to record a note in your Joy Journal about what you drummed with your fingers. Was your drumming slow and methodical or rapid and energetic? What embodied sensation did you have as you did it? What feeling might be associated with what you drummed? What thoughts? Were you free from thinking altogether? You are a living work of art, and you just manifested your life as artistry via drumming.

Now continue to let your fingers drum. As you do so, think about the last time you witnessed something racist and drum what that felt like. Drum it out. Literally let it out through your fingers for thirty seconds.

When you are done, take a moment to consider this question: *From the pace and rhythm I just embodied, what can I notice about how I felt about racism in that moment?*

As I did this practice, it was rapid drumming followed by stops, slows, and more rapid drumming. I interpret that to mean that for me, racism in this moment feels like running in the movement for Black lives, catching a breath, and more running! What did your drumming tell you?

There are many ways we can pause to connect to our embodied, moment-to-moment experience of life, the oppressions that infuse and surround us, and ever-present joy. Pausing is a way to extract wisdom from the pain of everyday living. Meditative practices are inherently intended to help us remember to pause and see all the possible responses we could greet life with if we only stopped to notice our thoughts and develop a clear view of reality, set our intention—our resolve—and then mindfully guide our thoughts, words, and actions to respond wisely.

## Storytelling and Mindful Speech

We humans tell stories in verse and song, through art and dance. We have stories about birth and death, about hunts and floods. We tell stories about American "pioneers" and stories of "invading refugees." We sometimes tell stories to remind ourselves that we are connected to something bigger than us. We may tell stories about "man versus nature." We sometimes tell stories about "us" and "them." Stories can connect us or they can alienate us. In many cases, we relive our parental or ancestral stories. Or we may be trying to live a story like "the American dream." Sometimes we live our lives in *reaction* to a story.

When we find meditative practices, we might heave a sigh of relief. Finally, we are not at the mercy of every thought and feeling. We are not drowning in that chowder of emotions because we can slow down and observe the mind and decide where to put our attention. Great! Yet those stories remain in us. The metaphor typically offered in meditation classes is of a glass of water with mud in it. When we allow the water to settle for a while, the mud drops to the bottom, and we think we have a clear glass of water. The mud (our unexamined stories) remains at the bottom, waiting for the next "jerk" to stir it up. Then off we go again, launched into the stories that feed our anger, greed, and ignorance. Fortunately, there are practices that can help us reframe and release the stories that no longer serve us.

Mindful speech can shift our relationship to our inner stories. When we use language that offers a more authentic, inclusive depiction of reality, we are using mindful speech to embody justice. Since a shared and progressive vocabulary helps us enlighten our stories and work together more effectively, and since some of the language in this book may be new to you, I will offer a brief introduction to some useful language and concepts. As you read through this section, breathe deeply and notice what thoughts and feelings arise. Welcome both the comfort and the discomfort that arises when we play with language to liberate it—and to liberate ourselves through it.

## Useful Terms and Concepts

**People of the Global Majority (PGM)** is a term that emerged in dialogue under the leadership of social justice educator Dr. Barbara Love. It was coined as an alternative to the term *People of Color.*[4] I introduce this term to meditative practitioners as a way of re-cognizing (thinking again) about Indigenous, African, Latinx, and Asian heritage people. Using the term *People of the Global Majority* (PGM) can itself be a reflective practice, a language liberation practice that invokes a more just worldview. Saying PGM frees us from using the language of enslavers and colonizers who labeled humans by color and judged people's worth based on their proximity to whiteness. It is also a way of shifting our collective awareness to notice that African, Latinx, Indigenous, and Asian people are not "minorities" when viewing humanity in the global context. *People of the Global Majority* is a term that reminds us that although the ancestors and kin of PGM may not reside in the privileged realms of the West in large numbers, they are present everywhere and have been intrinsic to the stewardship and development of every part of the world we now live in. In using this term, we remind ourselves that the majority of the world's population is not of European descent (i.e., white or global minority). This can help shift the cognitive distortion that white people are entitled to more resources and more space in the world. It also reminds us that humanity is a global community and that anytime we decide to, we can undo the racism that has cleaved distance between us by naming us "white" and "colored." Also, we can undo internalized racism, such as the created devaluation and hierarchies among PGM based on phenotypical and behavioral proximity to whiteness. Throughout this book you'll notice that I refer to Indigenous, Asian, Black, and Latinx heritage people as global majority people or PGM.

**Oppression** refers to the systematic mistreatment of an individual or group of people based on the devaluation of some characteristic of their diversity. For example, the oppression of older people—ageism—is based on the devaluation of our aging selves. Ageism treats youth as a virtue, but of course, being younger does not make us better or more valuable. Later in the book we explore releasing ageism and coping with grief as we reflect on how to age joyfully. After all, if we are not aging, that means we are dead!

**Adultism** refers to how young people often experience oppression. Consciously or unconsciously, our families, schools, and societies often devalue the thinking and behavior of children and young adults. It is also due to adultism that many of us gave up being playful. Later in the book you'll explore your own stories of adultism and consider how you can reclaim playfulness as you release adultism and many other types of oppression that you may have absorbed as a young person.

**Privilege** refers to membership in a cultural group that receives preferential status. For example, people who have no mobility challenges have able-bodied privilege. Privilege is not something we should be ashamed of having. The important thing is to not allow our privilege to obscure the realities of the world and to use our privilege to create resources for those who do not have it. Checking our privilege means examining our lives to make sure that we are not using our privilege to oppress or exclude those who do not have it. When we examine our privilege—the ways we "benefit" from the preference given to our ethnicity, economic status, educational level, ability, sexual orientation, and so forth—we can use it to be allies with ourselves and others in ending oppression. The reflective exercises in *Joyfully Just* are designed to help us become aware of our unique experiences of privilege and oppression. I offer practices for us to kindly yet rigorously and reiteratively remove the dirt of unexamined privilege from the clear water of our essential being. When we clean ourselves this way, we naturally feel lighter and more joyful.

The term **Human Revolution** was coined by the Buddhist educator and teacher Josei Toda, who described it as a process of developing ever-clearer awareness of our purpose or mission in life and positively transforming our way of living.[5] Toda explained that human revolution is a means to cultivate an unfaltering perspective based on an understanding of the eternity of life. Rather than the shortsighted pursuit of worldly goals, doing one's human revolution means aiming for a way of life that maximizes meaning and value creation. The only way to fundamentally transform humanity's inclination toward inequality and destruction is through increasingly engaging in this wise and contributive way of living. We cannot legislate change in people's hearts no matter what laws we change.

Elaborating on this topic, Daisaku Ikeda, who was directly mentored by Josei Toda, states,

> There are all sorts of revolutions: political revolutions, economic revolutions, industrial revolutions, scientific revolutions, artistic revolutions . . . but no matter what one changes, the world will never get any better as long as people themselves . . . remain selfish and lacking in compassion. In that respect, human revolution is the most fundamental of all revolutions, and at the same time, the most necessary revolution for humankind.[6]

Wanting to become richer, more educated, calmer, or to develop any singular aspect of one's person reflects a desire for *relative* happiness. That is in sharp contrast to the goal of human revolution, which is to create a life condition of *absolute* happiness—an inner state of life where reality is seen clearly and engaged with in contributive, restorative, justice-oriented ways. This is what Buddhists refer to as *right view* and *right action*. Human revolution also involves and facilitates the development of an interior life condition that cannot be defeated by external influences. The freedom we access in our contemplative practice can create enough interior spaciousness to face the good, the bad, and the ugly of life (all of which are intricately interwoven) with enduring equanimity and courage. This way of being in and with the world is the actualization of the process called human revolution. As we do our human revolution, we develop discomfort resilience.

**Discomfort Resilience** refers to the capacity to lean into discomfort with an interest in the growth to be gleaned from pain or difficulty. Getting comfortable with discomfort is a prerequisite for developing self-awareness and insight because it means we seek out and attend to the aspects of ourselves and our world that we find painful. We can develop curiosity about suffering instead of feeling defeated by it. Discomfort resilience enables us to experience joy from the pain of resisting negative influences. The practices in this book guide you to your own understanding of iconic author and activist Alice Walker's profound statement at the end of her book *Possessing the Secret of Joy*, where she declares, "Resistance is the Secret of Joy."[7] When we develop discomfort resilience, we know the joy of resisting our addictions, the joy of resisting pettiness, the joy of resisting cultural appropriation, the joy of resisting exploitation of any kind, and the joy of communities and allies in resistance.

**Fierce Compassion** refers to a type of compassion toward ourselves and others that allows us to challenge complacency. In the spirit of fierce compassion, we want growth for ourselves and others, and we act in ways that facilitate that growth. Compassion is often thought of as simply comforting. For example, "I will show compassion toward myself by getting a massage or a nice dessert." In the light of fierce compassion, though, we see that some uncomfortable things may *also* be acts of profound compassion toward ourselves—such as getting a breast exam or colonoscopy. Fierce compassion is what propels us to act justly toward ourselves and others. Facing injustice is uncomfortable, yet doing so with fierce compassion can lead to a deeper and more expansive sense of well-being. So, you can think of fierce compassion as the colonoscopy that helps us detect and remove the polyps of injustice that are a pain in the butt and threaten to destroy us! Dr. Murphy-Shigematsu writes,

> Embracing vulnerability, we cross borders within ourselves and between us and others. Cultivating humility, gratitude, and acceptance, we become more authentic and kinder to ourselves and all other beings. Seeing and listening to others we believe in our oneness and connectedness with each other and with nature. Taking responsibility for our own life, we seek to understand and realize our unique purpose in serving humanity.[8]

With a heartful practice such as this, we realize that our efforts to engage with others mindfully and to end racism are not charitable offerings. Rather, they are the means by which we recognize and enact compassion toward our own interdependent lives.

On this point, Daisaku Ikeda says,

> Compassion is often thought of as akin to pity, but whereas pity may be condescending, compassion springs from a sense of the equality and interconnectedness of life. Because genuine compassion is about empowering others, helping them unlock strength and courage from within their lives in order to overcome their problems, it may sometimes appear stern or contradictory.[9]

In contrast to the notion of compassion as something that always feels good when being offered or received, we can consider compassion as something meant to help us move past the limitations of complacency and privilege. It takes courage to treat ourselves and one another with fierce compassion, and it takes discomfort resilience to receive it graciously. For example, we may know that someone will be embarrassed if we correct them for using sexist language, yet our fierce compassion gives us courage to do so. If someone corrects us for using sexist language and we have cultivated discomfort resilience, we will be able to receive and be grateful for the correction and recognize it as a gift of fierce compassion offered by someone who cared enough to correct us.

Fierce compassion is rooted in respect for the inherent dignity and inestimable possibility of one's own life and that of others, and a desire to see that dignity and possibility triumph.

> It takes courage to treat ourselves and one another with fierce compassion, and it takes discomfort resilience to receive it graciously.

**White Supremacy.** When I refer to white supremacy, I am speaking of ideals that colonizers brought to the Americas and the rest of the world—ideals that privilege colonialist, Eurocentric ways of knowing and being. I am speaking of the fact that global minority (a.k.a. white) people are recognized and featured more prominently as leaders in almost every field of endeavor. Global minority people are still paid more than most global majority persons even when they have the same educational level.

White racialized people, people who grew up with the identity and/or privileges of being white, have appropriated most of the wealth in the world, although they are the minority. White supremacy is evinced by the overrepresentation of global minority people's experiences at every level and in every type of education. This overrepresentation of white racialized people also exists in arts and entertainment. It is important to note that this is not earned positionality: it is appropriated and maintained through economic, social, and political violence. These are all visible aspects of white supremacy. The less tangible ones are the beliefs that hold global minority power in place.

As noted author Resmaa Menakem writes, "When people hear the words white supremacy or white body supremacy, they often think of Neo-Nazis and other extremists with hateful and violent agendas . . . But mainstream American culture is infused with a more subtle and less overt variety."[10] Menakem quotes Robin DiAngelo: "White supremacy does not refer to individual white people per se and their individual intentions, but to a political-economic social system of domination. This system is based on the historical and current accumulation of structural power that privileges, centralizes, and elevates white people as a group."[11] For example, one of the first acts of white supremacy was dividing humanity into false categories called "races." So to cease reifying that, we can use the word *ethnicity* instead of *race*. Racism is real, as is the racialization of all people, but race itself is a construct of white supremacy.

Language helps us alter our conscious minds as much as it reflects that alteration. This is necessary to release the cognitive distortions we absorb from white supremacy and heteropatriarchy. US and European societies, alongside many other societies around the world, are heteropatriarchal in that they are hierarchical societies dominated by heterosexual males with prevailing biases against and oppression of LGBTQIA+ folx, women, and nonbinary people.

At the start of this millennium, when I was doing international research on the experiences of LGBTQI global majority people, phrases like "his husband" or "her wife" were not common parlance among the general public. Back then, it may have been hard to envision legally recognized queer families. The most common falsehood that was employed against queer families at that time was that there would be an increased risk of pedophilia if nonheterosexual people were granted legal rights to marry and have families. Even though all the research and data showed that heterosexuals make up the overwhelming majority of pedophiles, many people would not let go of the myth because it felt like their only armor against the changes they feared would ensue if nonheterosexual people had equal rights.

Dr. Frantz Fanon, the founder of decolonial psychoanalysis, often spoke about the cognitive dissonance that people experience when confronted with uncomfortable truths. Dr. Fanon observed that because our core beliefs are emotionally entrenched, we rationalize, ignore, or deny realities that discomfit us.[12]

Despite pushback, language continues to progress to reflect transformations in society. The evolving descriptions of gender identity are an example of this expanded understanding of how humans can exist and be in relationships with each other. New language points us toward a new reality. Our minds often resist truth and cognitive distortions based white supremacy abound. Language practices help us literally begin to speak white supremacy and heteropatriarchy out of existence.

Let's Practice!

## Mindful Speech

Practicing mindful speech—assuring that our words reflect our most fiercely compassionate intentions—is one means of invoking and embodying a heartful approach to life.

With mindful speech, we can stop speaking in ways that reify racism and other types of oppression. Inclusive, reality-based language is a means of speaking white supremacy out of existence. Mindfulness practices with language can help contradict unconscious notions of white supremacy.

Try this as a language practice: If you are a person of the global majority, say so: "I am a person of the global majority." If you are a European-descended person, try saying "African, Indigenous, Latinx, and Asian heritage people are the global majority; I as a European-descended person am part of the global minority."

Try saying it out loud. How does saying it land for you? Take note in your Joy Journal of any feelings, thoughts, or sensations that come up.

You could even practice using the terms *global majority* and *global minority* the next time you want to say "People of Color" or "white people" and notice how it feels to use them in conversation.

Whether you begin to use these particular phrases regularly or not, continue to play with language to try to be in a just and joyful relationship with whatever or whomever you are talking about.

## Connecting with Cultural Wisdom and Traditions

There are many spiritual and religious traditions, as well as cultural practices and rituals grounded in daily life, that lead us to a deeper awareness and help us to be present with our bodies, minds, spirits, and hearts in a way that is awakened to all life around us. Sufism, Islam, Judaism, Hinduism, Christianity, Buddhism, and many other religions and spiritual traditions have prayers and practices that ground awareness and foster insight. Any contemplative practice that allows us to closely examine and transform the underbelly of our psychological, emotional, and embodied processes will aid us in returning to our most awakened state of life and support us in releasing oppressive patterns. One of the reasons that I highlight Black wisdom traditions is that they help us transcend not only social oppression but also the sufferings of birth, aging, sickness, and death. This is one of the many ways Black wisdom mirrors Buddhist wisdom.

## Dance

Many African cultures, including African American culture, have rituals and practices that are uniquely contemplative and seamlessly integrated into everyday life. African dance is one example of this. African dancing is listening to the body, trusting the body to tell its story. In her video describing healing dance, African dance teacher Wyoma demonstrates that dance is praying with our bodies. She begins with words acknowledging the ancestors from whom the dances emerged, and this acknowledgment and gratitude is itself a practice of justice and mindful awareness of interdependence.[13] When we acknowledge the sources of our teachings and learnings, we are in conscious relationship with all those who taught us, and that awareness of being connected to and supported by our teachers deepens our joy. One of the most tragic harms racism and colonialism did to humanity was the diminishment and dismissal of global majority peoples' dancing as savage and primitive. Much of global majority peoples' dancing intentionally embodies the movements of water, sky, animals, and our relationships to these. This is why African, Indigenous, Asian, and Latinx dances are now coming to be recognized as deep contemplative practices and used in meditation retreats. We free ourselves from cultural appropriation and develop a joyfully just relationship with cultural traditions of wisdom that have been subjugated and exploited by participating in such dances only when we can summon reverence for and connection to the peoples who developed these traditions. By acknowledging global majority peoples' suffering and supporting their leadership through our compassionate, reparative action in the world, we can engage with their wisdom traditions justly.

There are dances that people do in healing rituals and dances that are done in celebration. There are also spontaneous dances done as communication with oneself: with the moment of life one is experiencing, with the people in a given space, and with one's surrounding environment.

And if you've ever celebrated by doing the Griddy, then you have Black athlete Allen Davis to thank for creating that celebration dance!

We often think of dance as being a total body movement, but we can dance the story of a single part of our body. We also don't need to dance for a long time to let the body's movement message resonate within us.

Taking a dance break is a way to mindfully infuse joy into any moment and do justice to your body. The blood, tissue, and bones of your body are almost always in motion. Dancing is paying attention to that motion and directing it. When you dance without music, the rhythm of your body, the song of your soul, comes through differently than when you dance with music. It is like the difference between a silent meditation and one where you have meditation music. Both are valuable.

You don't have to get up from your desk, bed, couch, or car seat to dance! Car dancing can help you be present with joy in traffic. Desk dancing can make Zoom meetings and computer work delightful. Many cultures have hand dances, shoulder dances, or head dances as their primary movement. We can dance with our faces and tongues, too!

---

Let's Practice!

## Shall We Dance?

Just for a moment (time it if you like), move only the upper part of your body to a rhythm that feels natural for you. Let the movements flow naturally, listening to your body tell you how it wants to move.

How was that for your body? Did your body guide you to move in a way that released some tension or pain? Did you notice any physical pain or restriction in your movement? What did you feel emotionally? What were your thoughts, or were you free from thinking for a moment?

Every time we do this, we connect to and transform our body's rhythm, so I invite you to dance often to enliven your joyfully just journey.

---

## Learning from Black Wisdom: Take a Page from the African American Spoken Word, Embodied Love, Activism, and Song Books—Justly!

I invite people of every ethnicity and origin to notice how much you already learn from the self-transcendent contemplative practices of Africans and African Americans. This includes Black-led justice leadership, Black language praxis, Black embodied practices, and praxis with all genres of Black music. Let's start with Black dialect so that from there we can understand it more thoroughly everywhere, including in songs. Toni Morrison states, "Language alone protects us from the scariness of things with no names. Language alone is meditation."[14] Dr. Morrison is not saying that language is the only type of meditation but rather that the way we speak both reflects and refines our insight. This is why nonculturally appropriative practices with Black dialect are featured throughout this book.

Like much of Black speech, the expression "you must be out your natural mind" is eloquent and precise because it captures how when people speak, we are often not coming from an authentic or relaxed state of mind. The notion of a natural mind is an insight from Black dialect. Colonization, enslavement, Jim Crow, police terrorism, and microaggressive racism were—and are—intended to drive all people out of our natural minds: to make us so obsessed with power via aligning with white supremacy or so crazed with fear and grief that we could not think, speak, or embody freedom. White supremacy has also created a context wherein we often doubt, distrust, and devalue our own minds and the minds of Black and other global majority people.

All of us can rediscover, reassert, relieve, and rejoice in our natural minds. Together we'll try practices that create an opportunity to pause before any reflexive, defensive responses triggered by discussing racism and internalized racism can take over and shape the thoughts and words we speak to ourselves and other people.

We have already practiced doing this through mindful speech. Creating some space via pausing allows us to sense and speak the language of our clearest and most expansive minds. Such practices contribute to an inner and interpersonal dialogue that reflects an elevated, integrated, and authentic appreciation of all life. I invite you to consider more language-related practices that contribute to your mental health, improved interpersonal relationships with loved ones, and empowered engagement with all people.

Intentionally contemplating Black dialect—including Black language in poetry and song as we hear it, speak it, read it, sing it—allows us to both *draw from* and *bask in* the laconic eloquence of Black people. Exploring Black dialect as a linguistic meditation helps us notice and appreciate the wellspring of wisdom that is contained in Black parlance. For Black peoples—whether we're African American or Trini, Bajan or Dominican—to speak our natural minds is to affirm not only our dialect but also our intellect. By invoking our ancestral and diasporic tongues, we are affirming them and embodying them for all time.

Black dialect is often simple, on purpose. For Black people in the US and many other parts of the world, intentional paraleipsis, wherein we emphasize something by saying little about it, is an organic way of speaking. Black breviloquence reflects extemporaneous creativity employed to describe circumstances as seen from a uniquely Black perspective on reality. So much of what is well said in Black dialect is poorly captured in conventional English. Consider how much more emphatic, embodied, and empathetic the statement "I feel you" is compared to "I understand how you feel."

> Intentionally contemplating Black dialect allows us to both *draw from* and *bask in* the laconic eloquence of Black people.

The creativity of Black language comes from an embodied and relational experience of living. African-heritage Black people have so many rich languages to draw from, yet even if the only learned and spoken one is English, it is constantly being updated by African Americans. There are many hypotheses about how and why this is. It is in part a creative, adaptive response to the egregious violations of our personal space and lives caused by racism, wherein we have to develop codes to say what we really think around white racialized people due to their fragility and our determination to get our needs of the moment met. Speaking to global minority people with deference and care for their fragility is often necessary for Black people to keep our jobs and maintain our safety. This is why many Black parents teach their kids to be submissive when speaking to global minority adults and police so that they may—possibly—stay safe.

> If you are not Black and want to be in a just relationship with Black dialect, pause and ask yourself why you are using it before or as you find yourself doing so.

Language and its arts are but one of the ways Black people have learned to translate, transcend, and transmute the suffering of racism. It is important to recognize the relationship between racism and the creativity of Black language because when non-Black people appropriate Black dialect, they often want our rhythm but not our blues, as the saying goes. Many non-Black people often skip the work of examining and addressing their anti-Black racism and use Black language to forge documents of alliance with Black people while making little or no effort to actually be allies. For non-Black people, the use of Black dialect is often just a shortcut, a way to appear to be multicultural or embrace diversity without having authentic, reciprocal relationships with the very people whose argot they emulate.

However, it would be a mistake to ascribe the ever-growing glossary of Black dialect solely to the ongoing transmutation of racism.

The theme of Black linguistic expression is our indefatigable joie de vivre. Black people are often resiliently joyful in ways that surface humor in the direst circumstances. This reflects the creative spiritual resilience that is the source of Black dialect. All of life's sufferings, illness, aging, death, and loss of every kind is addressed and redressed in Black idiom.

If you are not Black and want to be in a just relationship with Black dialect, pause and ask yourself why you are using it before or as you find yourself doing so. Are you trying to appear cool or current? Are you trying to seem connected to Black people and this is a shortcut? Are you genuinely experiencing the language as a practice in wise, precise speech? If it is the latter, it is useful to acknowledge the source when using it. So, if you want to use Black dialect and you're not Black, practice prefacing it with "As African Americans say . . ." Practicing acknowledging the source, even some of the time, breaks the culturally appropriative pattern of snatching the words out of Black peoples' mouths without so much as a nod or a thank you.

Say "*Yes!*" if you feel me so far! Call-and-response is another aspect of Black speech and Black song that shines as an interdependent embodied practice. Even when we can't hear each other with our ears, we can "hear" each other energetically. And as trailblazing musician and performing artist James Brown said, people feel you long before they hear you anyway, meaning that your life force has a vibe that can be felt by anyone who is attuned even before you speak.[15]

You may wonder why "be" often prefixes the use of other verbs in Black vernacular. I invite you to notice the use of conjugations like "I be," "she be," "he be," or "they be." Using *be* before another verb articulates Black awareness that we embody what we are enacting. When I say "I be writing," it means that I am not just performing the act of writing but that writing is transforming my being—who I be—as I write. The *be* before the verb also speaks to the regular and sometimes repetitious or constant nature of a thing I be doing. I be what I do regularly. This is Black wisdom saying, "What you do most regularly is who you are."

So, I am not simply writing this; I am enacting my existence through writing: I be writing.

# Connecting Through Black Kinesics: From High Five to Dap!

Did you ever wonder where the high five came from? Or the fist bump? You have seen it a million times and done it too. Let's explore its origin story.

As early as the 1930s, Black people began using the phrase "Give me five" to invite each other to slap palms in agreement or celebration. Giving each other five, high fives, and dap are all gesticulation practices created by Black people to affirm connection and recognize a truth: to share an insight in the present moment. These gestures have been copied worldwide and are now part of how almost all humans connect. Black kinesics fulfill a human longing for brief but meaningful ways to relate and affirm reality together.

"Give me some skin" is another way of saying "Give me five," and these expressions illustrate how Black people made touch natural and joyful through a simple gesture that can be done with a stranger standing with you at a bus stop, or a family member, a child, or an elder. These concise, embodied Black interdependence practices may be one of the greatest yet least appreciated aspects of Black wisdom.

Dap is another way that Black people, especially Black men, teach us to be affectionate while subverting narrow notions of masculinity that proscribe touch between men. Dap communicates much without words and transverses men's oppression—the notion that men can't show emotional and psychological bonding—by providing a powerful connective experience through symbolic, synchronized physicality.

The term *dap*, sometimes spoken of as an acronym for "dignity and pride," was coined by Black soldiers in the Vietnam War who were imprisoned in the Long Binh Jail (LBJ), a notorious US military stockade that reflected the racist disproportions of the American carceral system. While about 11 percent of American soldiers (and 2 percent of officers) in Vietnam were Black, over 34 percent of court-martialed soldiers and over 50 percent of the prisoners in LBJ were Black.[16]

"Long Binh [Jail] was the kind of place that from the moment you walked in, you were trying to figure out a way to get out. Here you are in a war zone, in a jail, just at their mercy," said veteran Scott Riley, who was sentenced to LBJ. The stockade was overcrowded, and the military rehabbed metal shipping containers into maximum-security jail cells referred to as "the box." "The temperature in the box was a hundred-plus degrees. The light was constantly on, twenty-four hours a day, and you were in there, naked," remembers Riley.[17] It was under these tortuous conditions that Black men created this enduring, internationally copied kinesic practice to show their support for and connection to one another. They created the dap in response to the military's ban of the Black Power salute.[18] Note the self-transcendence of developing an embodied, affirming symbol of solidarity while experiencing unjust and brutal imprisonment. Note the global impact that these men's practice has had. *Dap reflects the leadership of Black men, and it has informed how men everywhere now relate to each other.* And yes, women dap, too!

Black women have come up with their own styles of dap over the decades, most of which have some form of hand contact and sometimes shoulder movement. These have also been copied by women all over the world who are not Black.

Black queer and trans folx have added to the meaningful gesticulation repertoire of Blackness as well. Since the 1920s there has been a strong culturally engaged LGBTQIA+ presence in Harlem, New York, "so it should come as no surprise that Harlem was the birthplace of 'vogue,' a highly stylized form of dance created by black and Latino LGBTQ communities," writes historian Tsione Wolde-Michael. "Through dance, drag queens showed how gender is a performance."[19]

It is important to notice Black communicative kinesics that *all* people are encouraged by, so that we have insight into how Black lives enrich all lives. It's vital that we know who we have to thank for the practices that adorn our lives. It is also important to acknowledge the Black origins of your patterns of speech and behavior because otherwise you may not notice the self-transcendence that is being illustrated. So much of what Black people have done and do to enhance language and living is part of how we transmute suffering, and it offers a model infused with wisdom.

If you are reading or sharing this with someone, give each other five or dap it up right now!

## Black Social Justice Leadership: Enlightening the Way to Freedom

All Black wisdom traditions have justice at their core. Justice is the freedom and opportunity for everyone to actualize their most joyful, compassionate, and contributive self and to compassionately support others in doing so. Those who inhibit justice for others are also blocking their own access to their greater selves. Bhikkhu Bodhi, a Buddhist monk and author, points out that one of the "many nuances" of the word *dharma* means justice, in the sense of a belief that "all people possess intrinsic value, that all are endowed with inherent dignity and therefore should be helped to realize this dignity."[20] Buddhism and Black wisdom traditions support and guide us toward inner and communal liberation. In addition to developing the phonics of freedom via dialect, music, and gestures, Black people have also modeled how to subvert injustice and create social and political change, thus making the United States and the world more liberated spaces for everyone. I address this point in an article about Juneteenth:

Black people ended the enslavement of Black people. They did so through countless acts of daily resistance, from putting herbs in enslavers' food to make them too tired to rape or beat us, to the millions of heroic escape efforts we will never know of. One of the delusions of white supremacy is that white people ended slavery: that Abraham Lincoln was swayed by white abolitionists and together they freed the helpless Black people. This is absurd because abolitionists themselves were guided and inspired by the works of Black people to end slavery: from Nat Turner's resistance, we see the root of John Brown's rebellion. Frederick Douglass' eloquent rage moved and continues to move countless minds and hearts beyond the delusion that Black subjugation is anything other than brutal cowardice. Sojourner Truth led the way for all women to see their power and preceded the suffragist movement in America—even though Black women did not have the right to vote or any other rights until almost half a century *after* white women won that right. For context, my mother and grandmother never had these rights until the year of my birth—1965—and even then, trying to exercise their rights was often life-threatening because of white supremacist terrorism in the form of the Klan and violent police and government interference.[21]

Speaking of women, Black women have been leaders of protest in the US since its inception. Elizabeth Freeman was the first to sue for her freedom from enslavement in Massachusetts. Her case led to a bevy of freedom suits that would eventually result in Massachusetts outlawing slavery.[22] Charlotte Grimké, Frances Harper, Sarah Parker Remond, Mary Ann Shadd, and Harriet Tubman are some of the most noted female abolitionists; however, countless Black women facilitated the dismantling of slavery.[23]

---

Let's Practice!

## Contemplating Contributions

Let's practice reflecting on the contributions of these leaders. Close your eyes for a moment and cast your mind to envision what the world would look like now if Black people had not resisted and ceaselessly worked to end slavery. Take out your journal and note your responses to the following questions:

- *What would my mind perceive if I walked past auction blocks and whipping posts? How would I respond to these circumstances? How would I teach my children to respond?*

- *What would these circumstances make me feel?*

- *How would I act on what I think and feel?*

- *In this moment, can I notice gratitude for Black people ending enslavement in the US and so many parts of the world? What else can I notice that I feel, think, and sense as I contemplate this?*

Before and after the American civil rights movement that began in the 1950s, Black people were forerunners in the anti-war movement, labor movements, anti-poverty movements, LGBTQIA+ rights movements, and climate/environmental protection movements. Take a moment now and consider a Black activist who fought for something you value and modeled how to do so. If you don't know of any or you want to expand your connection to those who model resistance to oppression, contemplate this list to find your movement model! Say their names aloud to help you resonate with their powerful leadership. Look up any name(s) that intrigues you:

| | | |
|---|---|---|
| Ida B. Wells | Carolyn Finney | Lateefah Simon |
| Martese Johnson | Whitney Young | Anya Dillard |
| W. E. B. Du Bois | Julian Bond | Rae Wynn-Grant |
| Rosa Parks | Leah Thomas | Ernestine Eckstein |
| A. Philip Randolph | Thandiwe Abdullah | Genesis Butler |
| Haile Thomas | Rue Mapp | Marsha P. Johnson |
| Chelsea Miller | Pauli Murray | Marley Dias |
| Bayard Rustin | Dorothy Height | Phill Wilson |
| Marsha P. Johnson | Malcom X | Tarana Burke |
| Michelle Alexander | Jerome Foster II | Ibram X. Kendi |
| Ruby Bridges | Danielle Coke Balfour | Leah Penniman |
| Jo Ann Robinson | John Lewis | Corina Newsome |
| Vanessa Nakate | Mary Church Terrell | Sophie Ming |
| Ella Baker | | |

We all may have heroes and icons and yet we often don't empower ourselves to continue the good works they did. Once you find a movement model, answer these questions to help guide your learning from them.

- *What do I admire about who they were (or are)? What aspect of their attitude, their contemplative practice, their way of being, could I cultivate within myself?*

- *What do I admire about what they did (or do) in the world? What could I do in the world now that furthers that work?*

---

## Meditations on Black Music: Black Music as Meditation

Throughout our *Joyfully Just* journey we are accompanied by the sounds of Blackness! We will practice with Black music to expand our sense of joy and to justly acknowledge the source of much of the music that moves us through life.

Black music—the music created by Black people throughout the African Diaspora—is both the source and sound of the cultivation of our shared humanity. It is the expressed liberation of our humanity. The African drum beats out all manner of possibilities for the human heart. The drum sounds out communication, celebration, lamentation, invocation, and convocation. Djembe, udu, bongo, and more call us to the essential Africa, the cradle of our human species. Drumbeats call us to action, inviting embodied liberation through movement. We enact the pulsating aspect of our own lives as the beat reverberates in us, driving us to emerge dancing.

The Black American music called Jazz has encouraged us to live outside the lines just as the Black women and men who created it did—and still do. They invite us to join them and live the liberty in the music they play. As Thelonious Monk said, "The piano ain't got no wrong notes."[24] Liberating us into the joyful improvisation of our own lives, Jazz teaches us to learn from victory and defeat. Jazz arises from and articulates the ineffable suffering of racism even as it creates soundtracks of that suffering transcended. Jazz intones what is impossible to put into words: the nature of life and being, the confluence of courage and doubt, the joyous freedom that can only arise from escaping bondage and oppression of all kinds. Jazz's unmanaged notes score the disorganized nature of our human spirit, ruptured and rupturing—and then returning, always returning to mellifluous harmony.

Through Black Rock 'n' Roll music, we connect to our own disorganized harmonies. We rock out and into Jimi Hendrix's concordant discord and Prince's dissonant consonance. Reggae music, born in Jamaica, is the music that squashes the legacy of enslavement and colonization with soulful, easeful resistance.

Black Blues music strums our heartstrings as it intones our heartbreak. The Blues grew from and reflects the pain of racism, poverty, and lost love. Through the creative despair of the Blues, we learn from Black artists like Bessie Smith and Lou Rawls as they invoke humor and pathos, singing the irony of life's follies and failures. From Black people we have learned to sing and play our personal Blues and be easeful in the capricious nature of loss as it reflects life's impermanence.

Black Rap and Hip-Hop music assert the aggressive passion that resists subjugation. As Black Hip-Hop music is copied and emulated by every culture around the world from Australia to China, we honor the potency of Blackness that has helped all people to tap into their own power. Re-cognizing the righteous anger at racism, we learn to fight the power that would suppress our humanity. Polishing the diamond of Black anger to this shining gem of creativity, Black Hip-Hop artists from Queen Latifah to Kendrick Lamar teach us to stand up and stand out for justice, infusing our activism with poetry and passion. No other music so sonorously uplifts our rage and expresses our power as Rap and Hip-Hop music do.

Black Rhythm and Blues gives love and embodied movement back to us timelessly. Unbridled passion abounds from Maxwell's melodies and Lauryn Hill's lyrics. As we sing in our showers and dance with our sweethearts, R & B from Black musicians is the rhythm of our love affair with life.

Transcending the legacy of bondage and ongoing exploitation and violence against us, Black people lift all spirits with Black spirituals. Black Gospel music elevates the hopes of humanity and calls us to create an immovable resolve within, based on our inherent divinity and dignity and the determination to see that dignity and divinity triumph. Declaring that we shall not be moved, we hold firm to our resolve to be free. With Black Gospel music we invoke determination and commitment to and from our spiritual selves: the strongest aspect of our being that is timeless and eternal.

> Black Hip-Hop artists from Queen Latifah to Kendrick Lamar teach us to stand up and stand out for justice, infusing our activism with poetry and passion.

The profound global impact Black people have made on the lives of everyone on the planet is demonstrated in the ways that the music of Black people has seeped into the bodies, minds, hearts, and spirits of people of every nation. Black music at its core is freedom song. The songs speak Black resistance and Black commitment to complete liberation. Each genre of Black music contains elements of hope, despair, humor, and courage, and intones an expansive expression of our human experience. Black music in its multidimensional genres presents to us the totality of our possibility as human beings in lyrical and sonic form. Black music moves us to embody sound. We celebrate this nourishment from Black minds, Black bodies, and Black souls. In celebrating Black music, we celebrate our own humanity, which has been rendered back to us so creatively by Black musicians the world over and through all time.

Let's Practice!

## Reflecting with Black Music

For further reflection, let's sense into our musical mood! What type of music matches how you feel right now? Is there an artist or song that comes to your body-mind-heart? Let a verse or two of that song play within you. If you have the space and time, go ahead and play that song now on your phone or whatever device is handy. What does the song bring to your awareness? Does it remind you of certain people, places, or experiences? Why do you think that song came to you now?

Often the music we choose to play is our inner voice's way of celebrating, of exploring a path through a difficulty, or both. So, another practice you can work with is playing a song when you feel stuck or want to get clearer mentally or emotionally. The song you choose is something like an assessment of your mood, and it is also your inner artist creatively composing a way forward. Notice what songs you have in your Joybox and see if you can mood match and mood mix. What songs in there that are usually played when you are celebrating could also possibly be played when grieving? Music can be used to transcend a mood as much as it can to create one, so try playing the opposite of what you want to hear sometimes and notice how you relate to the music. Note any insights from this musical reflection in your Joy Journal.

## Practicing with Poetry

Part of what makes some of the music we love so compelling is its lyrical poetry. Reading, reciting, and creating poetry is a type of meditation that can expand our conscious awareness and help us feel into aspects of our experience that we did not even know were there.

For example, when reading a novel, hearing a song, or just listening to someone speak, language can strike us as poetic. To explore this further, let's drop into a reflective poetry reading practice with this excerpt from Zora Neale Hurston's classic novel *Their Eyes Were Watching God*. Although the book is technically a work of prose, this passage resonates with the rhythm and power of poetry. Write down your reflections in your Joy Journal as you read. What sensations, feelings, and thoughts arise for you?

There is a basin in the mind where words float around on thought and thought on sound and sight. Then there is a depth of thought untouched by words, and deeper still a gulf of formless feelings untouched by thought.[25]

Engagement with poetry is a wonderful way to notice what resounds in our being. Make a note in your Joy Journal of how Hurston's words resonate in you.

As we will discuss further in the coming chapters, poetry-based practices are one of many methods that can enable us to develop fierce compassion and discomfort resilience. This allows us to enjoy a more authentic engagement with our own interior life, with the lives of other beings, and with all that surrounds us, bolstering our efforts to end racism and other types of oppression.

Let's Practice!

## Journaling with the Spirit: Embracing Joy in Impermanence

With this final practice of the chapter, we are beginning with the end—embracing impermanence and communing with the ineffable aspect of ourselves we sometimes call "spirit." We'll do this by writing a letter to our own internal life force or energy—or it could be written to the Orishas, to Allah, to Krishna, Vishnu, Brahma, or Shiva, to God or to many gods; to your ancestors; to the universe; to your own spirit and inner divinity.

In a paragraph, just let the pen roll or the keys clack as you write whatever comes to mind to say to these divine aspects of, in, and with your being. Then, embracing impermanence, write briefly about the following questions: What would you offer yourself for this day if it was the last day of your life? Make a word offering, a request, and a brief expression of gratitude. You can also record your letter as a voice memo. Let it be brief—we've got both more and less time than we think!

Take about five minutes to do this. If you only had five minutes, what gratitude would you express? What request would you make? What words would say it all? We will probably live thousands more days and hours, but in these five minutes, knowing no more time is ever promised, what does your soul cry out? Let it shout onto the page!

# Chapter Two

## Resilient Compassion

Fierce compassion and discomfort resilience are mutually reinforcing pathways to freedom and joy. In this chapter, I'll be talking about how discomfort resilience allows us to develop and maintain compassion toward ourselves and others in difficult times. The fiercely compassionate mindset/heartset that we cultivate bolsters our ability to grow from pain and difficulty. As we grow fierce compassion that is resilient, all of life's experiences become fields of learning where we can harvest joy.

Loss and pain are part of growing up and advancing in life. There is no suffering that is not fertile soil for growth if we have the resources to transmute the pain into wisdom, which in turn helps us lead more meaningful lives. However, we often lack guidance or the internal, social, or environmental resources to do this.

The good news is that contemplative practices can help us develop internal resources like self-esteem, relational resources such as empowering support systems, and environmental awareness that allows us to be sustained by our natural habitat. Developing fierce compassion and discomfort resilience helps us build our internal and interpersonal compassion, which guide us as we transform pain into insight. Fierce compassion and discomfort resilience are our internal and relational resources for just, joyful living.

Shakyamuni Buddha taught about the four noble truths and the eightfold path. The four noble truths are:

- **The truth of suffering:** the reality that all existence in this world entails suffering, as represented by the four sufferings inherent in all life—birth, aging, illness, and death

- **The truth of the origin of suffering:** suffering is caused by our craving for the fleeting pleasures of the world

- **The truth of the cessation of suffering:** releasing cravings that come from our lesser self ends the suffering

- **The truth of the path to the cessation of suffering:** there is a way to release those cravings. The way or path to releasing those sufferings is traditionally interpreted as the discipline of the eightfold path:

  - Right views, based on the four noble truths and a correct understanding of Buddhism

  - Right thinking, or command of one's mind

  - Right speech

  - Right action

  - Right way of life, based on purifying one's thoughts, words, and deeds

  - Right endeavor, to seek the truth

  - Right mindfulness, always to bear right views in mind

  - Right meditation

"Right" in this context is not meant as a value judgment. Rather, the eight aspects of the path are "right" in that they are comprehensive and holistic. In teaching about the eightfold path, Shakyamuni used the word *samma*, which also connotes relatedness and wholeness.[1]

The four noble truths and the eightfold path reflect the basic attitude and approach that undergird Shakyamuni's early teachings, which concentrated on eliminating distorted views about life and the world. He called these distorted views "delusions"; I also think of them as cognitive distortions. The goal of Buddhism is to awaken us, both to life's harsh realities and life's capacity to attain, sustain, and reflect enlightenment.

The Lotus Sutra makes it absolutely clear that two aspects of Buddhist practice are indispensable if we are to attain enlightenment. One is directed toward perfecting ourselves in the sense that we awaken to our fundamental enlightenment and develop our inherent potential, and the other is the practice of leading other people toward that same development. We can engage with the eightfold path to purify our view, thoughts, speech, actions, way of life, work, awareness—and our meditative practices themselves.

## Life Is a Spiritual, Psychological, and Emotional Gym: Let's Get Our Inner Workout On!

You can always get a fierce compassion and discomfort resilience workout in, no matter where you are or what you are doing. Yet just like going to a health club, deciding to do your inner workout requires determination—a decision to take charge of your mind and life and grow your inner strength. As Daisaku Ikeda points out,

> When we change our inner determination, everything begins to move in a new direction. The moment we make a powerful resolve, every nerve and fiber of our being will immediately orient itself towards the fulfillment of this goal or desire. But, if we think, "This is never going to work out," then every cell in our body will be deflated and give up the fight. Hope, in this sense, is a decision. It is the most important decision we can make.[2]

Another word for determination is *resolve*. To fully engage the gears of self-compassion and discomfort resilience we need resolve. Resolve is one of the Buddhist paramitas, or perfections of mind, because, put simply, it helps us "perfect" our heartful, mindful engagement with the world. Resolve is always the starting place for me. In addition to cultivating resolve to embody my bodhisattva vow—my commitment to support the liberation of all beings—I also commit to return to that resolve when I find myself drifting from it. The bodhisattva vow is itself an expression of resolve.

Because our minds change from moment to moment, because life's challenges come hard and fast, and because we get discouraged and heartbroken, it is necessary to continually renew our resolve moment to moment. So, in addition to making resolutions at the start of a new year, I like to practice *new-moment resolutions* to remind myself that I can bring fresh determination, resolve, and energy to each moment.

---

Let's Practice!

## Make a New-Moment's Resolution

Take a deep breath to settle into the present moment. Allow yourself to land in this singular time and space. As you breathe deeply, consider what you would like the next moment or moments of your life to be like. Consider what your aspirations are. What are your wildest dreams for what your day or night could be? You are in charge of it, and your vision of this moment and your next moment is what you get to create. Would you like your next moment to be restful, fun, productive, social, or reflective? Try saying it either aloud or silently to yourself as a sentence: "I resolve to _____ right now."

For example, as I write this, I realize I need to get up and stretch, so this moment's resolution for me is to take care of my body—right now. You can even add to your resolution with some specific actions you will take in the moment(s) to come, such as "I resolve to take care of my body by setting the timer and stretching every twenty minutes." Remember that you can always hit the reset button on your state of mind by dropping into a new moment's resolution!

———————

Another resolution we can make is to experience and share fierce compassion and discomfort resilience. Fierce compassion is a growth-oriented approach to self-care. We grow discomfort resilience by leaning into the pain in our lives with an intention to grow our strength, courage, and wisdom.

> Fierce compassion when acted on becomes a skill, a response-ability, an ability to respond instead of reacting.

The Buddhist teacher and author Pema Chödrön reminds us that "the most fundamental aggression to ourselves, the most fundamental harm we can do to ourselves, is to remain ignorant by not having the courage and the respect to look at ourselves honestly and gently."[3] Living with fierce compassion means developing a habit of loving, candid self-reflection such that it becomes part of how we come to see and polish our greater self unceasingly. It is a reality-facing self-view and worldview that is consistently able to bring forth kindness and courage toward ourselves and everyone around us. Fierce compassion when acted on becomes a skill, a response-ability—an ability to respond instead of reacting. It is our practice that helps us pause when an activating thought or action occurs, and in that pause we can cultivate a response instead of just reacting on impulse. This peace-giving practice enables us to greet every situation, especially failure and disappointment, with a kind, brave spirit.

Without this response-ability we find ourselves stuck in react-ability, and that is just as explosive as it sounds. When we are in reactive mode, we blow up at ourselves or those around us. The internal blow-up may feel like stomach churning or headaches, which are actual biochemical markers of anxiety. Being in reactive mode may also show up as the deflated physiology of depression, which robs us of joy.

What distinguishes a response from a reaction is the wisdom we access when we pause. Pausing between the activating event or circumstance and the next thought, word, or action we express makes all the difference in our capacity to be just. For example, pausing when someone cuts you off at a traffic light might enable you to not think of it as personal, not shout curses out of the window, and not race ahead to cut them off at the next light. When we consistently pause to access wisdom, we cultivate response-ability.

## Self-Awareness and Affirmations for Fierce Compassion

Fierce compassion begins with self-awareness. In Buddhism, *right view* is the first step on the eightfold path because seeing ourselves and our environment, and noticing how we are relating and connecting to that environment, is the first step to enlightening our path.

---

Let's Practice!

## A Compassion Check-In

Let's do a compassionate self-awareness check-in. How does your body feel at this moment? What would be a fiercely compassionate action you could take toward your body now? For me, it is simply pausing to drink some water as I write. It is important to note that these practices need not be very time-consuming. In fact, they are time-restoring because rather than racing through our days, we are pausing frequently to nourish our bodies and minds and savor the time we have even more.

Continuing our self-compassion inventory, take an inward soft gaze at your feelings. How are you feeling emotionally? What would compassion toward your heart sound like or look like? What does your heart need? Take a deep breath, then another, and consider it. Sometimes just noticing your emotions and connecting to them is enough. Like smiling at a child who just needs to know you are present with them while they play or work, smile at your own emotional being now. Maybe take a moment to say, as African Americans say, "I see you" or "I feel you" to your own heart as a way of acknowledging to yourself that you are present with your feelings.

Or maybe your heart needs to hear an affirmation. Affirmations are a powerful means of positive self-talk and one of the most impactful ways to enact self-compassion. We are always in conversation with ourselves, whether we use words in that inner dialogue or not. Since we are the person we speak with the most, let's make sure that conversation is an affirming one.

What's something kind you can say to yourself at this moment? Is it something like "I am worthy of good care" or "I love myself"? Take a moment and say those words to yourself. You can say them silently if you are in a public space or aloud if you are in a sufficiently private space to speak aloud.

What are the words or sentiments you could offer yourself to make this moment joyful? Offer yourself those words or sentiments now. Is it a gratitude affirmation? Something like "I am alive and that is gift"? What are the words that you need to hear to make your day—this day—joyful? Is it something like "I am safe, I am loved, I am free"? Whatever compassionate words you need to hear, say those words to yourself now.

---

We can release the cognitive and verbal injustices we unwittingly perpetuate against ourselves by being just toward ourselves through right thought and right speech. If we can rely on ourselves for compassion, then we are more free. If we don't wait for other people to validate us and instead develop the constant habit of doing it ourselves, we become strong. When we justly affirm ourselves, we create a fragrant inner world of motivation, encouragement, and joy. To celebrate your self-affirmation, take a moment to breathe in an uplifting scent. It could be your favorite essential oil, or some cilantro or mint you have in the fridge, a breath of fresh air from your window, or the earthy fragrance of dirt in your favorite plant.

If we don't wait for other people to validate us and instead develop the constant habit of doing it ourselves, we become strong.

When our bodies and minds are redolent with the fragrance of fierce compassion, we act lovingly and powerfully on behalf of our greater self, anointing our lives and imbuing all that we touch with the balm of joy.

I love that sentence I just wrote! Sometimes we feel embarrassed or maybe even ashamed to appreciate ourselves when we do something well. We may struggle to say out loud what we are pleased with about ourselves or our work. Yet recognizing our right action, our good deeds—not just when we do service "for others" but with the understanding that when we do anything well, it serves everyone—is positive reinforcement that will train us to continue to take more right action.

A core tenet of behavior theory is that when we encourage and reward our own good behavior, our entire being gets motivated to repeat such behavior so that we continue to get the reward. Consider something that you have done well today that you are pleased with and offer yourself appreciation. Affirming yourself is a vital way to practice self-acknowledgment, which in turn deepens self-awareness. Did you brush your teeth? If so, you can acknowledge that as a beautiful effort you made to care for your well-being—and to share clean breath with those around you! Pause and mentally note three other things you accomplished today. Opening this book to access more joy is also a step you can acknowledge that you are taking toward your own growth.

Discomfort resilience helps us practice fierce compassion because it gives us the stamina to be compassionate toward ourselves and others in ways that may be uncomfortable. In many ways, we naturally practice fierce compassion, and we all have some level of discomfort resilience. The goal is to grow resilient compassion, which is consistent fierce compassion and discomfort resilience so that you can endlessly expand the realms of inner life and outward engagement that are possible for you.

This heightened capacity for response-ability—to increasingly be able to respond to the developmental needs of your greater self—is liberating. And we can start by noticing what we already do in this regard. If you have ever gone to the dentist, that was practicing fierce compassion toward yourself because you probably didn't go for fun.

The first step in developing resilient compassion is always acknowledging what you already do to develop and manifest your greater self. The next step is cultivating resolve or making a determination. What ways do you resolve to care for yourself and grow, big picture? Do you want to sleep more? Do you want to improve your financial literacy and money management? Do you want to try a new occupation? All of these require resilient compassion because we know that failure and mistakes will be part of achieving any goal and we need internal stamina to persevere.

Take a moment now and do a deep-breathing practice to summon resolve and set an intention. Note how the resolve feels for you and also jot down that intention in your Joy Journal.

---

Let's Practice!

## Making an Action Plan

Breathe in deeply; allow fierce compassion for your being to arise, then breathe out fully, exhaling a commitment to caring for your being fiercely. Next, try this meditation:

*Breathing in, I resolve to care for my being fiercely;*

*Breathing out, I reflect on how to care for my being fiercely.*

Now take a few minutes and list a few things in your Joy Journal that you resolve to act on out of fierce compassion toward yourself. You have already set an intention and meditated on resolve; now, let's make an action plan.

There are two relevant African proverbs you can use to guide your action planning. The first is "Dreams are the voices of ancestors." What dreams are your ancestors communicating to you at this moment? It is fine to start with the big dreams, the vision. For example, what is your vision and/or your ancestors' vision for your emotional well-being? Your spiritual well-being? Your cognitive or intellectual well-being?

Once you have these written down, then list at least one action you can take as an expression of fierce compassion toward yourself in each aspect of your vision or dream. Consider making these reflections part of your morning meditation or practice so that they can enhance and inform your daily routine.

The second proverb states "A plan is just a dream with a deadline." Journal as you reflect on the plan(s) that could help you realize your dreams. Consider one action step toward your dream/plan that you could accomplish *today*, supported by fierce compassion from and for yourself. Your action step might be creating a timeline for your plan, putting some inspirational reminders around your living space or office, or setting up a time to meet with your joy partner or joy squad to dream and plan together.

Maybe your dream is a health goal. If so, what might be the next step? Going to bed early? Putting something beautiful in or around your sleeping area? Or perhaps you might resolve to drink the recommended daily allowance of sixty-four ounces of water today or go for a walk with a joy partner (even virtually, if you are far apart). Resolving and acting with fierce compassion for your physical well-being is one way to enact personal justice. So go ahead and do yourself justice!

-------

In reality, there is no separation between self-compassion and compassion for the lives around us because we are always in relationship with all life. As Ikeda says, "Each form of life supports all others, together they weave the grand web of life. Thus there really is no happiness for oneself alone, no suffering that afflicts only others."[4]

Compassion is also relational because we have a natural biological inclination to empathize, sympathize, and co-experience reality with other beings. Have you ever found yourself crying because someone else was crying or yawning when someone else does? That is one of the clearest indicators of our interdependence. We perceive the sorrow, physical discomfort, anxiety, or fatigue that another person experiences not just intellectually but also viscerally. The African American expression "I feel you" captures this profound intersensory experience precisely.

One of the ways Buddhism teaches us about interdependence is through articulating *dependent origination*. Dependent origination means that everything is connected and interdependent. Nothing exists in isolation, and everything in the world comes into existence when the causes and surrounding environmental conditions are right. This is one of the earliest principles formulated in the history of Buddhism. In its simplest form, the Buddha expressed it as "This is because that is." He was enlightened to the truth that the whole universe is a living, interconnected entity and that nothing exists separate from the law of life. Buddhism offers this lens to help us transcend the lesser self, which tends toward egoism and separation, and develop a greater self, which is fused with the life of the universe. So, when we are practicing compassion, we are striving to cultivate this greater self—the aspect of our being that recognizes and can act on our inherent power and possibility. Enlightenment, which is the ultimate aspiration of Buddhism, means seeing one's own limitless capacity as well as the limitless capacity of other human beings and all life. Limitless capacity means we have incalculably more mental, emotional, physical, and spiritual potential and power than we know of or use. The practices of Buddhism—from adherence to the eightfold path, to chanting mantras like Nam Myoho Renge Kyo, to mindfulness meditations of all kinds—help us access more and more of that power every day.

Fierce-compassion practices are part of the canon of Buddhist practices and teachings that help us access our greater self. For example, my lesser self might be saying, *You're feeling tired, Kamilah. Stop writing for now and watch some television.* When that happens (every fifteen minutes or so today!), I take a deep breath, look at my altar with the pictures of my grandfather and mother, and I refresh my resolve. I do so out of fierce compassion for myself because I know writing is far more fulfilling and liberating than watching TV. Also, when I arouse compassion for myself, my sense of connection to all beings grows, and that sense of connection in turn enhances my compassion.

So, how do we arouse compassion when we are just not feeling it? We return to resolve and set a new moment's resolution that relates to manifesting our greater self. To the degree that we embody our greater self, we are free—free to liberate ourselves from oppressive thoughts and behaviors and free to help others experience that liberation as well.

bell hooks writes, "When we engage love as action, you can't act without connecting."[5] If love is just a sentiment for us, however—if it is the feeble anemic love that Rev. Dr. Martin Luther King Jr. decries—then it does not give us any power to act. However, if it is empowered love that works in the service of justice, then our love for ourselves and life around us has agency; it has the capacity to improve and enrich everything.

bell hooks further states, "Martin Luther King, Jr. was so profoundly prescient in describing how the work of love would be necessary to have a transformative impact."[6] The work of love she speaks of is compassion in action. The compassion we cultivate toward ourselves increases our frustration tolerance, our discomfort resilience, and therefore allows us to be in just relationships with everyone around us. Let's dive into discomfort resilience and more practices of fierce compassion to support it.

## Frustration Tolerance: Resistance and Courage

Fierce compassion and discomfort resilience nourish and fuel our growth. The more discomfort resilience we have, the more we can do, feel, know, create, and experience authentically without having to numb out or avoid and repress painful experiences.

The example I gave about winning the battle to write instead of zoning out with some television is a good example of how self-compassion helps increase frustration tolerance. Increasing our frustration tolerance leads to the development of discomfort resilience. *Frustration tolerance* is a psychological term that means exactly what it says: How much frustration can you tolerate? Of course, it varies from moment to moment and by situation. Factors such as social oppression, illness, privilege, and belief systems impact our frustration tolerance. For example, some parents can tolerate the frustrations of raising children but they have a lower tolerance for the frustrations that come with trying to advance their career goals. In my practice as a therapist, I had many clients with this struggle. They could spend hours patiently toilet training their children, teaching them to clean up after themselves or behave appropriately in public spaces, but they had a really hard time when I gave them short, time-limited activities to do that were related to their career goals.

I had one single father, Javier, who wanted to start an electronic device repair business, but he just did not feel comfortable promoting himself or his services. He would get frustrated whenever any of the businesses he wanted to partner with as an independent contractor said no to him, and for that reason, he did not reach out to potential business partners often. I told him that being uncomfortable can be a wonderful thing because the more you go past your comfort zone, the bigger your comfort zone gets. But if we never go past our comfort zone, we stay in its relatively narrow borders. When we reiteratively push past what we believe we can do or be and engage our resolve, what we can do or be expands. That repeated pushing is the psychological and emotional exercise that builds our discomfort resilience muscle.

Javier and I agreed that he would set a goal of reaching out to one potential business partner every week. He was already doing about one per month, so we agreed this would be a push. He said that because he knew he had to talk about it every week with me, that reminded him to try. That speaks to the value of an accountability partner.

I encouraged him to reward himself with every rejection. Every time one of the businesses he reached out to declined his offer, he had to do something he enjoyed for at least ten minutes, whether it was singing to his son, playing his favorite song, dancing, or just relaxing with friends. I emphasized how important it was to resist the urge to sink into despair or just lie down if it did not go well. *The point is to reward ourselves for trying, especially when it looks like we have failed.* When we do this, our brain gets the message that the act of trying itself is something rewarding that leads to joy. We automatically get that message when we get the desired outcome from our efforts. But when we don't get the desired outcome, we need extra encouragement to try again. In behavioral therapy, this is called "positive reinforcement." With Javier, it started to work immediately, and he began reaching out to two businesses a week after just a month.

Then to boost it, I added an affirmation related to his aspiration to make more money for his son's future. I asked him what it would be like to bequeath his son a never-give-up spirit. I encouraged him to say to his infant son, "It didn't work out today, but Daddy will never give up" every time things did not go his way. In this way, he affirmed his resolve each time he "lost," and his child became an accountability partner in Javier's developing resilience.

After two months of this, Javier didn't even care about the rejections anymore because he was happy to be able to try and to not be defeated when things didn't work out. He had developed discomfort resilience. Verbally affirming his resolve when speaking to his son became a regular part of his day, deepening his connection to and commitment to his child. He realized, as he put it, "Right now is the future I can give him. His future won't come from the money I can give him as much as the lesson to just keep going and grow stronger, no matter what."

This is an example of how we can use defeat and make it a cause for victory. One of my favorite poems by Kahlil Gibran is an ode to defeat. He says,

Defeat, my Defeat, my solitude and my aloofness;
You are dearer to me than a thousand triumphs,
And sweeter to my heart than all world-glory.[7]

Defeat is sweet when it strengthens our resolve, when we don't allow it to be a signal to give up, when we let it be a path toward the magnificent landscape of our own limitless capacity to keep going, to live as fiercely as we can.

In this poem, Gibran goes on to describe defeat as "my deathless courage," meaning that it is only failure and loss that show us how endlessly brave we can be, because it takes courage to keep trying. For me, the most vivid example of this courage is African heritage people enduring hundreds of years of brutality, failed escapes from and unsuccessful attempts to subvert slavery, and false promises of freedom after years of working to "buy" family members out of slavery. They did all this while maintaining the tenacious will to keep going despite being degraded and having previous and ensuing generations of their families violated for sport, sold, or murdered. From the trafficking of African people beginning in the fifteenth century throughout the Diaspora to the violations tragically happening today, the resilience of Black people throughout the world is indeed deathless courage. It is courage sustained by the resolve to not just endure but to also rejoice in life. That undefeated joy, Black joy, is itself victory.

> The resilience of Black people throughout the world is indeed deathless courage.

## Strong Spirit, Strong Faith, Strong Prayer

Ikeda states, "A strong spirit, strong faith, and strong prayer—developing these is victory and the world of Buddhahood."[8] But how do we make a strong prayer?

As the passages below illustrate, prayer can take many forms. Using your voice as you reflect on these insights can help you embody the insights viscerally. Let the following reflections create a resonance in your physical being.

## Meditations on Prayer

Recite these meditations on prayer from Ikeda and note the ones that resonate with you in your Joy Journal.

> Prayer is the effort to align the gears of our life with the movement of the universe. Our lives that have been passively embraced by the universe now embrace the universe in turn, make the entire universe our ally, and fundamentally redirect our state of life in the direction of happiness.
>
> Prayer is not a feeble consolation; it is a powerful, unyielding conviction. And prayer must become manifest in action. To put it another way, if our prayers are in earnest, they will definitely give rise to action.
>
> Prayers are neither light dreams nor vague wishes. They should be firm pledges of determination. Prayers made with such strong resolve invite clear results just as magnets attract iron.
>
> Prayer is the way to destroy all fear. It is the way to banish sorrow, the way to light a torch of hope. It is the revolution that rewrites the scenario of our destiny.
>
> Prayer is the courage to persevere. It is the struggle to overcome our own weakness and lack of confidence in ourselves. It is the act of impressing in the very depths of our being the conviction that we can change the situation without fail.[9]

## Song as Prayer, Prayer as Song

In the African American Christian tradition, Gospel music reflects strong faith. Gospel music is strong prayer. Songs like "Lord, Hear My Prayer," written by African American choral composer Moses Hogan, express an intimate relationship with the divine. And Black spirituals that were sung by enslaved people, like "I Shall Not Be Moved," became statements of resistance to racism in the American South and gained more popularity during the union and civil rights movements of the 1960s. Many Gospel songs reflect Black people's inviolable connection to nature, which enhances their impact as we hear and sing lyrics such as "Just like a tree planted by the water, I shall not be moved."

Songs like "His Eye Is on the Sparrow" and "Wade in the Water" also reflect this spacious ability to be meaningful across many social and historical contexts. These songs resonate with people of every ethnicity all over the world because they are a bequeathment of fierce compassion and discomfort resilience from Black American founding mothers and fathers, the enslaved who built the nation under conditions of inconceivable torture. The songs thereby forever educate humanity on how to sing amidst suffering, how to both cultivate and express self-transcendence, so it resounds throughout all time.

Many Hip-Hop songs both reflect and call forth our strong spirit as well, especially the spirit to defeat economic oppression, racism, and sexism. Hip-Hop has an extraordinary precision that is unmatched in any genre because it reflects the breviloquent insights of Black dialect. Consider songs like "Keep Ya Head Up" by Tupac Shakur and calls to collective empowerment like Queen Latifah's "U.N.I.T.Y." These songs also call us to resist internalized oppression. 'Pac sings to women who may devalue themselves based on disparagement from men and from sexism in general. For me, that entire song is, as Beyonce put it, "a whole mood"—meaning it depicts a state of mind I aspire to. First of all, 'Pac opens the song in connection, dedicating it to his godson and a little girl named Corin. Then he draws ancestral wisdom into the song with a Black aphorism—"The Blacker the berry the sweeter the juice"—to further affirm the richness of Blackness.

Throughout that song 'Pac allies women in multiple ways. In this masterpiece, he accomplishes all of the following with his lyrics: he makes a prophecy about how generations of youth will come to be misogynist if we don't change; he affirms the spiritual power of R & B (which also comes through in the Five Stairsteps song he samples); he expresses how he found peace despite the struggles of poverty; he discusses his youthful indiscretions; he protests against war and exploitative capitalism; he grieves his mother's substance abuse; he celebrates his mother's love and selfless dedication to him (yup, he is able to see and say that selflessness can exist right alongside the self-absorption of addiction); he shares his youthful dreams of being an artist; he cites Black economic resourcefulness and the challenges of making money legitimately as a Black youth; he expresses hopelessness against racism's magnetic pulling of Black people into the criminal legal system; he grieves his lost friends; he calls forth his own manhood to resist giving up; he offers metaphors about water; he encourages single mothers; he affirms his love for his own son and the importance of letting children know we love them; he reflects on the future for youth; and finally he returns to the directive to keep our heads up.

Only music can offer this kind of comprehensive encouragement in a form that makes our bodies as well as our hearts and minds thrum vibrantly.

Let's Practice!

## Your Call-to-Action Playlist

What is your song of bravery in the face of defeat? What is your song of resolve? List two of them and add them to your Joybox now so that when you need them, you can come back to them easily. Take a moment to identify what exactly the songs do for you, breaking them down just like I did with Tupac's song. This is a way of raising your awareness about the precise ways the songs encourage you, as well as developing insight into where you need continued encouragement. You can also name songs that call you to be an ally against some type of oppression or injustice, songs that affirm the worth of women, Black people, Latinx people, Indigenous people, LGBTQIA+ people, and so forth.

I was eight years old in 1973 when the song "Living for the City" by Stevie Wonder hit the airwaves. Let me tell you about what that song taught me. I remember hearing the compelling yet foreboding gravitas of the opening chords as they drew me to sit next to my mother in her room as she sat pensive, listening. Stevie's strong, insistent, indignant voice narrated the lack of opportunities and racist law enforcement encountered by so many Black people.

I didn't know then exactly what the chorus and title meant. I know *now* that Black bodies and minds and Black labor were and have always been used in America to sustain the cities and counties and indeed the country as a whole. I know that all over America and indeed the world, many Black people are living just enough to sustain the cities for privileged global minority people to live in comfort while Black people live on the fringes and are often compensated minimally, just enough to sustain their Black bodies and minds to work for the cities.

I understood this viscerally even as an eight-year-old. My mother did not scrub floors, but my grandaunt had done so for decades. I had read Ralph Ellison and Maya Angelou by this time, so I knew about the exploitation of Black labor. I had read *Incidents in the Life of a Slave Girl* by Harriet Jacobs, and I knew that as long as Black people have been in America, they have been exploited. I knew it was why we were brought to America.

Stevie Wonder calls out the racism that is often unnamed, the racism that is as ubiquitous as pollution, filling the space that opportunities should take and smothering the hopes of Black people. I saw the effects of this on the faces of loved ones struggling with addiction and on the faces of strangers, familiar in the desperation that I could not help but recognize.

At one point in "Living for the City," the beat changes with an ascent into the handclapping chorus where there is both uplifting Gospel music and a sorrowful wailing march to the jail cell—to the grave—singing and clapping hands as you face it. Then the vignette in the song begins and I can see the young man, the boy, described as looking with awe at New York City. That awe resonated with me because I could glimpse the Twin Towers in the far distance from my childhood bedroom. I knew how it felt to admire power and wealth even as it overshadowed us: power and wealth that towers over us, power and wealth built on us and of us, yet inaccessible to us. Then there's an ominous keyboard strum that prefaces the dialogue portion of the song. The words describe a young man being tricked into carrying something illegal. The stench of manipulation wafts in on the airwaves; the predatory is present.

I see the innocent, childlike mistake described in the song's vignette. He was a child, like me—a human trying to see the new and be in it wholeheartedly; honest, manipulated, exploited, and then suspected and prejudged. Harshly. He is sentenced to ten years in a court of injustice, shoved into a cell with one of the countless epithets he is to endure.

I know his fate is sealed as that cell door is heard slamming shut, closing out hope, shutting out all light.

Then Stevie Wonder returns, having transcended time to tell us of that young man's later life. Stevie presciently describes "the new Jim Crow" that was to mark the coming millennium just as the old Jim Crow scarred the twentieth century. In the last verse of the song, we learn that the man's body is now deeply wounded, he is likely unhoused, and there is no social or political protection for him. Stevie Wonder closes the song imploring us to face the sorrow he evokes and to act to create a more just and compassionate world. He reminds us that we face extinction if we do not.

As Stevie and the chorus sing, I can indeed feel the sorrow. When I was eight, that meant running to the bathroom where I sobbed uncontrollably as the chorus sang "da da da da da da da" in a way that is anything but light—in a way I had never heard it sung before.

When I emerged from the bathroom crying, I saw my mother smiling ever so slightly at me in a manner that was so kind and free of mocking that I ran to her. I asked her if this was real. If this really happened to a man. She said it happens to many men—many, many Black men. I asked why don't we do something about it? She said we are doing something. We are learning, she said. I insisted on something more concrete as a solution.

Memory does not allow me to recall what she offered in concrete terms at that moment. I know she comforted me without sugarcoating the brutal realities of racism. I know she said we had to work for justice, like the song exhorts, to be motivated to make a better tomorrow. I know she steered me to reading Frantz Fanon, Paulo Freire. I know that day led me to James

Baldwin. I know that from that day, I came to revere Stevie Wonder. I studied his music, came to know all his songs by heart, and allowed myself to be moved to and through the full gamut of human experience that his music expresses. Witnessing that song with my mother was an experience that built my discomfort resilience.

Play one of the call-to-action songs you picked a couple of pages ago to prepare yourself for this next part. Let your body sway or move in whatever way feels good. Dance with your resilient compassion!

## Discomfort Resilience

Next, we will learn about how to release delusions that weaken us and learn to build discomfort resilience to help us play and work together as allies. Attending to our right view by awakening to our interdependence, we can think of building resilient, fierce compassion as a way of cultivating what Dr. King referred to as "beloved community."

Developing the right view to engage in right speech and right action requires consciousness-raising. This is much of the work I do with individuals, families, and organizations. In particular, I help educators, mental health therapists, and social justice groups think about how they can have the most enlightened perspective reflected in their work and in all other aspects of their lives.

Everyone can benefit from Buddhist insights. You don't have to be Buddhist to do a mindful breathing practice or to learn about interdependence. Also, we can all learn from varied types of embodied practices such as dance, music, and art to help us pause, notice, and shift any oppressive, limiting psychological and behavioral patterns that impact our social institutional dynamics. I really see that pause as the ground, a creative space for us to self-actualize and grow, especially around emotionally and cognitively difficult areas like racism and other forms of bias and marginalization.

Have you ever had a moment when you're not sure whether something you are about to say is offensive or not? Try saying nothing! Just take a beat—a moment of silence for justice, if you will—to consider the most anti-racist, inclusive way of phrasing what you want to communicate. There is so much you can do in that thirty-to-sixty-second pause. You can ask yourself what your intention is and if it is an intention you respect. You can ask yourself if and why you have the right to impose a given question or comment as a means to achieve that intention. Finally, you can phrase the question or comment in a just, compassionate way. For example, you could ask, "May I ask?" so as not to presume you have a right to ask.

Cognitive distortions are irrational or exaggerated thought patterns that compromise our well-being. Becoming expert practitioners of pause allows us to create a little space between our cognitive distortions and any inappropriate statements or problematic behavior we might enact based on that distorted view. Pausing also makes space between cognitive distortions and their emotional effect—the feelings these thoughts might arouse. For example, believing that only written work is valuable might make us think that we are less smart if we prefer verbal communication over writing. Meditative practices increase our self-awareness and thus enhance our capacity for resilient, compassionate interpersonal engagement.

## Releasing the Cognitive Distortions of White Supremacy Culture

Activist and writer Tema Okun talks about the characteristics of white supremacy culture as the underlying ideas that compromise our capacity to have inclusive lives, institutions, and societies.[10] The work of becoming joyfully just is in large part about raising our awareness, bringing to consciousness the white supremacy–based cognitive distortions that cloud our most enlightened perspective. Our contemplative practices are a great resource to help us pause and reflect on the distortions that block our path to joy and justice. We can practice releasing them as we build discomfort resilience and fierce compassion.

Another way to think of these characteristics is as delusions, because they lead to befuddlement and unhappiness rather than clarity and joy. The goal of Buddhism and all meditative practices is to perceive reality more clearly. All the characteristics of white supremacy culture reflect illusions. Put another way, in cognitive therapy, problematic thoughts are known to be the cause of negative affect as well as dysfunctional behavior. That means that when we think in distorted ways, we feel and act unwell. Cognitive approaches to understanding mental health and behavioral health illustrate that we all have thought patterns that make up our cognitive schema. Our cognitive schema often reflects beliefs and expectations we have absorbed from a culture of white supremacy.

> Since we've all developed in the context of white supremacy, we've all internalized its ideas and strongly held beliefs.

White supremacy is ubiquitous. It's in science, education, health care, mental health care—it even gets into meditation communities. It's part of the legacy of colonization, enslavement, and subjugation of Black, Latinx, Indigenous, and Asian people. One important thing to remember about white supremacy culture is that it is no longer only perpetuated by white people! Since we've all developed in the context of white supremacy, we've all internalized its ideas and strongly held beliefs.

This means we all get to do the work of examining how white supremacy has created cognitive distortions for us. Okun very insightfully pinpoints some ways white supremacy culture presents in our lives, families, social contexts, schools, and organizations. These characteristics also have a negative impact on our interior lives. Okun says that the intention of thinking about these characteristics is not to be prescriptive or to assert that these are the only ways white supremacy shows up. The point is to get some handle on what we are all immersed in—what she describes as "the water in which we're all swimming"—so that we can work collaboratively to build and sustain a more just global community.[11] She invites us to use this list to understand our own conditioning and to use it collaboratively and collectively to guide our vision for the liberatory culture we want to build.

Now we'll explore these characteristics with some practices to help us remove them from our ways of being.

Let's dive in!

## Right to Comfort

Of course, if we want to develop discomfort resilience, the first characteristic of white supremacy we may want to explore is the *right to comfort*. We suffer unnecessarily when we cling to expectations of comfort, and we lose control of our lives when we assign responsibility for our feelings of discomfort to others. A "Why me?" approach to suffering is what we often see when this attitude is present.

Also, when we're faced with the possibility that we may have caused harm, our internalized right to comfort can make it very difficult to be accountable for our actions. For example, when accused of racism, global minority (a.k.a. white) folks may immediately seek to deflect the shame they feel about what they said or did rather than pausing to listen and learn from what occurred.

You may have heard global minority people say that they don't want to learn about racism or explore critical race theory because it makes them uncomfortable. That is an example of how white privilege makes white-racialized people feel they have an unreasonable right to comfort. Of course, Black and other global majority people, including children, *have* to learn about and deal with racism because we face it incessantly, so there is no such avoiding it for us. People with dominating identities like whiteness, maleness, Christian, straight, and the like are socialized to see their needs as primary, to expect deference to their "default status." When they are not the default, demands for the comforts associated with their privileged status often ensue.

All people can benefit from examining how we cling to comfort in ways that limit us. Clinging to comfort makes us fragile physically, emotionally, relationally, and spiritually. Joyfully just goals move us out of our comfort zone. What's great about that is that the more we step out of our comfort zone, the bigger it becomes, thus helping us experience more freedom. Kahlil Gibran beautifully describes how clinging to comfort and needing to be comfortable all the time is so compromising to our ability to be in touch with our own senses, to be awake. He describes how clinging to comfort steals joy:

> Or have you only comfort, and the lust for comfort, that stealthy thing that enters the house a guest, and then becomes a host, and then a master?
>
> Ay, and it becomes a tamer, and with hook and scourge makes puppets of your larger desires.
>
> Though its hands are silken, its heart is of iron.
>
> It lulls you to sleep only to stand by your bed and jeer at the dignity of the flesh.
>
> It makes mock of your sound senses, and lays them in thistledown like fragile vessels.
>
> Verily the lust for comfort murders the passion of the soul, and then walks grinning in the funeral.[12]

Let's Practice!

## The Fierce Compassion of Letting Go

Take a moment to note one way you could reclaim your joy by letting go of an unnecessary comfort as an act of fierce compassion to yourself. Maybe it's cutting down on how much you spend on fancy coffee or desserts and using that money to fund your dream/action plan. Maybe it's making a commitment to spend only twenty minutes of your free time on social media and using the time you get back for your dream planning. If you are reading this with your joy squad, text each other fierce-compassion goals so you can support each other in reclaiming the joy of releasing small or large comforts that consume your dream-planning time, energy, or other resources.

**Defensiveness.** *Defensiveness* can manifest as spending energy trying to protect a given position or maintain power over other people. We often see this when people exhibit white fragility or other types of cultural fragility. Robin DiAngelo describes *white fragility* as a type of developmental immaturity many global minority (a.k.a. white) people may get stuck in. An article looking at this phenomenon in medicine helps us understand the term, its relationship to defensiveness and the right to comfort, and how to distinguish it from related concepts:

> White fragility refers to feelings of discomfort a white person experiences when they witness discussions around racial inequality and injustice. For example, people of color may find it difficult to speak to white people about white privilege and superiority. The white person may become defensive, and the person of color may feel obligated to comfort the white person because we live in a white-dominated environment. White fragility differs from both white privilege and white supremacy. White privilege refers to the fact that white people have advantages in society that others do not. White supremacy is the belief that people with white skin are superior.[13]

We can work on our own defensiveness when we understand that defensiveness often comes from fear. We see this often when people want to avoid the uncomfortable feelings they have regarding factual information about the history of racism and colonialism. Our feelings are responses to facts, not necessarily facts themselves. Defensiveness deludes us into thinking we know the facts when often we only know how we feel about the facts.

We see defensiveness in fear-driven campaigns to protect power and property while denying the realities of racism. We see it when we fail to face ourselves and acknowledge, "Yes, that was racist, what I just said. Okay, let me learn from it and do better." We can be relaxed with ourselves about how we embody white supremacy and become resiliently, fiercely compassionate with ourselves. Admitting that you did something racist, sexist, homophobic, or ageist is not a condemnation of your being. It's an indication of your self-awareness that you're a work in progress. It's an indication of cultural humility, which itself reflects wisdom.

When we say something ageist, or we misgender someone and someone corrects us, we could take the lesson as a generous and fiercely compassionate offering instead of getting defensive. However, we cannot perceive the generosity of the correction when caught up in the fear, and then we can't arouse gratitude for the guidance we just received about how to be more inclusive.

> Admitting that you did something racist, sexist, homophobic, or ageist is not a condemnation of your being. It's an indication of your self-awareness.

**Power Hoarding and Fear of Open Conflict.** *Power hoarding* is another characteristic of white supremacy that reflects what Buddhism refers to as one of the three poisons: greed. The other two poisons—anger and foolishness—usually team up with our greed. Power hoarding reflects the delusion of scarcity. Dr. Toni Morrison speaks to this in her novel *A Mercy* when she describes how colonizers destroyed the natural environment of the United States with a single word—*mine*.[14]

Power hoarding often results from cognitive distortions related to the myth of scarcity, a belief that there is not enough to go around despite evidence of plenty. Power hoarding is often driven by our fear of losing control or comfort. Racism is very much based on this delusion of scarcity. We see this manifesting when global minority folks in the US express fears of immigrants taking "their" jobs.

Power hoarding manifests in many things we do. For example, when we collaborate on a project or when we're sharing a stage with other performers and have a tug-of-war about whose name goes first. Whenever the urge to hoard power comes up, we can choose to be honest with one another and say, "Oh, I'm feeling that tug of power hoarding and want my name to be first" instead of being so undercover about it. We can choose to face these feelings together instead of being ashamed about them and fearful of getting into conflicts. Conflict can be faced and handled in healthy ways. We don't have to be so confused or intimidated by the pull to hoard power that we can't have candid conversations about it.

---

Let's Practice!

## Power Sharing and Candid Conversations

Can you think of someone you need to have a power-sharing conversation with? Let's do a little psychodrama where you create a bit of dialogue, speaking first to yourself and to any feelings of greed or power hoarding as if those feelings were a person inside you that you want to help. Gently explore with yourself what your needs and issues related to power are.

Next you can role-play by practicing what you might want to say when you speak to the person who you want to practice sharing power with.

If we allow ourselves to notice tendencies to power hoard and explore them with courage, we can excise them from our minds and work openly with them in our relationships. We can figure things out together, building one another's resilient compassion. We can open to authenticity. And it works both ways, because being fearful about power hoarding can also make us give up power, resources, rights, or opportunities we genuinely need or have earned. Candid conversations like these with ourselves and others directly address our fears of open conflict and result in much more internal and relational freedom.

---

**Sense of Urgency.** The idea that "faster is better" and the urge to rush through complex or challenging processes can lead to catastrophizing and seeing danger where there is no immediate threat. An overdeveloped *sense of urgency* can also lead to overgeneralizations, which are another type of cognitive distortion. Our meditative practices slow us down so that we can think, feel, and sense into the situations at hand with insightful response-ability. As the philosopher and activist Dr. Bayo Akomolafe states, "'Hurrying up' all the time, we often lose sight of the abundance of resources that might help us meet today's most challenging crises. We rush through into the same patterns we are used to."[15]

An overdeveloped sense of urgency creates an enduring belief about the scarcity of time. If you have ever heard Black people use the expression "CP time" (colored people's time), that actually refers to a wise relationship with time wherein you attend to the needs of the moment more than the demand to be at any given place "on time." For example, if an important meeting is about to start, it makes sense to go to the bathroom even if it means you will be a little late to the meeting. When we live with an overdeveloped sense of urgency, we don't take time to care for ourselves well.

Urgency creates cognitive distortions that lead to poorly informed snap judgments. Oftentimes our difficulty being inclusive and our inability to get rid of bias occur because we're in such a rush. We just want to "get it done." I've worked as a consultant with researchers on projects where urgency was a real barrier to inclusivity. Together we were able to battle the urgency and slow down enough to notice the racism or trans-exclusion in the research design or in other aspects of the work. I invited them to dialogue with diverse stakeholders and experts from different ethnicities and backgrounds, especially people from the populations they were going to study. Makes sense, right? Let those whose lives the research is supposed to inform have an impact on your work before, during, and after the research.

Pausing to look for racism, bias, and lack of inclusivity can make us think, "Aw, man, this is going to take so much time!" We can work with that thought, though, almost like it's a recalcitrant young person inside us, and coach that inner child toward having the most inclusive experience we all deserve. Yes, it'll slow things down a little bit, but do you want it to be good and meaningful, or are you married to some arbitrary notion of time and urgency?

It's not that trying to do our best in a given timeframe is not useful. Paying attention to the needs of the moment is useful. Urgency becomes problematic when it is an inflated guiding principle that impacts how we feel about ourselves and others and how we do most things. Unbeknownst to us because it is so unconscious, these cognitive distortions impact and impair our capacity to think and act inclusively and to address racism and other types of oppression.

**Individualism.** Although we do walk through life as individuals, Western society has gone so far with a focus on *individualism* that we sometimes forget we are part of a collective human species and part of the ecosystem of the natural world around us. Over emphasis on individualism is a cognitive distortion that can lead to overwhelming feelings of isolation and loneliness. It's like having tunnel vision, perceiving ourselves as being alone even as we are surrounded by support.

Some of the most painful feelings of loneliness emerge from this distortion. Loneliness is valuable in some ways and fundamental to our being. Yet some of our exacerbated sense of loneliness comes from our marriage to a notion of individualism that disconnects us from our actual interdependent experience of life. The cognitive distortion of *personalization* can also come from this, because when we don't recognize the universality of suffering, we think, *I'm the only one who goes through such difficulties.* That belief could make us angry or depressed or drive us to addiction.

**Perfectionism and One Right Way.** Another characteristic of white supremacy that many of us internalize is *perfectionism*: the belief that there is some preset (nonculturally inclusive) notion of perfection that we must aspire to. Under the spell of perfectionism we become endlessly focused on how some aspect of our person (or someone else's) or our work (or someone else's) is inadequate and not meeting some unattainable standard.

Instead of hewing to that unreal standard, we can be fiercely compassionate and expect ourselves and everyone else to make mistakes. Those mistakes are part of the process of learning, right? Then we can all just relax the perfectionism and delight in any effort we make to manifest our greatest self. Dr. Toni Morrison talks about the "white gaze" in her documentary *The Pieces I Am* where she uses the metaphor of having a little white man on her shoulder, always saying something like, "That's not right, it doesn't reflect the colonialists' and enslavers' view, or it's not perfect according to some Eurocentric standard!"[16]

Perfectionism limits our capacity to be with, enjoy, learn from, and have gratitude for what *is*, because we get stuck on some idealized notion of what should be. Perfectionism can also lead to a lot of "should" statements where we are never happy or satisfied because we are "shoulding" on ourselves all the time! Can you think of one thing you would like to stop "shoulding on yourself" about? Take a moment and jot down one thing you could stop chastising yourself about.

Freedom from this aspect of white supremacy—the illusion of perfection—means that we get to just *be* and thereby be just to ourselves. We get to be authentic humans—who we are—and not pretend that we know it all. Because pretending that we know it all is another characteristic of white supremacy culture: the illusion of "one right way." My mother used to say "All roads lead to Cairo" to indicate that there are any number of ways to approach something; many elegant solutions to every problem.

**Paternalism.** *Paternalism*, another characteristic of white supremacy, can operate in a lot of ways. One such way is the *white savior complex*. The white savior complex is the belief that PGM are one-way beneficiaries of the largesse of those with white privilege. White racialized people may believe themselves to be charitable philanthropists saving global majority folx despite the fact that their privilege and wealth is inextricably linked to the legacies of colonialism and slavery. Any resources that privileged people, organizations, or countries share with communities that have been exploited is not charity or philanthropy, it's reparations. Also, "white saviors" and other privileged folks who see themselves as saving others often don't even think to ask marginalized folks what is needed. They just decide for marginalized people, which, whether done intentionally or not, further usurps power.

We see paternalism happening in relationships between people who are racialized as white and people who are Black, Latinx, Indigenous, and Asian. We also see it happening in older people's condescending relationships with younger people. Paternalism is how adultism or young people's oppression is often enacted. It's one-way teaching and one-way learning. There's no appreciation of the reciprocity of learning that happens in all interactions. Such limited thinking is an illusion that separates us from our own enlightened mind and from one another.

**Objectivity.** *Objectivity* is the erroneous belief that our emotions are not to be trusted, that emotional thinking and actions should be disregarded, and that we are "neutral" when we think logically. The myth of objectivity can lead to many cognitive distortions, including global labeling and oversimplifications. We see the myth of objectivity in science with the notion that unbiased and comprehensive knowledge is always obtainable and obtained rather than acknowledging that our preconceptions and expectations actually limit our gathering and comprehension of knowledge. Although having an objective viewpoint may be ideal in certain circumstances, it is important that we not be deluded into thinking we have gotten rid of all biases without having done any work to do so.

**Progress Is Always Best.** *Progress is always best* relates to the cognitive distortion of magnification and minimization: exaggerating or diminishing the importance of events or activities. If we have this cognitive distortion, we might believe our qualitative achievements are unimportant or that our mistakes are excessively important. We might value people who have more money, education, social media followers, and so forth.

The idea that progress related to industrial and technical advances is best for all is an aspect of white supremacy that has led to the destruction of our natural environment. This can also make us feel thoroughly unsatisfied because the "progress is best" belief prevents us from seeing the sufficiency and abundance of what we already have. When we constantly strive for more, and bigger—as opposed to thinking of progress from a qualitative perspective—we count our blessings in quantity instead of quality. Many of the current technological advances—from interactive social media platforms to artificial intelligence—also reflect how innovations that look like progress can have ethical implications that when unaddressed actually threaten our growth and collective well-being.

**Either/Or Thinking.** Also called black-and-white thinking, *either/or thinking* is a particularly limiting cognitive distortion. When we don't see nuance and the multifaceted nature of everything, that's a delusion. Take, for example, the belief that we are either racist or not racist. The truth is that most of us are on a developmental trajectory between being racist and being anti-racist. Some of our actions, ways of being, and behaviors simply reflect racism.

Avoidance is an example of how either/or thinking can affect our behavior. You might decide to avoid certain places where you feel your white fragility, or other kinds of cultural fragility, and that avoidance is a defensive response. You might avoid hanging out with people who have disabilities, people who are younger than you, queer people, or people who have significantly less money than you. It doesn't necessarily mean you're ableist, adultist, heterosexist, or elitist when you do that, but the avoidance certainly warrants candid reflection for your own insight and growth. You don't want cultural fragility to shape your relationships with diverse people forever. Instead of being hard on yourself or staying within the borders of your fragility, you can see yourself as someone on a joyfully just developmental trajectory and set goals to grow. The Buddha's teaching of the Middle Way—taking perspectives that avoid extremes, such as a moderate spiritual path between asceticism and hedonism— offers a model for subverting either/or thinking.

> The truth is that most of us are on a developmental trajectory between being racist and being anti-racist.

**Worship of the Written Word.** White supremacy has deprived us of a lot of wisdom with the oppressive notion that the most important ideas are written down somewhere. Worship of the written word erases the wisdom of embodied learning and leadership practices. It also erases oral traditions of wisdom transmission such as Black dialect, storytelling, and songs.

*Worship of the written word* refers to the ways that we devalue people's expressed stories, the richly varied narratives they either communicate orally or in other unwritten ways that are part of the profound wisdom of living beings. For some scholars, this manifests as the failure to value anything that's not in a peer-reviewed journal or published anywhere.

I have often shared an idea that someone found insightful, and they asked, "Is that published anywhere?" And I have often said, "No, but I just said it and you can cite me." We can actually begin valuing the oral traditions and citing them as sources that enrich our lives.

Speaking of citing, Black women tend to be the least cited knowledge or wisdom sources in every field; the least cited leaders or spokespersons. People tend to absorb and use what Black women say, but they rarely cite us. So, if someone of the global minority (like our white-racialized mindfulness teacher, for example) says something impactful, folks might write it down and cite that person—especially if they are famous (which global minority mindfulness leaders often get to be because of racism and white supremacy culture within mindfulness communities). But if someone hears a Black mindfulness teacher speak words that resonate, they are more likely to just write down what was said but not the name of the speaker. I have had so many people tell me they were so inspired by something I said that they put it on their website or in their book or elsewise marketed it to make money, but they never cited me—much less offered me any of the profits. This is a form of extractive exploitation of global majority thinkers called *citational injustice*. It's indicative of how common it is for people to absorb what Black people say, as is the case with copying Black dialect and phrases, without a thought given to acknowledging the source. We are trained to do this unconsciously via the power-hoarding nature of white supremacy. Yet if we bring it to consciousness, we can be more self-aware and less exploitative in our speech and behavior.

I wrote about this topic in an article for *The Arrow*, citing Rev. angel Kyodo williams:

> At the Embodied Social Justice Summit, Rev. angel Kyodo williams invited participants to "practice the magic of attribution" by naming the people whose words, thinking, or being enriches us. As I continue to practice with that teaching, I see that it really is magic

because when we honor those people, especially Black people we have learned from—when we say their names as we give our talks and write our articles—the magic of Black wisdom proliferates. *Cite Black Women*, the campaign focused on recognizing the contributions to knowledge Black women make to all fields, is one example of an effort to practice this magic.[17]

The campaign and hashtag #citeblackwomen are calling for citational justice. And because so much of what Black women and other global majority folks offer is shared orally, it's devalued or co-opted without attribution. If it's not copyright protected, we may think we don't have to even mention who we learned that from. And that compromises everyone's capacity to be awake to the contributions of Black women, thus entrenching the unique type of bias Black women experience known as "misogynoir." *Misogynoir* is a term coined by Black scholar Moya Bailey that articulates how anti-Blackness and misogyny shape how Black women are viewed and spoken of or to—or not spoken of or to—in ways that are harmful or degrading.

So, one of the ways we can step out of that overvaluing of the written word is to really be inclusive regarding whose thinking we value and cite. We can learn to respect and prize diverse ways of thinking, and to value the diverse ways knowledge and wisdom transmissions are shared, be that via Black dialect, Black music, or dance. Just because you heard it in a talk doesn't mean it doesn't deserve as much citation, honor, and valuing as something you read in a copyrighted article. The *one-right-way* characteristic of white supremacy culture mentioned above reinforces the overvaluation of the written word. In fact, all the characteristics of white supremacy culture are mutually reinforcing!

The characteristics of white supremacy can also impact how we do social justice work as well as how we conduct our meditative practices. Sometimes these distortions can cause those of us who are working toward justice and those of us who engage in contemplative practice to get very self-righteous. That's why it's wonderful to be able to notice these deluded ways of thinking in ourselves and say, *Hey, you know, there's that "one-right-way" characteristic showing up in my meditation practice or in my LGBTQIA+ rights advocacy. Let me use my meditative practice to turn toward myself and explore which characteristics of white supremacy create cognitive distortions that constrict my well-being and my efforts.*

---

Let's Practice!

## A Powerful Pause

Let's pause and center ourselves in silence for a moment and just take a few deep breaths. As you do so, see if there's a question floating through you or a thought about what has been said about white supremacy culture, and note that in your Joy Journal. We're going to have some time to reflect on the characteristics that are feeling alive for you—the ones that you see operating in the world and the ones you see manifesting in your life that you'd like to get some help with.

---

Stepping out of the rigidities of white supremacy affords us so much ease, so much inner peace and joy in our moment-to-moment existence. We'll get our footing back more readily this way after big and little stumbles. It's much better to be gentle with ourselves in the process of becoming inclusive rather than calling ourselves clumsy when we stumble. Instead of labeling ourselves a klutz, we can just say to ourselves, "Oops, come on, sweetie, watch what you're saying and where you're going." We can talk to ourselves in loving ways as we extract these characteristics of white supremacy from our ways of thinking and being.

---

Let's Practice!

## Releasing Cognitive Distortions

I'd like to create space now for you to reflect a little more on how these characteristics of white supremacy culture have landed or resonate with

you. Did one stick out to you? Was there one you jotted down as something you might invite your spirit, heart, mind or body to release? If so,
let's practice releasing it now.

I suggest trying this as a music practice. What is a song that helps
you think of letting things go? Maybe something with a floating feeling to it? As you reflect on the characteristics of white supremacy you'd
like to release from your mind and life, play a little bit of letting go
music. In written reflection, explore what stands out as an illusion or
cognitive-distortion contaminant of your heart, mind, or relationships.
What are the ways white supremacy might have polluted your most
enlightened view of your most expansive self? How does it impact your
view of your partner, your family, your work, and your world? Just free
associate. If you want a prompt, try this:

> One characteristic of white supremacy I may have internalized
> is _____. I can see it operating when_____.
> I could release it by _____.

Symbolically release the characteristic by writing it down on a small
piece of paper, tearing it up, and then recycling the paper. Let that paper
generate something new.

To conclude the practice, take a break and go outside. Breathe the
fresh air, exhaling everything that you want to release, so that nature can
help your heart and mind let it go!

---

Let's Practice!

## Our Identities

To deepen self-awareness and joy, it is good to know ourselves in the
fullness of our identities. We each have multiple aspects of identity, and
each aspect is itself an identity (for example, I am Black, I am female, I
am college educated). It is also helpful to be concretely aware of the privilege and oppression that shapes and is reflected in our lives. For example,
I experience racist and homophobic oppression, but I have privilege

# PRIVILEGE

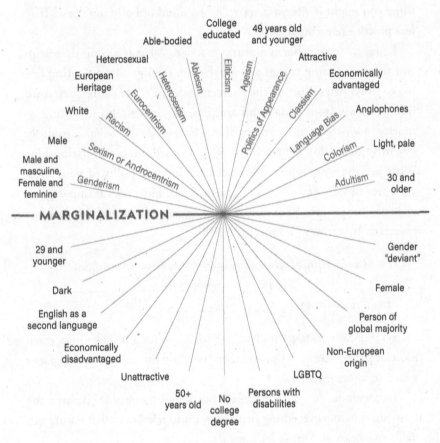

College educated
49 years old and younger
Able-bodied
Heterosexual
Attractive
European Heritage
Economically advantaged
White
Anglophones
Male
Light, pale
Male and masculine, Female and feminine
30 and older

Ableism
Elitism
Ageism
Heterosexism
Politics of Appearance
Eurocentrism
Classism
Racism
Language Bias
Sexism or Androcentrism
Colorism
Genderism
Adultism

## MARGINALIZATION

29 and younger
Gender "deviant"
Dark
Female
English as a second language
Person of global majority
Economically disadvantaged
Non-European origin
Unattractive
LGBTQ
50+ years old
No college degree
Persons with disabilities

## OPPRESSION

associated with being an English-speaking citizen of a dominant country. Let's practice mapping our intersecting identities with the identity and privilege map above. One of the exercises I do when leading workshops is to have folx work with identity, privilege, and oppression maps like this. Although these are best explored via discussion, you can try it out just to see your various privilege and oppression indicators. To use it, mark the areas on the map that correspond to aspects of your identities (you can snap a photo of the map and annotate it on your phone, redraw it in your Joy Journal, or write directly on this page). Feel free to fill in other identities, types of oppression, and privilege you experience that are not on this map.[18]

Now that we have some cartography of our own experience, let's hunt for racism in our lives so we can release it. It is impossible not to have absorbed racism. Perhaps play some music that puts you in the mood for adventure; something that gives you courage. Practice journaling with each of these prompts with a light and firm spirit of fierce compassion, making notes in your Joy Journal so you can let go of any ways racism is compromising your life. If you are a global majority person, use the first set of queries. If you are global minority, use the second. In your Joy Journal, take the time to note your answers as well as the feelings and thoughts you have about the questions.

## Getting to Know My Internalized Racism (for Global Majority People)

Discomfort resilience for addressing my internalized racism:

- *Do I have an expectation that other people of my ethnicity will think and act as I do? Am I ashamed or uncomfortable when they don't?*

- *Do I take care of global minority (a.k.a. white) people's feelings because that is an ingrained pattern? Is it sometimes hard to know when it is safe enough to tell them they are being racist or wrong on anything?*

- *Do I doubt my thinking around global minority people and often not speak up for fear I am not good enough or not three times as good?*

- *Do I think less of other global majority people (i.e., as an Asian person I have internalized racial messages about Asians, Indigenous people, Latinx people, or Black people)?*

- *How else would I describe my internalized racism? What does it look, sound, and feel like?*

### Getting to Know My Racism (for Global Minority People)

Discomfort resilience for addressing my racism:

- *Does my racism show up as a change in my demeanor around global majority folks?*

- *Does it look like relaxing into privilege and ignoring racism until there is an event?*

- *Does it sound like cultural appropriation?*

- *Does it look like performative activism?*

- *Does it look like the avoidance of global majority people?*

- *Does it sound like defensiveness when racism is discussed?*

- *Does it look like my life only consists of global majority folks who never call me on my racism and who soothe me?*

- *What else does my racism look, sound, and feel like?*

Congratulations! You bravely looked at an aspect of your heart and mind that was likely uncomfortable. Reward yourself with a nice walk or stretch as you do an affirmation. Perhaps something like, "Today I am pleased with myself as I bravely and vigorously develop fierce compassion."

———————————

For global majority people to develop healthy resilience, we must make commitments to resting, healing, and joyful living. We can cocreate spaces to grieve our losses together and release our rage and fear. We can continue to have joy as we celebrate what Dr. Toni Morrison calls "the exquisite wins of those forbidden to compete."[19]

All people can build resilient compassion. You can, for example, actively and daily subvert anti-Black racism and violence. Dr. King wisely instructed us when he said that "power without love is reckless and abusive, and love without power is sentimental and anemic. Power at its best is love implementing the demands of justice, and justice at its best is power correcting everything that stands against love."[20] You are reading this book because you have humanitarian love in your heart and mind. The question is whether or not it is the empowered love of which Dr. King speaks or some anemic, sentimental love for humanity that has no agency. Reflect now and continuously, in your solitude and in community, on how to act powerfully to correct any and all injustice against Black people. To do so is an active gratitude practice for all the ways Black wisdom traditions enrich your life. To do so is also an act of powerful love for yourself and for all of humanity.

These practices in building discomfort resilience and fierce compassion have already made you stronger and more just! Go you! And the more you practice with them, the more joy is ahead for you!

# Chapter Three

## Power and Playfulness:
## Mo' Joy and Mojo

This part of the book is about getting our mojo back and experiencing more joy as we do so. *Mojo*, a term drawn from African and African American spirituality, literally means "an embodied spiritual resource."[1] So, it makes sense to use contemplative practices to manifest it.

In this chapter, we do a deep dive to recover our youthful zest! We'll look for where we may have lost our mojo: our curiosity, freedom of expression, joy, and gusto for life. We may have also lost our ability to openly express feelings like sorrow or rage. If you are one of the lucky ones whose energy and joy match or exceed what you had as a child, and who can still cry openly or rage when outrage is felt, that's marvelous. Yet many of us are more repressed, pragmatic, less adventurous versions of our younger selves. We may wonder what happened to us and when. Here is our chance to find out and do something about it!

We'll also explore power and playfulness with the goal of reclaiming embodied freedom and joie de vivre. We will look at the dynamics of our childhoods, our families, our sexuality and relationships, and the ways we pursue pleasure and interact with nature. We'll examine how adultism connects to racism and other forms of oppression and constricts our interpersonal relationships. A key premise of *Joyfully Just* is that facing social oppression is necessary to access joy because oppression is one of our deepest sorrows, and if we don't weep through the sorrow, then we can't have the joy that exists in and beyond that weeping.

## Adultism: The Gateway Oppression

Young people's oppression, also known as *adultism*, is the oppressive use of the power older people have over younger people. It is the intra-personal, interpersonal, and systemic devaluation of the thinking and behavior of young people. By "young people," I am referring to children and adolescents as well as young adults who are often dismissed and devalued for their youthful, unjaded ways of knowing and being. Have you ever heard someone tell a twenty-one-year-old that they are naïve, that they will know better when they are older? That's young people's oppression. Have you ever heard anyone say children should be seen and not heard? That is adultism. Adultism limits youth autonomy and stifles young people's capacity to be in the world as they see and feel it. Adultism demands that youth experience the world from a more "mature" viewpoint. It is evident when we tell young people to "grow up" and see the world as some older people do.

I invite you to explore adultism with me as a gateway oppression. Adultism was the first form of oppression many of us experienced early in our lives. We may have quickly become complicit in our own oppres-sion and that of other youth, telling ourselves or other children to be more mature or to "grow up." Furthermore, the power adults had over us may have made it difficult to resist learning and accepting other oppres-sive ideas we were taught—such as racism or homophobia. Were it not for the unquestioned power adults wield over children and youth, our natural resistance to other types of oppression might have prevailed.

Most of us have experienced adultism and we unwittingly perpetu-ate it. We do this interpersonally in our families, institutionally in our schools, and socially in various contexts. Before you read on, take a moment to reflect on your experiences in the past day or week when you might have behaved in a way that is influenced by adultism. For instance, if you are a guardian or teacher of young persons, did you subtly or overtly praise them for being more "adult" or chastise them for being childlike? The popular phrase "being the adult in the room" plainly elevates the status of adults.

Our exploration of adultism does not deny that most adults have genuine experiential wisdom and effective ways to communicate and be in the world. When I talk about adultism, I am referring to the unchecked power that adults have and exercise in *unexamined* ways *simply* because they are older than the people they are engaging. This can include the power to make micro decisions about younger people's choices (such as when they can go to the bathroom or speak) or macro-level power to pass laws and make economic decisions that can be catastrophic for youth. Legislation inhibiting gun control is an example of this when we consider that it is youth who are often primary targets in perennial school shootings. Adultism has become startlingly evident when we talk about the climate crisis as well. When child climate activists made a case to US Senator Dianne Feinstein to support the Green New Deal, her response was, "I know what I'm doing." The *New York Times* headline (Feb 22, 2019) read, "Dianne Feinstein *Lectures* Children Who Want Green New Deal, Portraying It as Untenable."[2] Classic adultism! And when the Swedish environmental activist Greta Thunberg addressed the United Nations and famously said, "How dare you! How dare you continue to look away and say you are doing enough," she was confronting and refuting the adultism that is pervasive in discussions of the uncomfortable truths about climate change.[3] The extractive worldview and practices of generations of adults have led to the exploitation of the environment, and that has consequences that future generations will have to endure and try to address. That's why Thunberg exclaimed, "How dare you!" Adults made this mess and the young people are going to have to live in it while trying to clean it up.

Noticing our experiences with adultism is valuable because how we were met in our childhood may have set the stage for how we meet the world now—and for how we mete out justice to ourselves and others. The first instance of young people's oppression is often at potty training, when some children are taught that bodily functions are nasty.

Children are often punished for not having more control. More shaming via adultism occurs when self-pleasuring starts. Masturbation, or even exploratory touching of genitals, is often shunned in children. Then along comes sexism, which simultaneously glorifies and objectifies female sexuality while shaming girls and women for having it. Then along comes racism, which projects hypersexuality onto Brown and Black bodies as a means of deflecting the shame global minority people felt and feel about the predatory history and contemporary sexual exploitation of global majority people. The objectification and exotification of Asian, Latinx, Indigenous, and Black women is a prime example of both these oppressive messages intertwining in our perceptions of those around us, our self-perception, and our behavior.

When we use the phrase "good children" or more often "good kids," we are sometimes referring to children who don't say much ("seen and not heard"). Good children don't run wild. Good children don't cry or throw tantrums. Good children suppress sorrow and outrage. Notice the actual value judgment that we assign to youth is based on their silence and stillness at the very time of life when humans are most full of zest, curiosity, energy, and new emotions.

Also, youthful optimism, creativity, and vision for change are often viewed as naïve. This is another aspect of adultism. These are damaging perspectives and behaviors not just because they smash the vitality of the young people in our lives but also because we have internalized them. We might inadvertently smash our own youthful perspectives and attitudes, denigrating enthusiasm in ourselves as childish and immature. The message we may have internalized early in life is that the only worthwhile aspects of ourselves are those that reflect some rigid standard of maturity. Most importantly, it is via young people's oppression that we were and are encouraged to give up fun itself! We may have been told to play less because the quest for fun was deemed immature and childish. Such words imply that what is young and not yet mature—what is childlike—*has less worth.*

In devaluing what is young and playful, we sometimes reenact the period in our own childhoods when our playfulness was cut off, our assertiveness deemed disrespectful, our curiosity called "nosy" and "bothersome," and our joy called "foolish." I invite you to reclaim your youthful insouciance; to romp through life with the vigor of a "terrible" two-year-old, the inquisitiveness of an eight-year-old, the fearlessness of a teenager, the optimism of an eighteen-year-old, and the know-it-all swagger of a twenty-five-year-old. All these aspects of youth reflect valuable insight and embodied ways of being our authentic selves in the world.

> The process of becoming joyfully just involves the reclamation of our beginner's mind: the part of us that is okay with not knowing.

The interior dialogue of self-admonishment we may have learned during childhood because of adultism can continue throughout our lives. It can come out in the ways we talk to ourselves and one another. We might call ourselves silly for being hopeful or playful and limit the joy we allow ourselves to experience. The importance of play is diminished in value for us as adults due to the ideas we carry and perpetuate from internalized adultism. Thus, the process of becoming joyfully just involves the reclamation of our beginner's mind: the part of us that is okay with not knowing, the part of us we valued before we were taught to be ashamed of what we did not know.

Consider the refrain often hurled at young people, "You should be ashamed of yourself!" Most of us heard this at some point or another, and hence, we likely have some shame that is free-floating; it is not anchored in any particular action or inaction but rather shame about our very being. It's often hard for us to be just toward ourselves because of shame. When we make mistakes, shame is right there, shouting, "Give up! This mistake defines you!"

Also, many of us were inculcated with specific messages about the shameful, insufficient nature of a particular aspect of ourselves: our skin, hair, feet, breasts, height, weight, speech, gait, posture, and so forth. All of this we had to endure because adultism is enforced by power: power of size and also the power that comes with controlling all the means of sustenance. We could be denied food, housing, and sleep, or commanded to eat, sleep, or go outside at a whim. Our physical bodies could be beaten in the name of teaching or parenting. We had no means to resist, and when we tried, we may have been hurt more. Sometimes we may have been complicit in oppressing our peers because we internalized adultism and critiqued other young people as being "just kids." We may have projected the violence that was wrought upon us onto those younger or frailer than us and become bullies. Young people's oppression is often a formative part of our life experience and worldview.

"Good" stereotypes or characterizations that were thrust upon us can also be marginalizing. For example, boys are often lauded for being tough as children. This can and does launch boys into lives where they forever value themselves by how "tough" they are. I was often rewarded for being mature as a child and so I strove to be "grown up" all the time. I tried to be quiet and serious and often affected what I thought was a mature posture. Looking back, I can see how that diminished my playfulness. I stopped engaging in behavior described as "silly" or "childish" after the age of twelve. This was my internalized adultism, which I am delighted to shake off more of by writing a book about rejoicing in play!

Let's look further at young people's oppression in two places where it often emerges: home and school.

At home, adultism might have been demonstrated by those on whom we relied for all sustenance in life. Our caregivers may have often unintentionally and unwittingly oppressed us as part of parenting and socializing us to be in a family and in the world. They may have done this because they thought they were keeping us safe and whole. Examining our personal histories of young people's oppression is not meant to blame our elders and teachers. Rather, it is an opportunity to choose what we want to learn and keep from our elders while we honor and recognize the places where *they* could learn from *us* or where our ways of seeing and being in the world simply differ.

In schools, adultism is often administered by teachers on whom youth rely for guidance and affirming evaluations. If we teachers do not reiteratively examine our own adultism, we are likely to perpetuate it. Our oppressive patterns kick in when we don't feel we have the space to pause. Our predominant behavioral patterns are dictated by our sympathetic nervous system: the fight-flight-freeze-or-fawn mode. When we function from this state, our ingrained patterning—in this case, adultism—dictates how we behave toward younger people in our care. Teachers and parents sometimes find themselves reinforcing unexamined tropes that are completely at odds with their own best aspirations for their students or children.

Stressed and overworked, many parents and teachers not only diminish young people's valuation of their ideas but also their valuation of their very being. Shame and humiliation are frequently used in parenting, just as they are often part of the pedagogy some teachers use. This is often truer in under-resourced, disenfranchised schools where young people are policed rather than empowered.

Young people's oppression in schools has enduring impact since school is where we should learn to trust our thinking, decisions, intellect, and sense of social connection. Formal education from kindergarten through grade twelve and beyond may have been the place where we learned to judge and misjudge ourselves and other people; where we learned to oppress and bully based on perceived ethnicity, gender, sexual orientation, and other points of difference. Adultism in schools forced us to accept the racist and sexist content that informs and deforms our understanding of diverse peoples' contributions to the world. Consider how much (or how little) content you were taught about the contributions of Black and other global majority people in elementary school, high school, college, or graduate school. Education is the place where we learn to institutionalize hierarchies because hierarchical designations are thrust upon us and we are forced to reenact them. So, adultism makes racism in education the norm that we must accept and produces people who cannot think inclusively. We then become the conduits through which oppression and/or privilege continue to be enacted in the world.

> For us to become *upstanders*, we have to catch and release the embodied painful experiences that turned us into bystanders.

National data show that Black children are suspended at three times the rate of white children, and that children with disabilities are twice as likely to receive an out-of-school suspension than their nondisabled peers.[4] The words used to describe the misbehavior of white middle-class children are *goofing off, horsing around,* and *being naughty,* while words used to describe global majority children are *aggressive, hostile, threatening,* and so forth.

As children, we understood the importance of integrity; it likely pained us to see adults violate this value through unequal punishment. But because adults had power over us, we might not have resisted or supported our peers, and thus we were socialized into becoming bystanders. If we are white (a.k.a. global minority), then as children we may have seen African American classmates being treated more harshly than our global minority peers, and we didn't understand it. We may have been quiet because we knew something was off but we had little or no power to speak up. This is how we learn to be bystanders.

For us to become *upstanders* we have to catch and release the embodied painful experiences that turned us into bystanders. It takes courage to face our complicity, to love lavishly and forgive the childhood version of ourselves that did the best we could and then aspire to do better now. Social science researcher Brené Brown talks about how "power over" other people "is driven by fear," whereas courageous and innovative people share power and inspire others "to develop power within."[5]

It is through practicing becoming upstanders—in speaking up to affirm our most inclusive intentions—that we begin to develop *power with* other people. As we uncover the past, we see the ways in which we stood up for others, hid from others, betrayed others, or were simply unable to act. If we can witness this within the love and care of mindfulness practice, we can slowly start to let go of our pain, guilt, and shame. As we reclaim our own integrity and sense of justice, our resolve increases and our joy grows.

Let's Practice!

## Updating Our Messages

You may have already worked your way through some messages you were given as a child, such as "Girls can't do math" or "Boys don't cry." If so, try this: If you can remember one person who gave you that oppressive message (society often reinforces these messages, but it helps to have a face to associate with it), bring this person to mind, and as genuinely as you can, offer them understanding *and* a contradiction of the message that you were given. So, the message to a teacher who said girls can't do math might be, "I am a girl, and I can and did do spectacularly well at math." What contradiction would you offer to an adultist message you received? Say it aloud if possible or write it down. Then you can simply rest in the truth of that contradiction.

Or, if you're feeling supported, you might speak to the person who said oppressive things to you, adding something like, "I understand that what you taught me came from ignorance, and I offer you this truth to help you." Or "I understand your messages to me came from a place of care, and I thank you for that, *and* those messages are not right." Many of us have lived either in conformity with or rebellion to the messages we received as children. These reflections allow us to tease out who we want to be, independent of the oppressions we absorbed or were taught via adultism.

Let's Practice!

## Re-Collecting: Fill Your Joybox!

To prepare to jump into excavating adultism from our lives, let's enjoy a short breathing and grounding practice and notice some of the joys of our youth that buoy us.

Take a moment to get comfy and relax. If closing your eyes feels good, do so to turn your gaze inward. If you'd like to keep your eyes open, try looking down at a forty-five-degree angle, not focusing on anything but simply letting your eyes rest gently on the ground. Take three deep, diaphragmatic breaths. We don't usually breathe very well, so let's correct that. As you breathe in, give every single cell of your body the gift of oxygen. As you gently exhale, allow yourself to relax further. Take filling, big-belly breaths. Breathe like a baby breathes. Visualize babies with their round, relaxed bellies just rising and falling—deep inhalation and gentle, long exhalation. There is nothing more to do— just enjoy the oxygen. As you inhale, if your feet are on the ground, feel how your feet support you. Feel how the ground rises up to meet you, exhale gently, feel your feet again, then let go. *Thank you, ground. Thank you, feet!* Our feet work so hard to support us all the time. Breathe deeply again and relax further. Now, as you breathe, check in with your mind. Where is your mind? Simply pay light attention to it. Don't be harsh in any way or force it to do anything. Just simply rest in awareness of your mind.

Once you are settled, bring to mind a fun memory from your childhood: a tree you climbed, the fort you built, some artwork you created, or songs you sang. Experience that memory as fully as you can. If you can, hum one of your childhood or young adulthood songs to yourself. Hang out with it and sing like nobody's listening! Nice!

Now I invite you to remember some loving care you received as a child. Do you remember a particular instance in your life when an adult demonstrated great love and care for you? Try to recall one discrete instance when a parent, grandparent, aunt, uncle, teacher, or stranger showed you kindness, love, or just positive attention. Reinhabit that moment if you can and see how it still lives in you. What was the day like? Do you visualize any colors or scents, any textures?

What is the feeling that memory evokes? Marinate in the feeling and allow it to resonate in you as a loving care memory that keeps you buoyed in the sea of life. When it starts to slip away, just offer it thanks and let it go.

We can recall moments like these anytime. Doing so is a contemplative practice of calling forth and re-membering the love and care that sustains our lives. Re-collecting is the contemplative practice of gathering parts of our life experience that may have faded from our consciousness. It is a practice that can help us be present with the joy that already exists: the joy that undergirds each moment. Let's re-collect some of these moments using the suggestions below:

- **Your Songs of Joy.** *Think of two songs you enjoyed as a child and hum or sing one now. Jot down in your Joy Journal what that song brings to your heart, mind, and body.*

- **Your Joyful Nourishment.** *Recall three favorite foods you had when you were young that you can remember the taste, smell, and feel of. What does each of them bring to mind?*

- **Your Joyful Stories.** *What were the first stories you were told or read that made you joyful? What were the first stories you could read to yourself? How did these make you feel?*

- **Joyful Engagement with Art.** *Which art activities (coloring with crayons, painting, drawing with sidewalk chalk, playing with clay, etc.) do you remember? How did they make you feel? What lasting memories or sensations do you have from these?*

- **Joyful Memories: In-Joying Nature!** *What did you do outside as a young person to engage with nature? Think of three joyful moments in nature and write about them in your journal now.*

I invite you to "be" with these moments, objects, and experiences. This is *your* Joybox! Hum that lullaby, remember every mouthwatering detail of the red velvet cake or honeysuckle blossom or the light of the moon as you walked home. Allow yourself to truly discern, to truly appreciate all the wondrous gifts of your youth. Give your youth back to yourself. Through these re-collections you will be awakened to the full reservoir of yummies that have sustained your life.

These re-collections will also help balance the pain you may encounter as you traverse the path of justice for yourself and others.

Sometimes we bury happy memories because there is too much bad mixed in with the good and we would rather not look back for fear of seeing too much pain. But then we forget all the joy we had, too; we no longer have access to the good memories because the baby has been thrown out with the bathwater. Now that we have a collection of pleasant memories to balance our awareness, we can look at what was challenging as a young person. To truly understand the impact of adultism in our lives, we need to revisit memories that may be painful. Adults (often unintentionally) may have been verbally or physically harmful to us. These painful experiences inform our lives to this day unless we regularly shed the weight of that baggage.

---

Let's Practice!

## Catch and Release to Unseat Adultism

**Self-Care Reminder.** For some of us who suffered adverse childhood experiences, the following practice might arouse some painful feelings. Be kind to yourself and attune to your own experience. Please proceed with conscious awareness of emotions, thoughts, and bodily sensations arising as you explore this. Feel free to pause or skip to the next section and come back to this when you have the bandwidth and support to think about it. Remember, this practice, like all the practices in this book, can also be done in therapy sessions, with friends, or with other forms of emotional support such as music or soothing settings and scents.

When you're ready, allow your attention to float back to your early youth. Take out a pen and paper or your journal and gently allow your mind to fill in the following sentences.

- *When I was a child, the messages I received about my body were _____.*

- *When I was a child, the messages I received about my mind were _____.*

- *When I was a child, the messages I received about my feelings and expressing them were _____.*

Repeat this activity using each developmental stage of your life.

- *When I was a teenager, I learned _____ about my body, mind, and expression of feelings.*

- *When I was a young adult, I learned _____ about my body, mind, and expression of feelings.*

Next, consider the following questions and jot down your thoughts in your journal:

- *How do those early messages impact how I relate to my body, mind, and emotions now?*

- *How do they impact how I relate to the minds, bodies, and emotions of other people now?*

- *What would I like to keep from what I learned about my body, mind, and emotions as a child? What would I like to release?*

Feel what arises. If painful feelings come up, then turn toward them and welcome them. This is your body and mind telling you it is ready to work with this. You are ready to release it. If you couldn't handle these thoughts and feelings, they would not be emerging.

As you stir up these memories, notice what happens to your body, emotions, and mind. Where do these thoughts and memories live in you? Does your mind move away from them or is it able to explore them? If you can "be" with one of these memories, take a moment to be curious about the message you were given. If it arouses anything too painful for you, then pause and come back another time to do this exercise when you feel ready.

As you notice messages you received that you no longer want to keep, say to yourself, *I now release that.*

We can catch and release any shame we may have felt as youth by developing affirmations that contradict internalized oppression. For example, we can speak back to any negative self-concept by saying things like "I love how dark my skin is" or "I love how large my body is." Other affirmations include:

- *I am grateful for my body, mind, and heart. I release shame and embrace my youthful self.*

- *I commit to walking with and honoring my youthful self.*

- *I commit to reclaiming my youthful joy.*

Now I invite you to say more in your journal about your youthful joys. Use the following prompts to guide you.

- *What made you feel gleeful as a child?*

- *What was something you were curious about as a child?*

- *As a child, what was one way you felt connection with or curiosity about nature?*

- *What did you find joy in that you later gave up because you thought it was childish?*

- *How do your childhood experiences impact your experience of glee and curiosity now?*

- *What would you like to keep from what you learned about inquisitiveness and joy as a child? What would you like to release?*

## Messages That Socialized Us into Race, Gender, and Sexual Orientation

The next step is to expand this exercise to scan your earliest memories of noticing ethnicity, gender, and sexual orientation, or attraction to others. Noticing our earliest memories of racism, sexism, homophobia, and heterosexism helps us unearth them from the internal soil in which they were planted.

- *What are your earliest memories of noticing racism or the disparate treatment of people of different ethnicities?*

- *What were your earliest memories of noticing differences between boys and girls or men and women?*

- *When did you first notice different treatment of boys and girls, men and women?*

- *What was your first time feeling attracted to someone physically?*

- *What did adults say to you about that feeling?*

- *When did you notice that some people were attracted to people of the same sex, and what did the adults in your life say about them and that attraction?*

- *What joys were lost to you because of oppressive ideas?*

Write down one joy that could be reclaimed by releasing any oppressive messages.

To finish this exercise, you can reflect on messages about privilege:

- *When was the first time you noticed privilege?*

- *What messages did you get from adults about people with disabilities?*

- *What messages do you remember receiving about children with different learning styles?*

- *When did you first notice able-bodied privilege?*

- *When was the first time you noticed language privilege?*

- *When was the first time you noticed age privilege or age-based discrimination?*

- *What joys were lost to you because of these oppressions?*

Write down one or two joys that could be reclaimed by releasing these oppressive messages.

---

You can do these reflections regularly to clear and affirm yourself as often as you'd like. Some of what you unearth might be things you prefer to forget. But the journey to justice begins with being able to face the wholeness of your experience: the good, the bad, the painful! As the Buddhists say, "No mud, no lotus." It is the mud of our suffering that helps us transform into the flower of our greater selves.

## What's Lotus Got to Do with It, Got to Do with It?

The lotus flower is symbolic in Buddhism because it flowers and seeds simultaneously, symbolizing the reality that as soon as we make a cause, the effect already exists whether or not it manifests at that moment.

Nam Myoho Renge Kyo is the phrase many Buddhists (including me!) chant to invoke and evoke our enlightened minds and the enlightenment inherent in everything around us. The phrase is understood by Nichiren Buddhists to be the name of the ultimate law permeating the universe, in unison with human life, which can bring forth enlightenment. It is also the Japanese title of the Buddhist scripture often referred to in English as the Lotus Sutra. Because these invocations are embodied, their real meaning can only be understood by practicing with them to experience the invocations in an embodied way. Trying to define them is like trying to define love. Nonetheless, here is one translation of the words:

- *Nam* is often translated as "fusion with," or "devotion of one's entire being to."

- *Myoho* means "mystic law" (*mystic* in that it cannot be understood solely with intellect).

- *Renge* is the word for "lotus flower." In this phrase, it refers to the simultaneity of cause and effect because the lotus has flowers (cause) and seeds (effect) at the same time.

- *Kyo* is translated as "sound," "vibration," or "action."

Together the phrase can be loosely translated to express our fusion with the mystic law of cause and effect through sound and action. Nichiren Daishonin taught that all the benefits and wisdom contained in the Lotus Sutra can be realized by chanting its title, [Nam] Myoho-renge-kyo.

And yes, Tina Turner was a Nichiren Buddhist who chanted Nam Myoho Renge Kyo, so apparently the lotus has got a lot to do with it, LEL (Laughing Enlightened Laughter)! On YouTube, there are lovely videos of Tina Turner chanting Nam Myoho Renge Kyo and reciting the second and sixteenth chapters of the Lotus Sutra (this recitation is called Gongyo in Nichiren Buddhism). Try chanting it yourself and see if it helps as you release oppressive messages and reclaim your inherent joy.

---

Let's Practice!

## Chanting Nam Myoho Renge Kyo

At your own pace, try chanting Nam Myoho Renge Kyo as you envision releasing inner restrictions and expanding into your greater self. You can set a timer to do it for one to five minutes to start. Note any resonance the practice has in your body and mind as you chant.

———————————

## Ending Racism Begins at Home: Cultivating Anti-Racist, Non-Oppressive Family Relationships

We all want to be in non-oppressive relationships with ourselves and our families. We want to think well of ourselves and not suppress any aspects of who we are. Yet because of fear, self-loathing, and shame, we are not always able to acknowledge and embrace all of who we are. Likewise, because of fear, anger, privilege, and lack of insight about interdependence, we may squash the well-being of others by relating to them in a racist or otherwise oppressive manner. It is impossible to experience any enduring and heartfelt joy by causing others to suffer.

What would it be like to create families that were free from oppressive power dynamics? How do we achieve that? It begins with contemplating how oppression lives in our conscious and unconscious minds and shapes our notions of family. We can consider how oppression and privilege have impacted our family members' lives and losses. How has racism or internalized racism been transmitted intergenerationally in your family? Remember, internalized racism is when People of the Global Majority (PGM) have negative views of themselves and other PGM based on having absorbed racist ideas. What is the nature of the suffering racism caused in your family? What oppressive paradigms informed your grandparents' lives? For example, were your grandparents white people who had more economic opportunities during Jim Crow when Black people were not allowed to compete for higher paying jobs? In what ways was white supremacy culture present in your parents' and grandparents' lives? How is white supremacy culture present in your family now?

What coping mechanisms did your distant and closest ancestors develop to manage racism? What fears, diminished dreaming, hesitant hoping might you walk with daily because of the experiences of your forebears?

Certainly, the coping mechanisms handed down to us were the best our elders could figure out at the time. And for many of us, hating and rejecting the attitudes and behavior of our parental figures was not an option. We could not risk cutting ourselves off from our only source of nurturing, and so we sought some way to think and feel that we were aligned with power even if we did not have it ourselves.

Identification with the aggressor is part of how white privilege and racist attitudes get passed down through generations in global minority (a.k.a. white) families. Naturally, global minority children just want to love their parents, warts and all. Yet white peoples' hard work/heartwork of undoing white privilege involves examining and letting go of the idealized version of parents and other forebears who nurtured them and taught them the racism and entitlement they now embody and enact.

*Internalized oppression* (IO) drives PGM to devalue not only ourselves but also other PGM. Our (often unconscious) internalized racism compels us to favor and emulate global minority people to pursue the proximity to power that doing so—consciously or unconsciously—is perceived to offer.

Both racism and internalized racism reflect a compromised view of our most expansive lives, and both are nurtured and transmitted in our families. Exploring what precisely has placed doubt in our hearts about our inestimable possibility and worth is the starting point for reclaiming that possibility and worth. Our intrapersonal relationship with our family (the interoceptive or intrapsychic experience of family), as well as the actual inter-relationality with our family members, needs contemplation with reference to how racism and other oppressions have contaminated them so that we may have more liberated relationships with family.

## Family of Origin and Family We Choose

Our family of origin informs our self-concept, and that internalized sense of relationality impacts how we interact with family members. It also informs the conscious and unconscious choices we make about lovers, partners, friends, and our families of choice.

In my family, dozens of my cousins called my grandaunt, Aunt Essie, "Aunty Mommy" because she was both aunt and mother to many of them, as is often the case in Black families. My dear friend Vaishali refers to aunthood as a kind of middle way. Being an aunt now myself, I can say that aunthood is quite a perilous 'hood indeed; one where you are in danger of pissing off both your siblings and their offspring as you try to be an engaged resource in the lives of your nieces, nephews, and the non-binary children of your siblings. You want to share your wisdom without replicating the heavy-handedness of your siblings, which you understand from a different perspective than your nieces and nephews. You also have the space to see oppressive tendencies formed by the upbringing you and your siblings had.

The reality of what social scientists call "fictive kin" in Black families is our creative response to the ruptures caused by enslavement, kidnapping, and confinement via an unjust criminal legal system and racism in family and child services. Black people's families of origin are often ruptured by racism, so we make family of whoever is left in our communities. This also has pre-enslavement roots in that villages and tribes in Africa often raised children collectively as one family, hence the Nigerian Igbo proverb "It takes a village to raise a child."

We need to examine the historical trauma of our families so that we can understand its impact on our unconscious. That closer examination is precisely the goal of both therapy and meditative practice. We can use mindfulness practices to have well-considered, liberated, and liberating relationships with family of origin and chosen family.

## Mindful Sex: What Does It Mean to Be Joyfully Just, Sexually?

One place where I have had many opportunities to help people distinguish between momentary pleasures—which often lead to suffering—and real joy in their lives is in the realm of relationships and sexuality. As a psychotherapist working with people on figuring out what healthy sexuality is for them and how to be in healthy intimate relationships with others, I've seen firsthand how sexism and racism distort our relationship to joy such that our notions of pleasure itself are often suffused with unconscious motives of submission and domination. Mindful power play in relationships is possible, however, much of how we are socialized around sexuality reflects ingrained racism and sexism.

Let me give you an example: Richard was a self-identified white man who had recently come to terms with being gay. Having been attracted to males since he was a boy, Richard was very relieved when he finally came out to his Catholic family and they were supportive. The reason Richard came to therapy, however, was because he realized that some of what he enjoyed sexually had to do with racism. For most of his adult life, Richard had dated only Black men. This was something he had been proud of, thinking of himself as someone who easily transcended racism's limitations. He was proud of the fact that he appreciated the beauty of Black and Brown skin.

However, in a moment of sexual passion with his partner of two years, Richard made a very racist comment reflecting stereotypical notions he'd absorbed about Black male genitalia. His partner was so offended that he stopped having sex with Richard at that moment, left the house, and later asked for a break from the relationship. His now-former partner told Richard he needed to get some help looking at what was going on in his mind. Richard, hoping to get his partner back, decided to come to therapy to look at what indeed was going on in his mind when he made that outburst in bed.

As we explored this in session, we found out that, like many people all over the globe, a lot of what Richard learned about sex had come from the broader social context; music, media (TV, movies, pornography) that we all absorb to varying degrees. Since we know that media and our social context are riddled with racism, it is natural that these ideas get absorbed into our sexual notions and actions.

## Let's Talk about Sex: What's Hot, What's Not

As a regular, consistent contemplative practice, it is useful to ask ourselves, *How do racism, sexism, homophobia, heterosexism, and their internalized correlates inform who I want to have sex with and how I want to have sex with them?* The relationship between sex and power is itself worthy of contemplation. Being in touch with one's aggression often accounts for the engaged assertion of passion that is often experienced as "hot." However, unexplored aggression—or lack of any aggression at all—has roots in our unconscious that bear examination.

Racism sexually exoticizes *and* denigrates the beauty of Black, Asian, Latinx, and Indigenous people. Think of all the language around hot Black or Latin lovers, wild Native or Indigenous people, exotic Asians, and so forth. It is no wonder that the sex trafficking of PGM is exponentially higher than that of global minority people. Your fantasies and the type of pornography or non-pornographic sexual imagery you enjoy are windows to your unconscious. For white people, it is useful to thoroughly examine to what degree you may choose global majority partners because of racist ideas that live in the unconscious but are expressed all over the media we consume. A recent survey points out that "ebony" is one of the most searched for types of pornography, and in much of it, Black people are being exoticized and/or dominated.[6] How much of our selection of partners is based on choosing forbidden and exoticized fruit—sometimes consciously, and sometimes unconsciously?

Sometimes racism is in our sexual behavior and activities. Sometimes white people believe that having a global majority partner is a "get-out-of-working-on-racism-free card." We see this when white people say, "My partner (or child, best friend, etc.) is Asian (or Black, Latinx, etc.), so how could I be racist?" The answer is: easily! The earliest forms of racism involved sexual relations with global majority women and men and brutalizing global majority people into adoring and serving white people's beauty.

---

Let's Pause and Practice!

## Self-Soothing

This area of sexuality, especially as impacted by racism, is very tender. In your Joy Journal, make a note of what feels sensitive for you right now.

Put your right hand on your chest and left hand on your abdomen and focus on the rising and falling of your breath. Studies have shown that this self-soothing gesture can activate your parasympathetic nervous system and help you tap into your heart center.[7] Notice how reading this section feels emotionally for you and how it resonates in your body. Feel free to make a note of what you are feeling in your Joy Journal.

---

It's worthwhile to examine who we choose to love. If we have never been in love with someone of our own ethnicity, it is valuable to ask why. Likewise, if we have only been in love with people of our own ethnicity, why? If you are a person of the global majority, you could also consider the following question: *Is my internalized oppression calling me to be sexual with white people to feel worthy or better about myself? Do I subconsciously long for white approval and acceptance?*

Black women have long challenged Black men about choosing white (and more recently, Asian) women as romantic partners to help them advance socially and economically. As Black women, we get to ask ourselves, *Is some of that bemoaning about loneliness or jealousy?* It is certainly true that Black women want Black men to see them and value them. Black men who don't date Black women can benefit from exploring why, just as Black women can benefit from exploring their feelings about it.

> We can engage our contemplative practices to courageously explore all aspects of our lives.

White racialized people who desire global majority partners also need to take a long look at why they do and search out any unconscious exotification. I had one bisexual global minority client who exclusively dated Black men and women, and when I encouraged her to look at it as a way of not working on racism, as well as exotification, she backed away from therapy altogether. This is an example of how fear and defensiveness can keep us from self-awareness. We can engage our contemplative practices to courageously examine all aspects of our lives.

### Sexing Sans Sexism, Relations Rid of Racism

Now we'll explore some examples and practices to help us see how both subtle and overt forms of sexual exploitation seep into our thoughts and behavior. Whether you are a survivor of sexual abuse or not, pause and take a few deep breaths here and ground yourself in the present and in your body before you read on. As always, feel free to skip this section and revisit it when you have the support you need.

Sometimes women consent to sex in married or partnered heterosexual unions out of fear of losing their partner. We can see how this is influenced by sexism in popular culture. I remember how a global minority cisgender woman client, a working mom, processed how her husband regularly cajoled her into sex when she was too tired. She said she just allowed it because she got back to sleep sooner that way. With tears in her eyes, she asked me, "Is my husband raping me? I am saying no at first, but then I just give up. Wifely duties, you know?"

Notice what hearing about her experience brings up for you and jot it down in your Joy Journal before we begin this next practice.

---

Let's Practice!

## Getting Support

Have you ever had an experience of sex that you are not sure was consensual? If so, pause here and allow yourself to journal about it with these three prompts:

- *How am I feeling now?*

- *What support could I use now?*

- *How can I get access to that support?*

Once you have identified some resources to support you, journal about what that experience of nonconsensual sex was like for you. If you don't feel supported enough to do this now, you can come back to it when you feel more supported.

---

For more insight into racism, sexism, and sexuality, let me tell you about another client, a Black woman who exclusively dated white men. After over a year in therapy, she finally told me about how she got aroused when her white lovers would dominate her, sometimes using racist epithets. This is not unusual. *Race play*, wherein people act out racism in their sexual fantasies of domination and submission, is as common as any other type of domination fantasy.

This client shared that she felt degraded afterward but had the most intense orgasms from these types of interactions. We explored her early experiences around sex and she acknowledged that some of her earliest sexual memories were of movie scenes where white men sexually dominated Black enslaved women. She described how an actress looked coquettishly pleased to be whipped by the man behind her as he raped her. I explained to her that attraction is taught. We find things sexy because they were introduced to us as central to what hot sex is and thus we come to desire them. However, we can use our meditative practices to recognize and transform any desire that is harmful to ourselves or others.

Anyone who's ever had transcendent sex, where you feel your souls connected, where you laugh and play and have a physical experience of interconnectedness that resonates spiritually, knows how affirming that can be. The point is awareness, because without awareness you cannot truly be said to be consenting. If, for example, we are trapped by internalized sexism as heterosexual women, how can we say no when we're thinking, *If I don't give it to him at home, he's going to get it elsewhere?* The philanderer's trope is always, "My wife and I aren't having sex anymore," and women know this. Women often consent to sex out of fear of losing men or to validate their beauty and/or worth.

What if we were to pause before sex and reflect on how we want the engagement to go? We might be afraid that this will ruin spontaneity, but that's impossible because every moment is new. Reflection before sex allows you to set an intention and establish—or loosen—your sexual boundaries. Then you can have a thoughtful dialogue with your partner in which you actively listen to each other. What do you each want done? What do you want said? In what tone? It's not prescriptive but descriptive, so that the consent is for every sexual act and for the overall manner in which we are treated.

Let's Practice!

## Self-Reflection and Sexuality

To conclude this section, try this prompt for your journaling:

- *Do racism and sexism come to bed with me?*
- *In what ways can I see racism and sexism in my sexuality?*

Note your responses in your Joy Journal for continued exploration. You can always come back to these questions as you continue to reflect on healthy sexual and intimate partner relationships.

## Healing Our Connection with Elements of the Natural World

Nature can be a source of incredible joy (and mojo!) for many of us. We might also have some negative associations with elements of nature. If some aspects of nature are emotionally challenging for us, we can use our practices to reclaim and heal these associations and restore a joyful relationship with the natural world.

For example, some of us may have an unpleasant relationship with soil or dirt because of being called dirty or being punished harshly when we got dirty as children. This may be especially true for Black and Brown folx who were called dirty as part of a racial epithet. That slur reflects the colonialism that denigrates the soil and Brown- or Black-bodied people all in one insidious insult. Of course, everyone likes to get clean. Yet being dirty and in the dirt can also be joyful. We all get to reclaim dirt so that any painful experiences we had related to it don't block us from enjoying the richness of the soil that sustains us in so many ways.

---

Let's Practice!

## Natural Affirmations

If you have feelings about soil, try this affirmation practice using some of Black people's vernacular:

> *Despite the painful associations, I still dig you, soil! You are my kind of filthy! I welcome being dirty as I recognize that so much grows in dirt. Each time I wash clean, I will happily return anew to all the productivity that comes from and is reflected in the dirt.*

Likewise, many of us have fears of water from having been victims of flood, near-drowning, or other accidents and incidents related to water. If you have fears of water, try this affirmation to reclaim your connection to water:

> *Water, I know you have the power to drown, and you also have the power to buoy, to aid me in staying afloat. Like me, all bodies of water are full of all types of life. Just like my sorrows and joys, water, you ebb and flow. I am like you, water, learning to masterfully engage in the ebb and flow of life.*

If you have reactivity to fire, try this affirmation:

> *I recognize your power, fire. Like me, you have destructive and constructive qualities. With you I learn to manage the destructive forces*

*within me. I will use the fire within me to warm, to heal, and to light my own way and that of others.*

If you are a storm survivor and you need a wind reclamation practice, try this:

*Wind, wild wind, you blow like the storms raging through my own heart and mind, in union with the air that sustains my very life. I welcome your cool breezes as much as your fierce gusts, for in these I see the cool and fierce aspects of my own being.*

For a meditation with trees you might try:

*Dear tree, you stand so tall like me when I am proud and free, reminding me of who I am meant to be. Your leaves sway in communion with other elements just as I am always in connection with other elements. The rains and the sunshine nurture us, and we stand together, branching out ever farther and farther!*

------------

Trees have been degraded in the murderous, racist hangings of Black people in the United States for centuries. I lived in northern Virginia for many years, one of the cradles of the confederacy that sanctioned centuries of torture, and every time I saw trees and wooded areas, I would wonder if any of my ancestors or other Black people had been hung on those types of trees or on those actual trees.

The honest acknowledgment of the racist harms done in the wild and restorative reclamation of the natural world is a big part of the environmental work that Black people have been leading. Organizations like Outdoor Afro and Black in Environment offer all kinds of nature-engaging practices for Black folx, ranging from hiking the Underground Railroad in various states to meditating on beaches and flying kites on open plains.

Reflecting on how our natural environment has been exploited to harm people is part of how all people can deepen our awareness and reclaim a joyfully just connection to nature.

Black people have been terrorized in and through all types of outdoor spaces. The following quote from James Baldwin's novel *Just Above My Head* highlights how the landscape of a drive through Virginia and further south holds the memory of the ways Black people were hunted. It describes a real "Green Book" story, depicting why Black people needed, and need, safe houses on the road more accurately than the false, exploitative, white savior Hollywood movie *Green Book* did. As you read, sense into what the reality of simply navigating the lands can bring to mind and actually be like for Black people. Notice feelings and thoughts as they arise in your heart and mind and note them as you read this. Let these words from Baldwin be a meditation on creating justice in and for all people in the natural environment.

The landscape flew past, the land was flat, no cover. And I heard dogs yelping, yowling, barking through this landscape, looking for my ancestors, looking for my grandfather, my grandmother, looking for me. I heard the men breathing, heard their boots, heard the click of the gun, the rifle, looking for me, and there was no cover. The trees were no cover. The ditch was a trap. The horizon was 10,000 miles away. One could never reach it, drop behind it, stride the hostile elements all the way, to Canada?!? Round and round the tree, no cover, No cover. Into the tall grass, no cover. That hill over yonder? Too high, not high enough. No cover. Circle back, no cover.

Pissing as you run, no cover, the breath and the hair and the odor and the teeth of the dogs, no cover. The eyes and the gun and the blow of the master, no, no cover. And the blood running down, the tears, and the snot and the piss and the shit running out, dragged by dogs, out of the jaws of dogs forever and forever and forever, no mercy and no cover.[8]

I read this passage as a preteen shortly after my sister and I had been chased by dogs that were sicced on us as we rode our bikes through a white neighborhood in Georgia. I knew this had informed my family's decision to be part of the great migration of over six million Black people from the South, why they relocated to New York from Savannah in the 1940s. No cover.

Even when Black people are not terrorized outdoors, we are often ostracized and stared at, looked at as part of the wildlife and micro-aggressed with inappropriate questions. This happens to me often on the beaches in Monterey, California. I play with it lightly, saying to people, "You are staring at me? There's a whole ocean over there. You see the ocean, right?" In this way I lightly redirect white people who don't expect to see, and often don't welcome, me and other global majority people into beautiful natural spaces where they are not used to seeing us.

> Supporting global majority people and
> reclaiming our connection in the natural world
> is one way to interrupt environmental racism.

For these reasons, the work to support Black people in the wilderness and in all natural environments is so vital. This is also true for Native American people who because of *Caucacity* (Black people's term for the audacity of some white people's sense of dominion and rights to everything) are ostracized on their own land! Supporting global majority people and reclaiming our connection in the natural world is one way to interrupt environmental racism.

Environmental racism is a residual of the economic exploitation of global majority people and the commodification of their lands, which has created industrial, polluted, and otherwise unwanted land, to which global majority people are often then relegated. In these regions, PGM often experience disproportionate exposure to environmental health hazards.

Environmental racism also persists in the form of white people own-
ing and occupying most of the pretty, restorative places in the world,
while Black and other global majority folx are relegated to treeless, sun-
less, oceanless spaces. I have seen this problem globally because when
I travel to Africa and the Caribbean, it is always the native Black and
Indigenous people who live in the most dilapidated housing, while the
most beautiful resorts and residences are reserved for tourists or vacation
homeowners who are usually overwhelmingly white. All beings have a
right to engage freely in our natural world as this sustains our well-being
and puts us in right relationship with nature. This quote from Daisaku
Ikeda speaks to the way nature reflects life's own highest philosophy back
to us—human beings who are ourselves nature:

> Life contains the capacity, like flames that reach toward the
> heavens, to transform suffering and pain into the energy of
> value-creation, the light that illuminates the dark. Like the wind
> traversing vast spaces unhindered, life has the power to uproot
> and overturn all obstacles and difficulties. Like clear flowing water,
> it can wash away all stains and impurities. And finally, life, like
> the great Earth that sustains plants and vegetation, impartially
> embraces all people with its compassionate, nurturing force.[9]

We can release negative feelings about any spaces that cause us distress. Since my mother's death, I always chant Nam Myoho Renge Kyo
to release painful feelings and thoughts about hospitals before I go in for
a procedure or to visit someone who is hospitalized so that I can navigate
those spaces without a trauma load.

Let's Practice!

## Reclamation for Healing

Are there any environments that you would like to reclaim? Note them
in your Joy Journal. Then you can use the practices in this book to help

you move freely and joyfully through any and every space in the world. Exploring the painful places in our world for their meaning can help us heal and grow. Can you think of a time when you turned something painful into a source for growth? Pause for a moment and notice how you grew. In what ways can you tell you grew? Were any aspects of that growth joyful? Note that growth in your Joy Journal.

---

## Taking Our Joy on the Road: Pleasure, Power, and Place in Nature

We are almost always in a physical space that has something to teach us, no matter how we feel. Even in the grimiest, most pestilence-ridden place, there is and always has been the possibility for joy. And even in the most glorious places, there is and always has been suffering. The vast landscapes all over the world where enslaved Africans were tortured and forced to labor under brutal conditions were often also visually stunning with the bounty and splendor of the natural world.

In Toni Morrison's *Beloved*, one of the main characters, Paul D, is described as "listening to the doves in Alfred, Georgia, and having neither the right nor the permission to enjoy it because in that place, mist, doves, sunlight, copper dirt, moon—everything belonged to the men who had the guns."[10] With these words, Dr. Morrison demonstrates how racism robs global majority people of the right to be in a joyous relationship with nature. Nature itself was weaponized to subdue Indigenous and African heritage people. That's the legacy we are joyfully undoing.

Consider this: Sometimes we are in a strikingly gorgeous place physically or maybe we're at the end of a journey toward some success such as getting a degree or buying a house—and yet we are miserable. Have you ever been amid beautiful physical surroundings or you just achieved some success, and yet you were angry or depressed?

That may be due to arrival fallacy. *Arrival fallacy* is a term coined by the psychologist Tal Ben-Shahar to describe the false belief that once we get to a particular place we will become—and remain—happy.[11] Also, when we travel on vacation or even just go for an outing, we sometimes conjure a particular type of arrival fallacy that I call "wealth-fantasy tourism."

The prevalence of wealth-fantasy tourism, as demonstrated by social media posts of folks on yachts or posing with Bentleys or on luxurious beaches, is a good example of how we wind up so unhappy, even in lovely circumstances. There is nothing wrong with having nice things and being on luxurious yachts or in mansions. What trips us up is believing that these things are indicators of virtue or joy. Having a yacht cannot ever make us virtuous, and joy that is based solely on having material things always goes away. Worst of all, wealth-fantasy tourism encourages us to aspire to money and the trappings of wealth as if acquiring them will mean we have reached a state of lasting happiness. That incorrect view, like all illusions, will lead us to unnecessary suffering.

Wealth-fantasy tourism is fundamentally empty because wealth alone does not lead to joy. As Daisaku Ikeda writes, "There are many people in mansions who spend their days in tears."[12] Many economically rich people suffer from depression in part because of the pervasive nature of the wealth fantasy as a means to happiness. Note that I did not simply say "rich people" because there are many ways to be rich, including being spiritually rich, culturally rich, relationally rich, and so forth.

Wealth worshipping is problematic because it perpetuates the delusion that lives that are not financially wealthy are not as valuable. That idea gives economically privileged people the delusion that they have everything needed for life. It also gives economically disadvantaged people the delusion that they do not already possess much of what is needed to be happy. Wealth fantasies focus our attention on accruing financial wealth instead of internal wealth, and it is internal wealth that leads to joy.

Wealth fantasy and focus can intensify delusion and attachment to material things, and delusion never leads to joy. Illusions can lead to fun but not joy. The only time delusion can lead to joy is when it is transformed into enlightenment or insight.

## Choosing Joy over Pleasure

All joy contains pleasure, but not all pleasures lead to joy. Joy is an abounding spiritual resonance where we taste the beauty of life with the palate of our hearts and minds. Joy is a full-body, total sensory experience. No one is brought suffering by joy. True joy can only give birth to joy. Pleasure-seeking, a hedonistic desire to fill one or two of our senses with delight, can and does lead to suffering via addictions, including those that compel us toward substance abuse and exploitation of other people.

Take a moment here to make a list of three momentary pleasures that did *not* lead to joy in your experience. Next, list three things that were not necessarily pleasurable to do but that ultimately led to joy for you.

*Pleasure activism* invites us to be joyous while we transform the pain of oppression. It invites us toward pleasure that is just. It is not exploitative or based on the delusions associated with attachment to impermanent things such as health, beauty, wealth, or relationships. In contrast, wealth-fantasy tourism is ultimately joyless because it is so often built on injustice: on the idea of having more than others. No one ever poses with a scrub brush cleaning a toilet, but that can be as joyful as jet-skiing, depending on our inner state of life.

> Joy is an abounding spiritual resonance where we taste the beauty of life with the palate of our hearts and minds.

Think of the most unpleasant place you have been lately and then challenge yourself to notice one thing that was lovely about it—even if it was just the fact that you could breathe the air there. It is a very enriching skill to be able to notice the possibility for joy that exists in every context.

## Let's Dance It Out!

All joy is fun, but not all fun leads to joy. Some of what we call fun leads to immediate gratification and then almost immediately leads to more suffering. Distinguishing between fun and joy is an aspect of wisdom that will allow us to live more fulfilling lives. Some joy comes through fun, but much joy comes through growth and transformation. And some joy comes from self-transcendence. In one of his most clarifying statements about the incredible interior spaciousness that enslaved Africans demonstrated, the nineteenth-century African American abolitionist Frederick Douglass said, "I admit that the slave does sometimes sing, dance, and appear to be merry. But what does this prove? It only proves to my mind that though slavery is armed with a thousand stings, it is not able entirely to kill the elastic spirit of the bondman."[13]

The point Douglass makes here is important. He is saying that dancing and singing are misperceived by the white gaze—the perspective informed by white supremacy. Dancing and singing actually affirm one's humanity and call forth the humanity of others, and that is why they are such persistent parts of Black wisdom transmissions. Of course, some of it is "partying" in the celebratory sense of the word, but that is leadership as well. Racism would have us dismiss Black people as lazy hedonists who just party all the time. That is what prevents us from seeing the self-transcendence, the enacted neuroplasticity and highly cultivated resilience of which Douglass speaks. We can consider two ways that singing and dancing might be seen as "just playing." Sometimes the distinction between play and resistance, or play and spirituality, is indistinguishable. The enslaved people Douglass speaks of were perceived to be "just" (as in merely) playing. We can flip that notion on its head and allow "*just* playing" to mean that we play to be more just toward ourselves and others.

*Joyfully Just* prioritizes using meditative practices to enact anti-racist perceiving, thinking, and behaving. This is my intentional effort to address the ubiquitous prevalence and deadly impact of racism. Furthermore, racism is so transgenerationally destructive in the lives of PGM that it is appropriately a focal point. Racism doesn't do global minority (a.k.a. white) people any good either, despite the illusion of financial and social privilege. In efforts to get more of those, global minority people give up truth and being in right relationship with themselves, with the majority of the people in the world who are not white, and with nature itself.

Racism's power, which rests in our unconscious as much as it does in our interpersonal dynamics and institutions, also locks sexism and heterosexism in place. In 1988, political science scholar Susan Pharr described homophobia as a weapon of sexism in a seminal writing with that title.[14] Both the heterosexist perspective that obscures queerness and the homophobic one that fears or despises queerness are tools employed to keep people in strict confining gender roles. So, boys learned not to cry so as not to be perceived as sissies, and girls—myself included—were told to behave like "ladies" and not be manly so as not to be perceived as lesbians. The entire heteropatriarchy rests on racism, which asserts that PGM are already outside the bounds of normality. Just as adultism is the portal by which all oppressions are transmitted and learned, racism and internalized racism hold other forms of oppression in place.

## Suffering Without Being Insufferable

When we loathe suffering and unrealistically expect to have no or few painful circumstances, we increase our suffering by bearing it ungracefully. We can become bitter, mean, cantankerous, and just plain miserable. The next time you find yourself suffering, notice the different ways that complaint and gratitude resonate in your body as you contemplate the suffering.

If you are suffering in a way that you can notice right now, notice the difference in your body and mind as you try on these two responses. Say them aloud and note what you feel.

- *This situation is so messed up! I can't believe I have to go through this!*

- *I'm grateful to be alive to experience this. I wonder what I will learn about myself and others as I face this situation with courage. I can't wait to find out how this makes me wiser and stronger!*

This is not to say that we need to subvert our natural responses. I remain outraged, for example, about the killing of Ahmaud Arbery, Breonna Taylor, and so many others murdered in racism-fueled violence. Yet amid that outrage and the heartbreak, I find an unswerving, to-my-dying-day commitment to embody anti-racism and joy in my efforts to help others do likewise.

Learning to suffer well can also help us heal addiction. Our addictions often kick in when we're trying to soothe or distract ourselves from some woundedness or loss we feel. Addictions can also arise as ways to avoid feelings or sedate ourselves when experiencing conflict within or in the absence of our families. Consider the word *nurse* itself. Its etymology includes breastfeeding, of course, as well as anything we do to foster a condition—consider the phrase *nursing a grudge*. What if we could, as often as possible, decide to nurse our capacity to stay present with suffering, to peer down and look for the joy at the bottom of the suffering well? This is obviously not something we can do all the time, but practicing it is a portal to liberation because addiction enslaves us to our cravings and to escapism.

It's not our fault we have addictions, especially oral fixations like smoking and overeating. We are trained from birth to contain our cries by sucking or eating something. When we were babies and children, often when we started to cry or fuss and didn't need changing, when we started to weep for reasons we could not communicate—perhaps infant or childhood existential angst or loneliness—someone usually shoved something in our mouths. We got a breast, a pacifier, a snack, and so forth. Some studies even show that creamy substances—cheesy products and ice cream—are our preferred comfort foods because they resemble the breast milk that comforted us early in life.[15]

So many of us have learned to suppress our emotions via oral fixations. Yet food is just one of the many ways we can express addiction. All sorts of things can be addictive: coffee, gambling, sex, gaming, social media, television. We are openly encouraged by advertisements to binge-watch one show after another. And caffeine is so profoundly addictive that caffeine addiction is in the *Diagnostic and Statistical Manual of Mental Disorders*. For some people, substance addictions require both detox and therapy.

> Learning to suffer without being insufferable means
> we have less inclination toward complaint and
> thus we en-joy—engage joy—more in our lives.

Addiction is known to be both a genetic predisposition and a reinforced habit. It is both natural and nurtured. We know that by rehabituating ourselves, we can reverse or reduce the impacts of genetic predispositions such as addictive tendencies.

In a scene from one of my favorite books that I read as a child, *Daddy Was a Number Runner*, the author Louise Meriwether describes the maternal figure hiding the household money from a family member who is known to be stealing it to use drugs. The addicted family member cries when he discovers that he has no access to the money, screaming, "What am I supposed to do?" To which the matriarch replies, "Suffer! Suffer, like the rest of us!"[16]

This is the first truth of Buddhism, that there is suffering. Learning to suffer without being insufferable means we have less inclination toward complaint and thus we en-joy—engage joy—more in our lives because we are not dependent upon the pleasure of the absence of suffering in order to notice joy. We are able to access the more absolute happiness that comes from the wonder of being alive, including the wonder of how much suffering we can bear and grow from.

## Giving Ourselves Birthday Presence and Wishing Each Other a Present Birthday

In my work as a grief therapist at the Washington, DC, morgue, I learned that birthday celebrations were occasions that frequently led to loss. I witnessed countless stories of birthday celebrations gone awry. The actions people took to avoid suffering and immerse themselves in pleasure often led to overdoses and accidents that resulted in death. What if we could stop expecting to feel pleasure all the time, especially on days that are significant to us?

What if we could wish for each other—on our birthdays and at all times—the awesome experience of being present? This includes being present with the awe-ful! *Awful* and *awesome* have the same root. Pain can inspire as much transcendent wonder, as striking a sensory experience, as much awe as joy can. Life is such a wonder that if we pay attention, it is easy to have an awe-filled day where we notice the heights of both pleasure and suffering with equanimity and grace. This is the realm of joy.

Learning to give babies attention—to literally attend to their suffering—is a way to teach them that they can endure it and that we are with them in the human experience of doing so. At any stage of life, we can be present with one another's suffering so that we don't need to escape it. We can have someone bear witness and hold the suffering with us. This is the opportunity we have to enact our interdependent joy as members of the human family. All of us sharing our sufferings can be joyful.

## Humor as a Pathway and the Destination

The conflation of mindfulness with solemnity is often just a residual of colonialist WASP cultural norms. People often tell me how cheerful I am. I bring forth cheerfulness both as a cause for my own joy and as an act of resistance. I resist being defeated by suffering. For Black people and other global majority people who have been critiqued as "simple primitives," the reclamation of humor sans minstrelsy is another liberatory practice. Contrary to the racist notions of the happy darky, felicity is my faith. Humor is my heft—my gravitas.

Joy is an embodied practice, an enacted decision, as is evidenced in the songs people of African heritage sang in enslavement. The good cheer, kindness, and soul-stirring songs of Black people during enslavement were seen through the lens of the white gaze as evidence that the enslaved Black people were too simple-minded to even know they were oppressed. In reality, the singing was an expression of self-transcendence, of their capacity to both embody and share a resilient joie de vivre that had nothing to do with pleasure, joy that was completely liberated from the avoidance of suffering.

Smiling is not always an effect. Often because of the pain we are in, it does not come easily, but it is not about pretense, either. Weeping is also an expression of enlightenment. Think of the weeping Buddha. Christ's joy and the Buddha's sorrow are often unmentioned yet they are intricately related.

My smile is a cause, an invitation, to encourage myself and others to choose to put our attention on what is working, what is well; to decide to feel better, to smile at fear and pain and disparagement and dismissiveness, and keep on moving. A smile can and does signify an undefeated life condition, evidence of how our deepest joy comes from insight, wisdom, and triumphs over the lesser self, as we help others thrive.

---

Let's Practice!

## Re-Collecting Joy

When have you tasted absolute joy or absolute freedom? Let's re-collect those liberated moments! Take two minutes in silence to notice what today's joys are. Not just the superficial ones, like a nice meal; also reach for genuinely enlivening and liberating experiences. If there has not yet been one today that you can notice, go back to yesterday or last weekend and fetch it. Catch your joy! What's in your joy and freedom cart as you check out this singular moment? Share your joy and freedom in one of these ways:

- *Make a note in your Joy Journal of the day's joys or if you have time, note the joys you have had this week.*

- *Try an active listening dyad with a partner or friend, wherein you set a timer and take two minutes each to simply listen to each other talk about today's joys. Do your best to not interrupt each other: just pay attention and catch your partner's joy and freedom!*

- *Give four 30-second shout-outs to your sources of joy! Feel free to laugh at the timer going off, too. The timeframes we live within are absurd, and laughing at the absurd is enlivening!*

# Chapter Four

## Joyfully Just, Conscious Cultural Engagement

I am suggesting that we pay as much attention
to our nurturing sensibilities as to our ambition.
You are moving in the direction of freedom, and the
function of freedom is to free somebody else.[1]

**Toni Morrison**

Our sensibilities are the conduits through which we come to discern
truth and beauty. As Dr. Toni Morrison indicates in this quote, our
sensibilities or ways of perceiving can be liberated from oppressive paradigms and that will enhance our capacity to help others experience freedom.

In this section, we're bringing together chords of wisdom to form our
own life symphony of joyous liberation. We will explore art, music, and
mindful media practices to conceive the set, dialogue, and score of the
ever-unfolding play that is our joyous existence.

To experience the vastest sense of self-actualization and freedom, we
need a thorough awareness of our own cultural influences. We need
to note the influences that strengthen us and the internalized negative
influences we would like to reform. We also want to assess the impact of

all these on our worldview, choices, actions, and inactions in the world. Insight about our intersecting cultural perspectives can help us continually refine our inner and outer lives.

By empathically engaging with the cultural diversity within and around us, we are enriched and empowered.

You already took the first steps of this process earlier in the book, thinking critically about messages you received in youth about your ethnicity, body, gender, sexuality, and other aspects of your life. You also explored what you learned about people of various sexualities, genders, ethnicities, and other differences. The practice of iteratively reexamining our own perspectives is what allows for the purification of our perceptions. This is the profound insight Buddhists speak of when we reference viewing the world from an enlightened perspective. Enlightened, we are aware of the limitless capacities of our life force and that of others; deluded, we doubt our own capacity for enlightenment and we doubt that of others as well.

## Cultural Humility

Cultural humility is resourced by our fierce compassion and our discomfort resilience. Our psychological, emotional, and spiritual growth can help us develop a prosocial cognitive and behavioral schema. *Prosocial* simply means we engage with the world in a way that is vibrant and reciprocally enriching. A cognitive behavioral schema is the way we view and engage ourselves, the world, and our future. That schema forms our perspective on life and the action or inaction with which we live it.

Releasing or transcending cultural fragility is part of how we develop this empowered prosocial way of thinking and being. We can recognize cultural fragility in ourselves when we feel fearful, angry, or defensive about being immersed in cultural contexts different from our own. Just like white fragility reflects the emotional and psychological reactivity that evinces a lack of heartiness and hardiness, cultural fragility is the guardedness, defensiveness, or emotional and psychological shakiness we feel when we engage with cultural settings that are unfamiliar to us.

> When we are truly humble, we are aware of and at ease with our own unique being as an expression of extraordinary cosmic life force.

Our internalized white supremacist cultural characteristics, like the right to comfort, may contribute to our feeling put out when we are immersed in media or among people with whom we do not identify. We may feel this tremulousness or discomfort happening when we are the only able-bodied person in a room full of people with disabilities, or when we are the only young person in a room full of older persons or vice versa. That feeling that we are out of place is really nothing more than a bit of our cultural fragility separating us from the truth of interdependence and impermanence. Cultural fragility itself reflects a level of cognitive distortion, where we are unable to think clearly about our inherent connections to people who differ from us.

Cultural humility is a vital social engagement skill for all people, no matter what types of privilege or oppression we experience. We may think that humility has some kind of obsequious, servile, or disempowered meaning, but humility actually allows for our most empowered relationality. When we are truly humble, we are aware of and at ease with our own unique being as an expression of extraordinary cosmic life force.

Try saying that as an affirmation, amending it as it suits you:

*I am a brilliant, beautiful expression of limitless cosmic life force!*

Remember, affirmations are how we speak back to and calm that loud inner critic who has all the cognitive distortions. Black people have an expression about this wherein we say to cognitive distortions or untruths, "You are loud and wrong!" *Loud and wrong* applies when someone is equal parts incorrect and adamant that they are right.

With cultural humility we sense into our interdependence and the impermanent and imperfect nature of our being. Cultural humility allows us to show up authentically and be joyous in the opportunity to learn from everyone and everything around us. With cultural humility we are empowered by our freedom from delusions of perfection and liberated from the need to pretend to know "the" right way. We know that when we make a mistake, our resolve to be inclusive will make that mistake a valuable learning experience. When our fierce compassion and discomfort resilience is strong enough to bear regular correction and redirection, we absorb the corrections and redirections such that they augment our lives. When we live with cultural humility, mistakes and failures become stepping stones to growth on our joyous path of conscious prosocial engagement.

Let's practice growing our enlightened awareness with some activities to help us jump into the world of human diversity with wisdom and courage.

Many of us enjoy graphic arts—paintings, photography, sculpture, and so forth. We may not realize how our perceptions of art reflect some of the cognitive distortions or delusions we have absorbed via white supremacy culture and other types of social oppression. We need to clean our perceptions to engage art in a more just and connected way. For example, many of us have been taught to view African sculptures as exotic or as collectibles that make us appear worldly without needing or having any appreciation for or connection to African people. Much of the African (and Indigenous) art in museums is stolen goods. So, one of the ways I invite people to be in right relationship with African art is to consider the means by which it is/was acquired. If it was acquired unjustly, we can advocate and work toward its return to the people from whom it was stolen. If it is in the home or museum of someone who stole it, that art is devalued, not honored.

About five thousand pieces known as the Benin Bronzes were stolen by British colonial soldiers, and the largest collections of them are still in Britain. Some have been restored to their original home, Nigeria. The United States and Germany only just began returning what they have of this stolen treasure in 2022. In a statement about the repatriation of the art, Lonnie G. Bunch III, the secretary of the Smithsonian Institution, said, "Not only was returning ownership of these magnificent artifacts to their rightful home the right thing to do, it also demonstrates how we all benefit from cultural institutions making ethical choices."[2]

When we consider that the entire West African kingdom of Benin was destroyed by European invaders with countless Africans killed, tortured, and enslaved in the process, it seems incredible that any museum could proudly display these without even acknowledging how they acquired them or what happened to the people who created the works of art in the first place. What we are seeing when we witness the Benin Bronzes in the US or Europe is pride about theft and pillaging. It says, *Yes, we killed them, we destroyed their kingdoms, and we brought home their art as souvenirs.* This colonial legacy of stealing global majority artistic creations—usually after a genocide—has impacted how many of us view and display African art to this day. We have been socialized to develop a "Look what I have" attitude rather than appreciation for Africans who made it; to exploit the art for our own prestige rather than regard it in a way that reflects gratitude and insight.

---

## Let's Practice!

# Your Collection Connection

We do not have to stay in an appropriative relationship with global majority art. If you have any art made by Black people from anywhere in the Diaspora, here is an affirmation practice you might use to begin to be in a joyfully just relationship with that work:

> *I offer gratitude to the Black person(s) or African person(s) who created this art. I offer fierce compassion for their struggles, and this means that I will honor and support Black artists in the following ways: _____.*

Fill in the blank by letting your mind flow with whatever comes, allowing yourself to consider how you might support justice and joy in the lives of Black artists. Then try the following:

> *Reflecting on the origins of Black art and expressing appreciation for it helps me because _____.*

There are many ways that we benefit from appreciation and gratitude practices, and some of the ways are unique to us as individuals, so journaling about it helps you see how you personally are enriched by the art around you. This way it is not merely a possession but rather a part of your community of artistic teachers and muses. Free-association journaling such as this, where you let your mind make its own connections, can help you grasp meanings and significances that are currently vague or elusive in your conscious mind.

---

You can have a joyfully just experience of art and artists by first doing a consciousness-raising practice that lands you in the awareness of interdependence and then engaging the art with a spirit of fierce compassion. Consciousness-raising, as it is articulated in the wisdom of Black activists, refers to becoming aware of helpful and harmful cultural influences. The goal of consciousness-raising is to discern what is valuable and what is harmful in your own worldview. From the Buddhist perspective, raising one's life condition or elevating one's consciousness refers to purifying our perception, which also involves awakening to know which of your ways of thinking reflect delusion and which reflect enlightenment. Hence, the wisdom of Black activists and the wisdom of Buddhism are aligned on the need to refine our worldview.

> Stay woke is an invocation to call forth
> and maintain a discerning mind.

Woke means arousing critical consciousness and a commitment to seeing clearly. The misuse of the word, wherein it is bandied about to mean "politically correct," is an example of the delusion caused when Black dialect is appropriated or demeaned. The original expression stay woke was created by Black people for Black people, decades ago, inviting one another into consciousness and wisdom. Early usage of this language to describe Black consciousness dates at least to 1923 when the Black liberation leader Marcus Garvey issued calls to Black people of the African Diaspora to "wake up" and become more conscious and thus empowered socially and politically. Then the Blues musician Huddie Ledbetter, a.k.a. Lead Belly, used the phrase "stay woke" in a recording of his 1938 song "Scottsboro Boys," a protest song about nine Black teenagers wrongfully accused of raping white women and sentenced to death.[3]

I remember hearing and using this expression forty years ago as a teenager in community with other young Black activists. Saying "stay woke" is how Black people reminded one another to not internalize racism or exploitative capitalism. It was and is a call to stay true to our most discerning awareness. "Stay woke" is a dialect practice from Black wisdom that reminds us not to be fooled by all that would have us doubt our value and significance or all that would prevent us from seeing oppression in the world.

The brilliance of the use of the word as a state of being—*woke* instead of *awake*—is that it speaks to the constant vigilance Black people have had to maintain due to the tricky, slippery, shifting impacts of racism on everything from finances to self-concept, from health to child-rearing. *Stay woke* for Black people is an invocation to call forth and maintain a discerning mind. People may choose not to be conscious or woke when they are fearful or defensive about acknowledging racism and other types of oppression and fear losing privilege.

So, if *woke* is a word that you use, consider what you mean when you say it and how you might be truer to its actual meaning. How might you be in the right relationship with this wisdom word from Black dialect?

## Ending Cultural Appropriation with Reparative Relationality

Oftentimes when people think of reparations, they think of things like giving back land that was stolen from Native Americans or paying financial restitution to African Americans for the brutal exploitation of enslavement. However, we do not need to wait for government bodies to legislate us being in right relationship with those to whom we and our ancestors owe reparations. We can engage our interdependence and thrive more joyfully by being in just relationships with one another, by participating in what I call *reparative relationality*.

Reparative relationality means that we relate to one another in ways that repair the harms of social oppression. When we are trying to repair human relationships, we share power, opportunities, and resources with people who have been denied these by white supremacy or other types of oppression. Reparative relationality can exist between any people whose connection has been thwarted by social oppression—which means all of us. Cisgender men who have historically been positioned to be dominant in relationship to women can engage contemplative practice to be relationally reparative by following the leadership of and listening to women and noncisgender folx. Global minority (a.k.a. white) folx can deliberately and intentionally contradict white supremacy by declining leadership positions and instead backing the leadership of global majority people.

All people have privilege of some sort, which means that anyone can be oppressive. For this reason, we can contemplate reparative relationality from whatever social locations we find ourselves. We can also consider this from the standpoint of contradicting internalized oppression. For example, women sometimes internalize sexism and are harshly critical of other women based on sexist standards. Reparative relationality in this context would mean women contemplating how to be better allies to other women. We can further consider what economic reparative relationality looks like for us on personal, interpersonal, and institutional levels.

Let's Practice!

## Developing Reparative Relationships

In your Joy Journal, write the name of one person you work with who is marginalized in some way that you are not. Consider how you might be in a reparative relationship with them. This can be as simple as how we speak to one another. For example, instead of being directive in communications with young people or people we supervise, we can ask what they think of whatever we would direct them to do. Or you might be a white-racialized (a.k.a. global minority) woman and a Black colleague's accomplishments have been overlooked. If you are selected for a leadership role, you can ask that your colleague be offered the opportunity instead or that you share the opportunity. These types of small actions can create ripples of inclusive joy in our lives as we personally take on the challenges of healing the harms of an oppressive society.

Let's Practice!

## Taking In Some Art

Now that we know a bit about consciousness-raising, let's take it to the streets! More specifically, the streets with art! I encourage you to plan an art-viewing day, either alone or with children and/or family, with this joyfully just plan in mind. First, look online to find out which museums or murals near you feature the work of Black or other global majority artists. Then let yourself journal a bit about what thoughts, feelings, or preconceptions you might have about going to this exhibit. Do you feel proud of yourself, like you are doing something exceptional? Do you feel obligated? Do you feel fearful that you might say or do the "wrong" thing? What are you hoping to learn? Explore this in your Joy Journal. If you are going with other people to view the art, talk with them about what preconceptions and feelings they might be having. Then bring your Joy Journal with you to view the art. It may be easier to let this be an audio journal so that you can speak into your phone or other device as you view the art.

What do you feel in your body as you view different pieces? What emotions arise? What thoughts? Are there any thoughts that surprise you? What areas of personal growth does your engagement with Black art or global majority art point you toward?

Next, explore what the art means as described by the artists. Often our sense of feeling connected with art is limited because we don't quite understand what the work is meant to convey from the artist's perspective. Fertility symbols are a perfect example of this. Fertility symbols in African art are meant to illustrate and invoke reverent appreciation for the regeneration of life and the aspiration of African people to see their lives continue. In this way, fertility symbols could be said to say "Black lives matter" and deserve to be treasured. Perhaps saying "Black lives matter" or "Black lives inspire" is another practice you might offer, silently or out loud, when you witness Black art. Play with it to see what affirming messages about yourself and the artists can emerge from these contemplative practices with art.

For this next cultural engagement activity, I invite you to explore the wisdom and self-transcendence depicted in other forms of Black or African art via some of the most famous Black artists you want to know. Being familiar with the incredible spectrum of Black artists in the United States alone will expand your understanding of Black wisdom and self-transcendence. Fortunately, because of the internet, we have broad access to extraordinary images from African American artists. Witness the work of Kehinde Wiley, the first Black person to paint a presidential portrait (Barack Obama). Look at Wiley's work and journal about what it says to you about Black people and about yourself. Try that with other famous Black artists such as Kara Walker, Titus Kaphar, and Charly Palmer. Explore the work of Amy Sherald, who painted Michelle Obama for the National Portrait Gallery in Washington, DC, or Jacob Lawrence's work entitled *Migration of the American Negro* that chronicles the great migration—an aspect of North American history that affects everyone living in the US.

Bisa Butler and Faith Ringgold do amazing work with fabrics. Their creations are part of the legacy of quilting in the African and African

American artistic contemplative traditions. If you like sculpture, explore the work of Augusta Savage. If you enjoy photography, immerse yourself in the extraordinary worldview of Gordon Parks.

For a dip into artistic Black joy, explore the waterpark scenes in the work of the painter Derrick Adams, who in his discussion on Hip-Hop and relaxing while Black states that he "wanted to see paintings of Black people having fun." He paints about the "types of acts that can be radical without being purposefully radical. Because we are multidimensional, we have areas of life that are not just about combat; we have experiences where we need to refuel, regenerate, spend time with family, and these are equally important as protest."[4] In a message to Black people, he shares that we may not want to show this side of our lives because it looks like we are not working hard, either to advance our own lives or end racism. This reflection is useful to Black people to see if any of our internalized racism—messages from colonizers, enslavers, and white supremacy about us being lazy—get stirred up when we view Black art. If so, then we can decide to release that internalized racism, knowing that the more we recognize it and release it, the less it informs our worldview and behavior.

These contemplative art exercises can be done with global majority artists of every ethnicity so that you begin to undo how racism has informed what you see as art and who you know as artists. Whatever your ethnicity or cultural point of view, remember to do the reflective journal exercise as you experience art (or afterward) and consider how the work contributes to your understanding of your interdependent relationship with people from various cultural and ethnic experiences.

Sometimes the art we are viewing is painful to experience. If you have ever viewed depictions of Black people being whipped or chained, burned or hung, then it would be useful for you to consider what those images communicated to you and what they made you feel. Take a moment now and make a note or voice memo of what you felt when you saw that. What did you take away from the experience? For those of us who are Black, we may have numbed out to disassociate from our own vulnerability, or we may have felt a deep sense of connection. We may have felt inspired to protect Black bodies, or angry, or sad. Whatever the experience, it is important to note what we felt and what action or inaction we felt drawn to. From there we can set an intention about how we engage with art about Black experiences henceforth.

_____

Since throughout the world, depictions of brutality against Black bodies are so ubiquitous, we may have become desensitized to them. We may have come to view them as an unfortunate fact of life that we have no control over and thus it does not even warrant an emotional and cognitive response for us anymore. This is one of the instances where we can see our nonreaction as a reaction. If we are numb or indifferent to Black suffering, then a part of our own consciousness is dormant and our perceptions are limited, to say nothing of our capacity to authentically and empathically engage with Black people. I remember being on a flight and the woman in front of me was watching the movie *12 Years a Slave*. During the part where Lupita Nyong'o is tied to a tree naked and whipped until her flesh is bloody and tearing, the woman in front of me was eating potato chips and drinking her soda. I remember thinking that she was either socialized to be indifferent to this type of brutality toward Black people or she was using the food to help her have a detached and escapist approach to it. In either case, when viewing images of Black suffering depicted in art and film, we get to notice what feelings or absence of feelings arise for us. Notice your thoughts to see whether you are internally compelled toward justice by what you see or if you have a kind of *Ah well, what are you going to do?* thought. Noticing and developing empowered engagement is one way to cultivate a joyfully just approach to art and life, wherein we greet oppression with vigor and commitment rather than disempowered apathy or resignation.

This same vigor and empowerment can inform how we respond when we know that art has been unjustly acquired. For example, most museums have comment cards or suggestion boxes. On numerous occasions, from MoMA in New York City to the Louvre in Paris, I have left encouraging, positively framed notes to the curators and museum officials inviting them into authenticity by asking that they consider repatriation of stolen art. I further suggest that until they repatriate it, they can at least post a statement acknowledging the theft and the violent circumstances under which the looting of the depicted art took place. I have also participated in protests educating visitors outside of museums when the institution refuses to acknowledge or return stolen art. This type of advocacy is deeply meaningful and impactful. Some museums in the United States, Germany, and France have begun to return a very small portion of treasures stolen from Africa and from global majority people around the world because of such advocacy.

Many people think of protest as negatively disruptive, but if something harmful is happening and you disrupt it, that is very positive and life-affirming. Protest simply means to object, and we can do so with as little as one word or even a glance. Challenging ourselves to express our objections to oppression in positive, productive ways is how we develop our most agentive self and create a most just world.

Your protests can take the form that suits you best. You might start small, with simple gestures when you see or hear something oppressive: throwing side-eye or raising your eyebrow is a form of protest, right? The wisdom is in knowing that it is *you* who is empowered when you decide that social problems are not beyond your capacity to address. Remember that popular quote attributed to the cultural anthropologist Margaret Mead: "Never doubt that a small committed group of individuals can change the world. Indeed, it is the only thing that ever has." When we engage in protest practices, we can enjoy art and indeed all of life without deluding ourselves, numbing out, or being silently complicit with oppression.

> Challenging ourselves to express our objections to oppression in positive, productive ways is how we develop our most agentive self and create a most just world.

## Do You Know What Time It Is?

Some Black dialect practices take everyday expressions and imbue them with a reflective or insightful undertone. You may have heard Black people say, "I know what time it is," and you knew they were commenting on the issues and energy of a given moment rather than the hour on the clock. So, when we "know what time it is," we are aware of the unique challenges and opportunities in this moment in history, location, and relationships.

I invite you to consider "what time it is" with respect to aspects of human diversity that are recognized during certain months or even days. Heritage months and identity recognitions are ways to make visible those in our society whose lives and contributions have been rendered invisible by social oppression. Acknowledgments such as Black History Month or making Juneteenth a national holiday are absolutely not enough to end racism or any other kind of oppression. Yet the proliferation of events and activities during these months can provide meaningful opportunities for conscious cultural engagement.

Allowing fierce compassion and discomfort resilience to strengthen us each day, let's set the stage on which we enact our joyfully just present and future. This begins with the future that is today and this coming week. Sometimes we plan the future too distantly with no intention for immediate action. While it is always wise to plan for the near and distant future, we also get to know the joy of living immediately, acting in the moment. As Daisaku Ikeda says, "Leave behind the passive dreaming of a rose-tinted future. The energy of happiness exists in living today with roots sunk firmly in reality's soil."[5]

## Put Joyfully Just, Conscious Cultural Engagement on the Calendar!

Many of us want to be more cross-culturally engaged but sometimes we don't make any time to do it. Just as you tend to your physical health by making time to exercise, you can attend to your social well-being by making time for culturally conscious engagement with the world around you.

There are always abundant opportunities for cultural engagement. What is the current acknowledgment or celebration month? For example, if you are reading this in March, look up Women's History Month events in your area. To be as inclusive as possible, try to find events that acknowledge global majority women's or transgender women's history. April is Black Women's History Month, so there will be activities and events where we can learn about the contributions of Black women then as well.

The best activities allow you to reflect on your present-day realities and the personal implications for you. For example, going to a Women's History Month event about Native American women in your region could connect you to a deeper understanding of the region you call home. During Black History Month, you might learn what contributions Black people made to your favorite hobby or arena of work. What are local activities you could engage in this week to connect with and support the diversity around you? Take a moment and do a quick search to add at least one activity to your joyfully just, conscious cultural engagement calendar!

We know that these monthly designations are arbitrary. Black people often joke about how February is a cold, short month, so it figures that, because of anti-Black racism, it would be the designated month to acknowledge Black history. It is also useful to note that Black History Month is celebrated in February in part because the renowned founding American abolitionist Frederick Douglass was born on February 14. Abraham Lincoln, who acquiesced to freeing enslaved people after Black people and their abolitionist allies resisted and worked to end slavery for centuries, was also born in February. These monthly designations are also often politically motivated efforts for pseudo-recognition of marginalized populations without creating meaningful change. Nonetheless, even when heritage and identity celebrations are overly contrived and commercialized, they can be opportunities to explore aspects of our diverse human cultural experience. When Black people coined the phrase "Make a dollar out of fifteen cents," we were speaking of being resourceful!

Make your explorations of diversity relevant to your life. Here's a handful of examples of achievements by Black innovators so you can choose the ones you want to explore further: If you are a refrigerator repair person (or simply have gratitude for your fridge), explore the over forty patented refrigeration inventions of Frederick McKinley Jones. Jones also invented the first portable air conditioning unit. Pretty cool, huh? If you are a teacher, you could explore the works of Fanny Jackson Coppin, the Black educator and advocate for women's education for whom Coppin State University is named. If you are a nurse, you could explore the work of Susie King Taylor who, in addition to being the first recognized Black nurse during the American Civil War, is also the first Black woman to self-publish a memoir. If you work in publishing, you could explore the life and work of John H. Johnson, who formed the first Black publishing company in the United States. There is no field of endeavor that Black people have not substantively enriched.

By finding out who the Black and other global majority folx that have contributed to your field of endeavor are, you increase your understanding of your own field as well as your awareness of interdependence. You can practice this cultural engagement with all the monthly celebrations not as an observer but as someone who is continuously waking up to the ways in which your life is enriched by all types of people. Try engagement with the varied celebrations of diversity in your country or region. In the US, we have:

- African American History Month—February

- Women's History Month—March

- Black Women's History Month—April

- Asian Pacific American Heritage Month—May

- LGBTQIA+ Pride Month—June

- Disability Pride Month—July

- Black Business Month—August

- Hispanic Heritage Month—September 15–October 15

- LGBTQIA+ History Month—October

- Native American Heritage Month—November

## Conscious Engagement with Media

> Popular escapist fiction enchants adult readers without
> challenging them to be educated for critical consciousness.[6]
>
> **bell hooks**

For many of us, including children and youth, much of what we learn about people is from various forms of media, especially social media, television, and movies. Our intentions are often good. We may feel a longing for human connection, and in that sense, we are trying to engage our interdependence through media. Have you ever turned on the television just for company or felt a bit lonely and decided to scroll through social media? These are common responses to the call for connection that we all feel.

Just like all other aspects of our lives, it is worth attending to our intentions *before* we act on them to make sure we "stop and clean" the intention and act in a way that accords with our greater self. When I say "stop and clean," I am speaking of pausing. Pausing allows us to raise our consciousness and gain awareness of all the motives, conscious and unconscious, that may be driving a choice. For example, we often want to distract ourselves from work or something difficult in our lives. That is not always a bad idea. All our psychological defenses—including denial, which can manifest as escapism—serve a purpose at different points in our lives. However, if we are always in denial about the hard truths that impact our lives, such as sexism and ageism, then we never face them and do not develop the strength or wisdom to overcome them.

We can apply our practices to be joyfully just in regard to social media. Surveillance capitalism via the collection and commodification of all our searches, likes, and follows operates in a manner that reinforces an addictive pull toward overindulgence in social media. Have you ever lost an hour on Facebook or Instagram? That is not entirely due to your lack of self-control. Your "feeds" are algorithmically designed to keep you engaged. So, getting control becomes a real battle in which your fierce compassion and discomfort resilience must be engaged in the same way these are needed with other addictions. If we are to defend our own minds and protect our precious attention from those who would exploit it via calculated psychological and emotional bait, then we need to engage our contemplative practices to build the musculature for resistance. The word *resistance* has many meanings, and in this context, we resist all that would keep us from being just toward ourselves. We resist anything that would steal our joy.

Sometimes the theft of our time happens via distractions that, although cute and compelling, are somewhat less important than what we need or even really want to be doing. How many times can you watch a cat play with a ball? Hundreds of times, of course! But to be in command of our own attention means we do not get hooked that often or for that long.

> If we are to defend our own minds and protect our precious attention, then we need to engage our contemplative practices to build the musculature for resistance.

### Let's Practice!

## Social Media Self-Awareness

The next time you think of checking your social media feeds, try these queries as "pause practices" so that you can make conscious decisions about how you engage:

- *What is my intention as I open this app?*

- *What am I looking for?*

- *Is this the best place to find it?*

We can also try to get control of our social media engagement by timing it. If you are going to open an app, try setting a timer for fifteen minutes. Stop at the fifteen-minute mark and ask yourself how your life and well-being have been enriched by the time you've spent on the app. Be careful not to use this as a reason to beat yourself up, though. Instead, appreciate yourself for taking the time to notice and acknowledge how you might best use your precious time and attention.

---

Disturbingly, some of our most just intentions can be co-opted by unaware social media engagement. Because social media feeds the ideas we feed it, we can come to delude ourselves into white supremacy culture's "one right way" of thinking, even as we work for justice. Furthermore, because social media is so much about performance, we have begun to see a proliferation of performances of authenticity and performances of social justice engagement. For example, although some people participate in Black Lives Matter protests out of genuine commitment to protecting Black life, for others it is just a fashionable photo op where they get to pose for the camera at the protest.

In *Unfollow Me,* her book with candid critiques of this type of performance activism, Jill Louise Busby talks about the disingenuousness that many people, including Black and queer people, can unwittingly slip into if we perform static representations of identity instead of presenting our ever-evolving true self. Her book invites us into being in conscious control of our social media engagement. She describes frantic engagement with social media as "giving in to motion above everything else. As if things that are still or quiet can't change."[7] Slowing down to engage mindfully and with the fiercely compassionate intentions that flow from our greater self is one way to develop a joyfully just relationship with social media.

In addition to connecting us with people we feel an affinity for, media and entertainment offer windows into the lives of people we do not necessarily have contact with but with whom we share experiences of life's ups and downs. Sometimes we watch certain shows or films to join in community with people who we rarely get to be in contact with. That makes sense; it's part of our natural inclination to know one another.

Where this gets problematic is that much—if not most—of the media we engage with reflects oppressive delusions of racism, sexism, ableism, and other types of oppression. For example, I decided to watch the television show *Modern Family* because it was touted as a cutting-edge example of openly gay and multiethnic families being increasingly represented on TV. It turns out that the show is riddled with stereotypes not only about queer people but also about Latinx people. The Colombian woman in the family plays into those stereotypes, exhibiting internalized racism. There are multiple episodes where the Vietnamese little girl, Lily, is referred to as a "potsticker" or a "fortune cookie." They even make jokes about her ability to pronounce her own name. There are also "jokes" about the Native American genocide. That show is an example of how efforts at inclusive programming often wind up perpetuating microaggression and untruths.

Another example popped up in one of my favorite shows, *Grace and Frankie*. Former civil rights activist Jane Fonda, who plays Grace, utters an ageist and ableist line in an episode where she and Frankie are considering internet dating. She rules out one dating prospect by pointing out that he uses a wheelchair and only has one foot.

You may be wondering, *What's wrong with little jokes like this? Why do we have to be so sensitive? After all, they weren't meant to be hurtful; the writers and producers were trying their best to acknowledge the diversity while still being funny, right?* Well, when we mock some aspect of people's diversity, we continue to ostracize not only them but also ourselves. We miss the real differences and similarities we have as humans when we only depict and watch depictions that devalue one another based on oppressive ideas. We also deprive ourselves of the humor and insight that is possible when we don't use the old tropes and stereotypes to relate cross-culturally.

What can make this even more challenging is that many of us who are from marginalized cultural or ethnic backgrounds have internalized the oppressive views of ourselves, so we, too, find the stereotypes compelling, funny, or accurate. One example of this is the popularity of the *Madea* movies, which depict Black grandmothers as buffoons. Even though in most Black families, grandmothers are stalwart, dignified, and wise, that is not what the Madea image depicts.

This disparaging misrepresentation of Black grandmothers invites us to consider how some white racialized people are comforted by the familiar notion of a foolish and thereby impotent depiction of Black womanhood. In what ways are Black people so eager to have any representation of ourselves in the media that we settle for images that are demeaning? What internalized racism can be said to exist among us as Black people when we can tolerate such a proliferate misrepresentation of the nurturing figures who have been central to the preservation of Black life?

Rather than having a cancel or calling-out approach to ourselves, or to Black writers and filmmakers, what if we call ourselves and one another *in*, inviting more anti-racist, nonsexist, and inclusive media representations? This can be done in playful, community-building ways like having critical-consciousness watch parties.

---

Let's Practice!

## Plan a Conscious Watch Party!

We can actually plan our own consciousness-raising media gatherings! Send an invitation to anyone you want in your Joyfully Just squad. Remember in the beginning of the book when I encouraged you to consider inviting one or two people to read this with you and do the practices together? Well, this is a fun thing you can do together! Let everyone know it's going to be a conscious party (like Ziggy Marley's 1988 album). That means that there will be pauses, which can be called by anyone, to note important strengths, challenges, issues, or insights in what you're watching. Let the pause button serve a contemplative role as you take a moment to notice thoughts or feelings about a scene or ask other conscious party participants if they'd like to discuss what was just depicted.

Then everyone gets to take a five-minute individual reflection break after the show. This will be challenging because you will want to rush to discuss, but if you let your inner conversation happen first, the discussion with the group will be richer. Reflect on your reactions for a few minutes before discussing them. Look for your own biases as you go outside for a walk, stretch, journal, or do something that helps you integrate your perceptions of what you watched and consider where your cognitive distortions, defenses, privilege, and biases may be impacting your perceptions.

After your break, discuss! Set a timer so everyone has an equal share of whatever amount of time is allotted for discussion. If someone wants to cede their time, they can; consider sitting with them in silence while they reflect or journal. Not all communication needs to be written; maybe some of you might sketch how you received and experienced the show. Discuss what you watched using these prompts or any other questions you wish:

- *How was this inclusive? How was it not?*

- *What did racism look like from the director's or screenwriter's presentation of the material?*

- *How could you notice the white gaze?*

- *What did internalized racism look like? Internalized sexism?*

- *Was there heterosexism or genderism in the show? Ageism much? Adultism?*

- *Did the humor rely on oppressive ideas?*

- *Was Black music used in scenes that did not include Black people? Why and how was Black music used?*

- *Was violence or other suffering sensationalized and glamorized?*

- *Was Black or global majority suffering glamorized most or depicted blithely?*

After your discussion, create encouraging, positively framed posts on different social media platforms. Most shows and movies have a social media presence, so let them know what you think. Give yourselves a group name, so no one gets trolled. You can come up with a name that describes your unique group of viewers. Have fun making up a name that suits your group, or just call yourselves the Conscious Gazers or the Joyfully Just Gaze (tag me and cite this book if you use those). I will also be hosting some *Joyfully Just* Zoom conscious-watch parties, so stay tuned for those (pun intended)!

Posting or elsewise sharing your feedback allows you to be in an empowered relationship with the programs you watch. We can really revolutionize programming with supportive yet consciously critical calling-in of media developers and providers. Media developers and providers are welcome to dialogue with us as we do the respectful, encouraging, playful, and fiercely compassionate work of mutual development.

As we engage with television and film, we also get to think about who we see cast in different roles. Use the queries below to look for common stereotypes the next time you watch a film:

- *Is Black suffering trivialized? (For example, does the Black character suffer most graphically and/or die first?)*

- *Is Black dialect or expressions appropriated by non-Black people?*

- *Is the hero white?*

- *Is the Black or global majority person cast as a sidekick?*

- *If there are global majority folks in the film, are they being rescued by a white savior? (The white savior myth refers to the paternalistic characteristic of white supremacy in which white people are mistakenly perceived to regularly rescue or guide global majority people.)*

- *Is there a "magical negro" (a Black or global majority person who sacrifices their well-being or ignores their own difficult circumstances to aid or guide the white main character)?*

- *Are the Black or global majority characters depicted as having only white friends and partners? (For example, a tokenized Asian character, wherein everyone in their lives is depicted as white, promotes the message that white racialized people are central in Asian lives.)*

- *Are the Black, Latinx, Indigenous, or Asian women hypersexualized?*

- *Are the Black women depicted as sassy but not smart?*

- *Are the Black men depicted as dangerous?*

- *Are Asian men depicted as weak or as nerds?*

- *Is everyone in the show the same body type or are those with different body types cast in stereotypical roles?*

- *Are there gender and sexual orientation stereotypes?*

- *How is the plot, cast, or dialogue inclusive and anti-racist? How is it not?*

- *What other stereotypes or non-inclusive aspects can you notice in what you watch?*

---

Asking ourselves these kinds of questions allows us to develop a deeper level of discernment regarding what we do with our precious free time. It also allows us to step into empowered viewership wherein we vote with our choices for the kind of programming that supports and depicts justice.

Developing critical consciousness can support us in refining our awareness of and engagement with everything from art to education to the workplace, in ways that help us make healthier choices. Critical consciousness can also help us make empowered and empowering decisions about media and entertainment.

## Who's Watching?

Criticality is the capacity to read, write, and think in ways of understanding power, privilege, social justice, and oppression, particularly for populations who have been historically marginalized in the world.[8]

Dr. Gholdy Muhammad

Have you ever been watching TV and at some point asked yourself, *What am I watching?* or *Why am I watching this?* Sometimes the part of us that chooses to watch a given program is unclear to us. So, the question of who's watching becomes something of an existential one, because we can lose sight of who we are when we get lost in watching things that don't align with our values or greater self.

When you first open a streaming app, sometimes it asks, "Who's watching?" So, here's another way to work with that question. We know when a streaming app asks, that is about surveillance capitalism, which monitors our engagement and preferences to market products and services to us. However, we can use everything as an invitation to practice consciousness-raising. In this case, we can ask ourselves: *Who, indeed, is watching? Is it my inner child who needs comforting? Is it my traumatized mind that needs to work through something by watching trauma depicted externally? Is it my angry self that needs a place to rest my anger? Is it my overwhelmed self, looking to escape? Who in me and of me is watching, indeed? And is that part of me truly being fulfilled by what I am watching?*

We get to raise our consciousnesses and wake up to the many ways racism is reflected in what we watch so that we are not absorbing racism-infused content mindlessly and letting it pollute our unconscious perceptions and expectations of the world. Nichiren Daishonin writes, "If the minds of living beings are impure, their land is also impure, but if their minds are pure, so is their land. There are not two lands, pure and impure in themselves. The difference lies solely in the good or evil of our minds."[9] If we are constantly ridding our minds of racism, we are also ridding our lands of racism and other types of oppression. We are all responsible for being constructively critical as we engage—or disengage—with various types of television and film.

Here is another example of extractive, appropriative racism intrepidly at play on our television and movie screens: Have you ever noticed how some non-Black characters in shows are scripted to use Black dialect without ever acknowledging that it is Black dialect they are using? It is as if there is some tacit agreement that the cultural appropriation of Black dialect is just fine, that although the phrasing does not come from the speaker's cultural context, it is perfectly fine for them to use it indiscriminately with no recognition of or relationality to the Black people from whom the language practice comes. When you start to pay attention to it, you notice that most shows use Black dialect in this way and can benefit from some examination of why. The next time you hear it, ask yourself if they are using it to sound hip and edgy. Are they trying to feign cultural inclusion or connection to Black people that they have not actually developed? Does it seem as though they are using the language to connect to Black people? Or are they just using it in an entitled way?

You might notice that many movies and TV shows that have non-Black characters speaking Black dialect often don't actually have Black people in significant roles at all. They are implicitly saying, *Appropriating Black dialect is enough; we don't actually need Black people to make the show diverse.*

When Black people use Black vernacular, we are often seen as uneducated or "ghetto." Using our own creative language practices can place us in danger of not being accepted into schools or jobs when our qualifications are stellar. However, a white person could use the same language or phrasing and be viewed as worldly and witty. This is similar to how Black people are often not safe when we play our own Black music in our homes or when we are driving, but non-Black people get to do so without being targeted.

Racism causes Black people to be judged and harmed for engaging in our own cultural practices even as white people and other non-Black people enjoy and appropriate them without a word of gratitude.

Furthermore, the appropriation of Black cultural practices often results in financial and social gain that is almost never shared with Black people. One of the clearest and most disturbing historical and contemporary manifestations of cultural appropriation is the use of Black wisdom traditions to make wealthy those who have no real commitment to Black liberation.

One place where we see this phenomena, which I have dubbed "linguistic blackface," is in comedy. Some of the wealthiest white and other non-Black comedians owe so much of their popularity to the performance of this form of linguistic blackface or *blackvoice*. I admit that when I first started to see and hear this, I thought what many Black people did: I appreciated the use of Black dialect by non-Black people because it made me feel like our language practices were being valued. I thought that maybe we were being heard and recognized for this contribution, for how our ways of wording things shapes culture and reflects cultural shapeshifting. After all, imitation is the best form of flattery, right? However, when you cannot even safely use the dialect practice you created without being demeaned or when that dialect practice is not acknowledged as yours, then you're being devalued and robbed of the cultural resource you created.

This is not to say that we need to be overly obsessed with expectations of acknowledgment every time people use Black dialect, but we do get to start questioning why it is *never* acknowledged and appreciated when people benefit so much from it. We get to think critically about this and not allow ourselves or other people who are appropriating it to bypass gratitude and meaningful connection to and upliftment of Black lives.

Yes, it's nice that the British-American comedian John Oliver, the host of *Last Week Tonight with John Oliver*, is using our dialect, and it is very cute with his English accent. But what makes it more compelling than a Black person using the same phrasing? What would it be like if Oliver decided that instead of continuing to keep all the acclaim for his genuinely insightful and well-researched comedy show, he actually had Black cohosts regularly so that we could hear the Black dialect he loves from Black comedians? That sounds fun *and* funny to me!

Why do we glamorize or fawn over non-Black people when they speak Black dialect? It's almost as if we're so grateful that they use it that we don't even expect any kind of acknowledgment. Where is the expressed gratitude for using Black linguistic creativity? Black people may often feel we don't even need to be recognized in this way, and that might be Black internalized racism. When non-Black immigrants use Black dialect, they're often trying to settle in an American language or find a way to be fluent in American parlance. They too get to consider their appropriation and the lack of recognition of it as African American parlance. Everyone benefits from this type of critical self-reflection and consciousness-raising.

We can further explore cultural appropriation and exploitation by looking at the racism in the entertainment and sports industries. Racism in sports is an international reality.[10] From the way Black athletes are targeted by media and fans with racist standards and comments, we see the legacy of enslavement. That legacy is also evident in the idea that Black athletes are owned and must comport themselves by more conservative standards than their non-Black counterparts.

Movies and television are quite ensconced in the legacy of racism. Arguably one of the best American actresses, Viola Davis discusses how she is not paid comparably with other actors of her standing. She also points out that white supremacy impacts casting in that lighter-skinned Black people are cast as more attractive and intelligent characters in primary roles while darker-skinned folks are often cast as evil, as irrelevant, or as fools.[11]

For a deeper dive into the entertainment industry, take a look at late-night television. Have you ever wondered why all three of the major network late-night talk show hosts are white men (a.k.a. global minority)? If you have never wondered about that, then wonder about that lack of wondering as you wonder now! The late shows have become a necessary stop for anyone who wants to get significant public notice, whether for their creative works, their political campaign, their social justice efforts, or anything else. At the time of this writing, these gatekeepers of fame are all white men. Most comedians would agree that they have been influenced by Black comedians, and I know they also recognize the long history of only white men having the privilege of lengthy tenure as late-night hosts. Yet I wonder if they intend to share the helm with any global majority cohosts or alternate hosting with global majority people—ever? Obviously hiring a Black musical group to support the show is nice, and it benefits them to have such immense talent accompany the show. However, only having Black people as musicians is also on-brand with the racist idea that the white guys are the face, brains, and leaders of the show and the global majority folks just play the music.

One night while watching Jimmy Kimmel on his late-night show, I noticed how having a Black host or cohost would have really been ideal. Michelle Obama was on the show, and Kimmel asked about her reaction to her husband being called "fine" by a Black member of the audience while he was giving a speech. As much as I love Kimmel, I think even he would agree that the Black woman referring to Barack Obama in Black dialect as "finer than a muhfu*h" could have been a great moment to have a Black host explore the funny, concise expressions of admiration reflected in Black dialect in a way that only a Black host could have. The whole lovely exuberant exchange between Barack and that fan could have been unpacked for the layers of meaning it had. The public affirmation of Black male beauty that is enriched by inner beauty and commitment to justice was among the things that moment captured in simple Black parlance.

In any case, having white hosts speak Black dialect with no acknowledgment of doing so says two things: (1) It is fine to literally take the words out of Black people's mouths without acknowledging where the words came from; (2) Using Black dialect is inclusive enough; we get to hear all the Black wit and witticisms without any of the dreaded actual Blackness. One of the ways late-night hosts like Stephen Colbert, Jimmy Fallon, and Jimmy Kimmel can share the power and wealth that Black people have helped them accumulate is to share that stage—literally—with Black comedians as regular cohosts. They can engage those who have the talent but don't have white male privilege—similar to what *The Daily Show* did with rotating hosts. I am calling these comedians in to beloved community so that they can actualize their obvious good intentions to have comedy be a healing force that ends racism instead of perpetuating it. I am calling them in to consideration of how to be in a joyfully just relationship with the Black dialect they so clearly and dearly love and profit from.

> The point is for us to wake up and notice who is informing our speech.

Here are some ideas for non-Black people to contemplate being in just relationships with Black dialect. First ask yourself, *In what ways can I and my loved ones be more conscious of and critical about our engagement with Black dialect?* Take a moment and journal about it now. Try on some short acknowledgment and gratitude statements and work them into your communication just as you have worked in many Black expressions. You can adjust the phrasing to suit your own voice. You might try using an acknowledgement comment like "As African Americans say" or "I appreciate Black people for expressing this so concisely" before or after you use Black dialect.

The point of this is not to be prescriptive or to expect that every time Black dialect is used it must be acknowledged as such but rather that it should most certainly be acknowledged often since it is used often. The point is for us to wake up and notice who is informing our speech. Another important growth point is to notice the discomfort that comes up at the thought of verbalizing these small acknowledgments. Does it feel awkward or like it will take too much time? Notice how small acts of inclusivity can stir our clinging to comfort. We can invite ourselves to consider the discomfort Black people feel when we are judged for using creative speech from our culture while others are lauded for using it. Non-Black people get to contemplate this with an intention to raise awareness of and develop gratitude for interdependence with Black people.

You can also consider how you could respond when you *witness* folks falling into the trap of using Black wit and witticisms without any acknowledgment or appreciation of Blackness. Maybe you help them with their awareness and lack of acknowledgment lightly and without criticism, saying something like, "Oh, you really like using Black dialect, huh?" Upstander gentle nudges like this are one way of enacting our interdependence to support one another's conscious cross-cultural engagement.

# Chapter Five

## Joyful Suffering

In this final chapter, we will explore grief and loss to learn how to surface joy as we experience sorrow. This will help us to have a balanced awareness even in times of great pain. Buddhism elucidates the hindrances that block our capacity to manifest our greater self. The hindrance of death refers to how fear of our own death, fear of a beloved's death, or the actual death of a loved one can cause us to be defeated in the quest to manifest our own enlightenment. Overcoming the hindrances of overwhelming fear of and sorrow about death and other types of loss allows us to maintain joy as we grieve and to have an enlightened experience of life's inevitable losses.

The coming pages may evoke some challenging feelings. Those of us who already know we have unresolved loss and grief issues might consider setting up an appointment with a therapist or counselor so that if you need some support processing the emotional work we are moving into, you already have that resource lined up. As I tell my students, the worst time to shop for a therapist is when you are in a crisis, because you may not have the bandwidth or time to choose well; also, it may be a while before you can get an appointment. You can use this chapter as a companion to your grief therapy. If formal therapy is not your thing, then consider which friends might read this section with you. Maybe you could have a reading or listening party where you go through this chapter supported by one another, pausing to process your experiences. Our sorrow is diminished and our joy multiplies when we engage our interdependence and navigate life's difficulties in community.

To help you regularly awaken to joy as we navigate this topic, I invite you to bring along your Joy Journal and your growing Joybox of resources. Those essential oils you love, that soothing music? Put some on now! Open your Joy Journal—whether it is an audio diary you are creating or a physical one—and title this page "I Can Grieve Life's Losses with Joy" or something like that worded to suit you. You are going to unearth a lot in this chapter about how to have joy in all situations, so note your insights! As always, if you need to take a break or return to a self-soothing exercise in this book, please do so. Also consider pausing occasionally and reciting that Lotus Sutra mantra, Nam Myoho Renge Kyo, the core contemplative practice of millions of people worldwide. The invocation itself may create a soothing resonance in your mind and body.

---

Let's Practice!

## Joyful Suffering

Here is a practice for when someone asks how you're doing and you are not doing so well. Consider saying something like, "I'm suffering well," "I am suffering joyfully," or "Oh, you know me, suffering with determination." Try to qualify *how* you are managing your suffering in a way that recognizes the courage and resilience you are facing the difficulty with. This is a good way to be authentic and not just say "Fine" or "Good" when you're really stressed or in pain.

Being authentic *is* being just toward yourself. Your authenticity also invites authenticity from whomever you're talking to, since now that you are being real, they can step out of the "fine" pretense, too. This does not mean you have to elaborate on your suffering. If you are speaking with someone in passing, you can end the conversation with that one comment and an encouraging smile and wave. Or you can share with them that you're reading *Joyfully Just* and they can learn more about suffering joyfully from the book, too. This type of practice lets us speak the truth of how we feel and keep on moving.

---

## Our Timeless Dance with the Four Sufferings: Birth, Aging, Sickness, Death

The Buddhist teachings about the four sufferings—birth, aging, sickness, and death—offer us a framework for understanding the pains and losses all people experience.

Anyone who has ever witnessed childbirth understands why birth involves suffering. We know the birthing mother's body thrashes with pain, and we know the tumult of the fetus as it leaves the dark warmth of the womb and enters the cool light of the world. Should the new-born survive and age, aging is almost always accompanied by physical changes in appearance as well as aches and pains and even more likelihood of illness.

> There is a world of difference between being ill and allowing illness to change your self-concept and outlook on life.

Illness may lead to suffering because it causes physical pain and often deprives us of doing that which we enjoy. Illness may also separate us from ourselves when the sickness impairs our ability to function emotionally, cognitively, or behaviorally—when we lose our memory to amnesia or dementia, for example, or when we lose control of our emotions or behavior due to anxiety or addiction. Or we may lose our connection with reality itself and develop psychotic disorders. Illness may deprive us of the ability to be as self-sufficient as we'd like, to be the self we once knew. When we can no longer run or walk as we once did; when we can't eat the things we once enjoyed; and when dancing, sex, and other life pleasures become physically difficult to do, we suffer.

However, there is a world of difference between being ill and allowing illness to change your self-concept and outlook on life. This chapter will discuss navigating illness joyfully. The goal of some of the practices we will explore is to release internalized ableism and maintain our self-esteem and joie de vivre as we fall ill and age.

Death is considered a form of suffering because we fear our death and/or the deaths of those we care about. Death can also be considered a suffering because we fear that the manner of our death will be painful. In Dr. Toni Morrison's novel *Beloved*, the character Paul D asks whether his friend's mother died "hard," and Sethe, the main character, says no, she went "soft, soft as cream."[1] Most of us hope that we and our loved ones will have a soft death, but we can still use our practices to grieve joyfully, even when a loved one dies "hard" or in a way that is violent or excruciating.

Of course, these four sufferings are interrelated. Sickness often leads to death, and death can occur anytime, including close to or before birth, as is the case with many Black women who, because of racism, have higher maternal mortality rates during childbirth.[2]

---

Let's Practice!

## Finding Joy in the Four Sufferings

Excising oppressive ways of thinking that inform how we grieve or fail to grieve will allow us to know joy in grieving. Each aspect of existence—birth, aging, illness, and death—also contains great joy. What was the last childbirth that you celebrated? Note in your Joy Journal what was joyful about that birth. Next, write one aspect of growing older that you actually love and enjoy. Then consider the last time that you were ill and note one good thing that came from that. For example, did you get to rest? Did someone take care of you? Illness reminds us of impermanence and interdependence, and in that way it connects us to the meaning and the beauty of life.

Okay, now the big one: What is joyful about death? Think back to a celebration of life, a funeral, or a memorial where something joyous happened or was recounted and make note of that. It may have been a song or a story that was shared. In death we remember in sharper relief the joy of those who lived, because of their physical absence. Note something joyful you realized only after someone you loved died. That is the joy that emerges from death. Also, death gives us and our loved ones a break from all the hard work of living! According to Daisaku Ikeda,

Cycles of life and death can be likened to the alternating periods of sleep and wakefulness. Just as sleep prepares us for the next day's activity, death can be seen as a state in which we rest and replenish ourselves for new life. In this light, death should be acknowledged, along with life, as a blessing to be appreciated.[3]

Staying spiritually strong and joyous amid pain is part of the legacy of wisdom transmitted to us from Black people the world over. The great Nigerian musician Fela Kuti has a song called "Suffering and Smiling" that is a brilliant musical exegesis on how Black people all over the world transcend the sufferings of racism and maintain joy. Although both can manifest simultaneously, there is a difference between the suffering and smiling that global majority people enact as a shield against white fragility—so that white people don't further abuse us when discomfited by our rage or sorrow—and the suffering and smiling that is self-transcendence. For Black people, the work is to practice discernment to ensure that we do not smile through suffering racism when it is safe enough to interrupt it. For allies, the work is to practice releasing fragility so that our authentic outrage at racism, especially when allies enact racism, is welcomed and used as a point of learning. As we work to end racism, we can learn from the ways Black people exhibit discomfort resilience and maintain joy amid suffering injustice.

When most people bring to mind a significant loss, they think of the death of a loved one. We know that due to health disparities caused by racism, Black and American Indian and Alaskan Native (AIAN) people have a shorter life expectancy. This means that there is more grieving of deceased loved ones in these communities even as there are fewer resources to support that grieving.[4] Part of how we ameliorate this is to create space, time, and resources for Black and AIAN people to heal from the relentless assaults of racism as well as its historical and intergenerational residuals.

The stress of racism has cumulative effects associated with adverse mental and physical health outcomes. It also causes additional losses of loved ones. We lose our loved ones via stress on relationships that lead to divorce. We lose them to desertion or abandonment because of hopelessness. We lose our loved ones by hard choices we must make, such as abortion, separating ourselves from abusive parents or partners, or even our decisions to travel, serve in the military, or take jobs far from home. Whether we choose the loss or it chooses us, all losses of people we love or tried to love must be grieved.

## Understanding Grief and Loss

Our experiences of loss are more challenging when we lack understanding of the natural processes of grief and loss and when we are influenced by society's unwritten and oppressive rules about grieving. We may be discouraged from talking about our grief because it is often stigmatized as weakness or self-pitying. Sometimes we are discouraged from even *feeling* grief. How many times have you heard someone say, "Don't cry"? Well, you don't have to listen to them. When people tell you not to cry, it is usually because they are afraid that they will start to cry or elsewise feel vulnerable and unable to "fix" the pain. Since all humans are vulnerable to loss, sometimes people respond to the tears they see welling up in your eyes as indicators of the dam within themselves that will break if they begin to confront their own losses and fear of loss.

Nonetheless, emotional release is vital. Crying can be likened to the sweat of the heart as it does the emotional work of processing and releasing painful feelings. The dam holding back our tears must break, over and over, so that the flood can wash us clean of despair and prepare us for the new life that begins after each loss. It is not only our loved ones who transition when we lose them. We too transition. We move into the unknown and unknowable world of life without them.

In grief, sorrow isn't the only emotion that we experience. We can also experience a lot of fear because grief plunges us into that realm of the unknown. We don't know what life is going to be like without the person, capacity, place, or objects that we have lost. Another unwritten rule in society is that we shouldn't trust and value our own experience as we grieve, that we should not listen to what our own heart, mind, and body are telling us as we grieve. We often fear our own natural responses and thus delay our healing. Additionally, we often don't trust other people enough to talk about how destabilized we feel when we're grieving for fear that they will think we are "crazy" or weak. Because of the stigma and even criticism people often face when we show our emotional pain or mental health strains, we often have a compounded experience of grief due to self-isolation or ostracism. At the very time we need to enact our interdependence and share the pain of loss—the most universal suffering that every living being undergoes—we may have few or no others with whom to shed our tears, to accompany us through the emotional release that is so vital for healing.

> Crying can be likened to the sweat of the heart as it does the emotional work of processing and releasing painful feelings.

Part of my work as a mental health therapist is to encourage people to show emotions and reiteratively contradict that devaluation of their experience. It is important to understand the broad spectrum of grief processes and the ways that loss has a lifelong impact on us. The truth is that a lot of our past losses and separations have an impact on current losses and separations. Our experience of loss impacts the attachments and choices that we make or do not make. All those factors bear on future losses and separations.

Let me give you an example: If someone has an affair in an exclusive intimate partner relationship, the person who is cheated on experiences a loss. They experience the loss of the person, because their partner is involved with someone else. They also experience a psychological loss: a loss of trust that will impact the current relationship even if the infidelity ends. They may not be able to return to their prior level of trust with their partner, if they remain with them at all. This loss may also impact their future relationships, because it may be difficult for them to trust again. They may constantly worry about their next partner cheating on them, and that worry may put more stress on the next relationship and actually cause another lost relationship because they became clingy or overly vigilant and suspicious.

The key point here is that loss must be faced and healed. If it isn't, it will often lead to more loss in the future.

## Coming to Terms with Grief and Loss

People tend to mix up grief and loss. *Grief* refers to our emotional reactions to loss: the raw feelings that are present at the center of the whole process. Grief is a description of what we're feeling. Grief can include sadness, anger, terror. It can include a lot of anxiety. *Grief* is a word that is meant to encompass all our emotional reactions, although truly the experience is beyond words.

Grief is also the process of individually experiencing the psychological, behavioral, physical, and social reactions to our perception of loss. Not only do we think and feel differently in the face of a loss but we also behave and interact differently. We have a somatic, embodied response to loss. We may have tightness in our chest or a lot of sweating; we may yawn a lot or vomit or tremble. There are many forms of release that allow the body to discharge, to loosen the grip, to release the hold grief can take over our physical being. We may have sleeplessness or feel exhausted and sleep more. Grief is emotional labor, and that is why taking a bereavement leave or finding some way to give your body, mind, and heart time to orient itself to the new painful reality is necessary. Grieving is work, and it is hard to do other work when the grief work is demanding your attention. This is why we may feel cognitive disorientation, fuzzy-headedness, or an inability to think clearly. If we do not discharge the grief regularly, we are not letting ourselves do the emotional work we need to do to be present.

Grief can affect our social behavior in that sometimes people become isolated, feeling that others don't understand. That's correct in a way, because loss is so personal. Even if you have had the same kind of loss as someone else—the loss of a child, for example—every person's experience is so singular that it has to be honored as a uniquely agonizing experience that no one else can fully understand. This is in part because every relationship is different, but also because each person is likely to have had other losses that may be uniquely compounded by the current one.

Additionally, very few people truly turn toward the pain of grief and allow themselves to experience it. Most of us numb out or ignore the grief via various escape methods. Prescription or nonprescription drugs, alcohol, and food are often used to escape the body's aforementioned visceral sensations of grief, and that numbing can and does change our social interactions. Sometimes we become hypersocial in the face of a loss in a desperate effort to escape the feeling of disconnection. We may be hypersexual or just try to spend all our time with people to avoid the lonely feeling that being without a particular beloved causes. It is vital that we have lots of social support during grief so that we do not lose sight of and drift away from the precious loved ones we may still have. Sometimes when we lose someone of great importance to us, we throw up our hands in defeat and give up on staying connected to the other meaningful relationships we have. This, of course, leads to the unnecessary loss of people we could still have in our lives.

Yet even as we must work to share our grief with those who can stand the pain with us, we must also allow for the particular heartache and healing that can occur only in the solitude of our spiritual union with ourselves as we adjust to the loss or the impending loss.

*Disenfranchised grief* refers to when our loss is not even acknowledged as a loss. For example, when my gay client's partner of thirty years died, his partner's family did not include him in the memorial planning. They considered him a friend because his deceased partner never formally came out to them, and the family chose not to see them as a couple. As another example, the losses that accompany migration are often unrecognized. Through my work with UndocuAlly, a program that supports undocumented university students, I have been advocating for grief support for parents separated from children and children separated from parents due to migration. Unsupported grieving often makes it impossible to make good decisions and can also lead to depression, substance abuse, and suicidality.

Disenfranchised grief can also result from losses we are ashamed of, such as abortion or stillbirth. I once had a client who, after she miscarried her three-month-old fetus while at home, was told by the doctor to just throw the remains in the trash and come in for an appointment the next day. This failure to acknowledge a loss as a meaningful experience exacerbates and complicates our grief and mourning.

*Ambiguous loss* refers to the grief we feel when someone is either physically absent but psychologically present (such as a parent who works around the clock and is not physically there for the children) or physically present and psychologically absent (such as a loved one who has dementia or is constantly high on substances). All types of ambiguous loss also cause grief and deserve attention to heal.

*Mourning* is a process that describes how we respond to grief. Mourning consists of rituals and processes held in private, with our families, or in public. Mourning rituals allow us to bring the experience of loss to our conscious minds. In mourning we go through the process of recovering and adjusting to loss. Conscious mourning can involve various rituals, such as funerals, burials, memorials, celebrations of life, repasts, or other gatherings that we as families, communities, and sets of friends might organize to honor someone or something. Lighting candles and meditating with pictures or other memorabilia can be a private mourning ritual. Mourning helps us make the loss concrete so that we can begin to live with it and honor the value and meaning of what has been lost.

Elisabeth Kübler-Ross, who studied and worked with people who were dying, identified some key phases of grief that you may have heard of before: denial, anger, bargaining, depression, and acceptance.[5] Denial comes from that initial feeling of shock in which we believe (or try to believe) that the loss isn't happening. It's a reactive "hard no"—a last-ditch effort to make the loss untrue. Anger is that sense of outrage we feel when we can't deny the truth of the loss. It is when we cry out, "Why?" in rage or rail against how such a thing could be happening to us or our loved ones. After that, bargaining sometimes ensues: we promise to try to do something to reverse or minimize the pain of the loss. It's when we make a deal with God as someone we love undergoes life-threatening surgery, promising to treat them better or give up a bad habit if only God lets them live. Depression is the stage where we start to sink into the reality of the loss, when we have no choice but to see that this *is* reality. Acceptance can begin to occur once we realize, *This is what I've got to work with. It is what it is, and I can live with it and learn from it.* The stages are not linear; we cycle back and forth through them. It's possible to be in acceptance one day and anger the next day. It can be a maddeningly circular process, especially if we aren't getting enough time or support to really face the grief and recover from the loss.

Kübler-Ross applied these phases to *anticipatory grief* as well. When we or someone we love has a terminal illness, we may experience anticipatory grief acutely. The fact is that we all have a terminal condition: it is called living, and it always ends in death. Facing this in good humor rather than letting fear control us makes room for more joy in life. Fear is the driver of the anticipatory grief truck. If we are overwhelmed with anticipation of the grief we might go through when we lose this or that or him, her, or them, we often lose the peace of this moment. Anticipatory grief means we are consciously or unconsciously wrestling with the fact that loss is not just inevitable but also unpredictable.

In a way, anticipatory grief is just a natural part of living. It's a low vibration or hum of awareness that operates for most of us on an unconscious level most of the time. That is why bringing it to conscious awareness through our contemplative practices makes sense, so that we are not unconsciously preoccupied by it and it does not become the reason for excessive anxiety. Part of the reason that we frequently joke about dying and part of why we describe laughing so hard as "literally dying" is because at every moment we actually are literally dying! Humor is how we deal with the anticipatory grief of that fact. Also, part of why we watch so much TV and film about injury, accidents, loss, and death is that we are trying to manage the anticipatory grief we already feel as we know any of these can happen to us at any time. We can consciously work with anticipatory grief and worry with some light affirmations that acknowledge the presence of the anxiety or anticipatory grief without letting it run wild.

> If we can welcome our feelings as natural psychological and emotional impermanent states that pass eventually, we can know great peace.

Try an affirmation like this: "I see you, anxiety; you are welcome to pass right through as I notice all that is going well at this moment." We tend to let anxiety steal the moment, and it can lead to a particular kind of cognitive distortion or irrational thought pattern known as *filtering*, where we filter out the delightful aspects of our experience at a given moment and only focus on the troubling thoughts, feelings, or sensations. So, we don't ignore the grief; we welcome it to be with us and pass through us as we also welcome the other aspects of this moment in our lives. For example, you might be having anticipatory grief about losing your job. Try an affirmation like, "There is anxiety floating through me about losing my job. Welcome, anxiety. Feel free to float through as I notice that I have a job now and many other good things in my life, such as . . ."

It is important to develop friendly relationships with our painful emotions so that we don't become anxious about feeling anxious or depressed about feeling depressed. If we can welcome feelings as natural psychological and emotional impermanent states that pass eventually, we can know great peace. It can also be useful to not identify with a painful feeling, because at the same time you are experiencing it, you are also experiencing other feelings. So instead of saying, "I am depressed," you might say, "I can notice some depression moving through me." What other feelings are moving through you? Are there any pleasant feelings in there? These kinds of reflective practices can help you balance your awareness and be more connected to the possibilities for peace and joy in each moment.

All anxiety is about fear of losing something. Seneca, a Stoic philosopher in first-century Rome, is quoted as saying, "We suffer more in our imagination than we do in reality."[6] This is how anticipatory loss generates delusions or cognitive distortions that cause us to suffer by blocking our awareness of our fundamental enlightenment and capacities. We can also use a meditative approach to the *three-question technique* used in cognitive therapy as a practice to dismantle irrational fears. The three questions we get to contemplate are:

1. What is the evidence to support the fear or worry?

2. How else could that evidence be interpreted?

3. If it is a true or a rational concern, what are the actual implications?

This practice can help us diffuse the energy of worry and look more closely at situations to see not only threats but also opportunities present in every moment. That way, when actual loss happens, we have more energy and resources to deal with it because we haven't wasted as much time and energy worrying about it. Worry is the opposite of planning to prevent or manage a loss. When we use our practices, we can plan for loss management!

---

Let's Practice!

## Put Your Worries on Trial with the Three-Question Technique

Let's apply the three-question technique to an actual worry you have now. Get out your Joy Journal and pick a worry, any worry! Now, consider question 1: *What is the evidence that what I fear will definitely come to pass?* Really try to make a case for the worry, almost as if you are a prosecutor trying to prove that what you're worried about constitutes a real threat. This corresponds to the Buddhist practice of making friends with suffering, investigating it, and exploring its aspects in detail in order not to be overwhelmed by it.

Question 2 gives you a chance to speak for the defendant, which is your most rational, balanced, enlightened mind: *How else could I interpret that evidence?* Interrogate the worry to see how it could be a result of overgeneralizing or catastrophizing. What are the holes in the worry's story? Is the worry leaving out any alternative scenarios or possibilities? How does the worry reflect delusions about the nature of reality? Once you have explored it, then hand over the worry to the jury (your more balanced and less partial mind) to find out what the verdict is. If the verdict is that the worry is not such a big, overwhelming threat, then the case is closed and the worry can easily be dismissed!

If the worry is found guilty—if what is being worried about is definitely going to happen—then you move on to question 3: *What are the implications?* Does that worry being fact mean all is lost? What is still joyful about your life even if that worry is bound to manifest as reality? Remembering that your life force is bigger than any worry, especially when you strengthen it with practice, will help you not be a prisoner of worry-based thoughts.

Putting your worries on a playful trial in this way will lighten them and help you have a balanced view of whatever worries are breaking into your mind and heart and stealing your mental energy and joy.

---

## Let's Plan for Joyful Grieving

Because loss and grief are heartbreaking, they are also vast pathways to joy. Even in the throes of gut-wrenching grief, we can know great joy if that is our intention and resolve. Joy emerges from manifesting our varied strengths and potentials as humans, and grief reveals capacities we would've never dreamed we had. In grief we experience the vastness of our hearts—our vast capacities to love and mourn, both of which require our attention and intention to develop fully. All four sufferings can lead to joy when we set the intention to grieve well. This is what Nichiren Buddhism refers to as *changing poison into medicine*.

The reality of all life is death. The cost of all relationships is paid in the coin of loss. The price of having anything and everything is losing anything and everything. All that we love and cherish, including our relationships with ourselves and our own bodies, we will lose. Cheerful thoughts, right? Well, the good news is that by contemplating loss and grief, we can prevent unnecessary loss and grief and awaken to the miracle of all that we have right now. Daisaku Ikeda states, "An awareness and understanding of death raises our state of life. When we are cognizant of the reality and inevitability of death we begin to seek the eternal, and become determined to make the most valuable use of each moment of life."[7] Hence facing and exploring death and all types of loss helps us wake up to all that we have. Using our practices to contemplate loss and death can help us make wiser choices. We can develop more joy-filled appreciation for all that remains in our lives now and for our lives themselves.

---

Let's Practice!

## Planning with Loss

Practicing with the reality of impermanence can help us release anxiety. You can train your mind to be less fearful of loss through contemplative planning exercises. Using this strategy, write your own eulogy, being sure to include all the things you hope will be said about you when you die. A quick gratitude practice is a good way to get started! In your Joy Journal, list the first three things that come to mind that you appreciate about your life. Then set a timer for two minutes and continue to write in your Joy Journal. What qualities, characteristics, or achievements come to mind? Show yourself some love! Your eulogy could be full of memories, aspects of your life that are currently unfolding now, or future goals. Write or dictate as freely as you can, and remember that what you write is just for you, unless you want to share it with loved ones.

## Characteristics of Loss

Grief, loss, and mourning do not refer exclusively to our experiences around death. Grief can be caused by many kinds of loss. Loss can be sudden, as in racial violence, or more gradual, as in chronic debilitating stress. Loss can be prolonged, as in detainment in prisons and camps. Loss is always personal. No one can decide what constitutes a loss for another person.

Loss cannot be viewed as a single, unitary experience because it often has many dimensions. Loss remains forever in the unconscious. Past losses are aroused when set off by a current loss or even a reminder of the past loss. The truth is our past losses and separations have an impact on our current losses, separations, and attachments. In turn, all these factors bear on future losses and separations and our capacity to make future attachments.

Some losses are subtle. When they occur, we may be aware of having gone through a painful experience but may not recognize the experience as a loss. For example, when someone humiliates us or causes us to lose face, we might not recognize that the feelings we have afterward have to do with grieving. Minor failures, events causing shame or embarrassment, and disappointments are all losses that we can turn toward in order to heal and to grow our wisdom and resilience.

We can think of loss in four distinct categories (with some subcategories, presented below) as described by the author Bertha Simos:

- loss of a significant person

- loss of a part of the self

- loss of external objects

- developmental loss[8]

## Loss of a Significant Person

The death of a loved one can strike us as the most permanent and devastating loss possible. For many people, miscarriage and abortion is loss of a significant person, too. However, we can lose people who are important to us in other ways. Illness, accidents, and aging can change a loved one. As we move through different life transitions, we can lose significant people, such as through divorce. It's important to realize that just because we have a choice about ending a relationship doesn't mean it's not a loss. You may be the person filing for the divorce, but you still are going through a loss. The same clearly is true for a woman, a couple, or anyone who makes the decision to have an abortion: that is also an undeniable loss.

It's a loss, too, when we extend ourselves for friendship and are rejected. When we don't get a desired job where there are people we'd hoped to connect with or when we have to leave a job where we've developed relationships, that's another loss of significant people. Military service and deployment can also cause loss; we get separated from those we love. We lose contact with significant people when we travel. It may not be possible to be in touch with them, even if we're traveling for something enjoyable. We may experience a sense of loss whenever we're not connecting with the folks who are part of our everyday life.

The same is true for geographic moves. When we move, we don't have the same people around us any longer. There may be a lot of new opportunities and new people to meet, but we may lose close contact with some significant people.

Putting our loved ones in developmentally supportive environments is another example. If someone has a debilitating health or mental health issue or they're aging and unable to care for themselves, it's a painful loss for families to put that person in a treatment facility, and it is a loss for the person being placed there. This also goes for taking children out of violent or neglectful homes or placing children in foster care or in adoption. It may be a safer environment, but the child still grieves. Even if the change improves the life circumstances of the child, the separation from and longing for the original family is often still present.

## Loss of a Part of the Self

One aspect of loss that we often don't notice is the loss of parts of our being. Buddhism refers to these as the sufferings of illness and aging. We can think of these sufferings in categories, such as cognitive or psychological losses, structural losses, and functional losses. Let me put on my Buddhist psychotherapist hat and tell you all about how these work.

Cognitive losses refer to the difficulties we may begin to experience with comprehension, memory, and judgment. We experience psychological loss when we lose aspects of our functioning such as our ability to regulate our emotions. Successful emotional regulation does not mean suppression or repression of feelings. It means we are in a moment-to-moment endeavor to cultivate awareness of what we feel and express it in ways that lead to our growth and well-being. This is why meditative practices are so regularly used in emotional regulation. The practices engage the body's parasympathetic nervous system to help us be present and grounded in the moment and not let our emotions drive us into unnecessarily painful or dangerous situations.

Structural losses occur when we lose parts of our actual body. Whether it is a tooth, our hair, or a limb, structural losses always come with a sense of grief. For example, a client of mine came to the session one day in a veil because they had fallen and one of their front teeth fell out. The grief and panic they felt at this loss was expressed more visibly (in this case, with more sobbing) than their grief at the death of a beloved person, which is what they were in counseling for to begin with.

Bodily losses are challenging not only because we mourn what we miss of ourselves but also because they can confront us with our internalized ableism. *Ableism* is the social injustice that causes the stigma associated with losing parts or functions of our body and mind. Baldness and other bodily losses are regularly viewed as failures and labeled as unattractive. This can be especially hard for women who, because of sexism, often find our worth being estimated in accordance with our appearance. However, devaluation based on changes in appearance that reflect aging also happens for men and people of all genders.

> Bodily losses are challenging not only because we mourn what we miss of ourselves but also because they can confront us with our internalized ableism.

The overvaluing of physical appearance may also increase ableism among Black people. One of racism's functions is to denigrate the physical appearance of Black and other global majority people. So, when we lose physical functions or aspects of our appearance that are socially valorized, Black people are targeted with a particularly nasty strain of racism that's combined with ableism.

Also, since Black skin tone and smoothness, along with other aspects of Black people's physical appearance, often last into old age, we may sometimes feel additional shame as Black people when our Black *does* crack. The African American expression "Black don't crack" is about the long-lasting nature of Black people's physical beauty. However, to deepen our wisdom about this, I invite Black people to decide to value our Blackness in all its changing phases and stages and allow the new meaning of "Black don't crack" to refer to a resilient sense of self-love and an ever-growing appreciation of the beauty of our entire being. Let's allow *self-love* to be what never cracks. This perspective will enrich us as we inevitably become ill, age, and get injured, in that it allows us to remain unbroken in our resolve to love ourselves.

Structural losses can also lead to functional losses. For example, severe bladder disease means a loss of the bodily functions of that organ. Not only do you have to grieve that loss but you also have to grieve social stigma if you tell anyone or if you have an accident in public. Part of the reason to work for a less ableist world is so that we can all stop being stigmatized for moving through natural stages of life such as illness and aging. One study found that the highest suicidality among seniors and people with chronic illness is among those with uncontrollable urinary incontinence.[9] Another study found even higher suicidality for those with fecal incontinence.[10] A simple loss in muscular control can cause incontinence, yet people often cannot enjoy the remaining abilities they have because of social stigma and shame.

Whenever we lose one function, we can do a gratitude practice that raises our awareness of our remaining functions and all the ways that they augment our lives. Contemplative practices can help us face these losses in good humor. Even when life feels like it is literally full of shit due to our own incontinence or that of an elder, adult, or child we are caring for, it still contains so much to be grateful for and joyous about.

### Time-Out for a Laugh—Seriously! What Is This Shit?

Shit, both literally and figuratively, has value. Shit represents successful metabolization and offers a resource for fertilization and is thus an inexorable part of the cycle of life. That is true of literal shit as well as figurative shit such as the difficult and unpleasant aspects of living. Those difficult and unpleasant aspects also fertilize our growth when we tend to our shit properly.

Have you ever heard Black people say, "Handle your shit?" That's what we mean: work with it to see what value can be created from it. Black people also coined the expressions "That's the shit!" and "That's that shit right there!" in appreciation of something amazing. Same principle: saying "That's the shit" is an expression of discernment, a way of appreciating something beautiful or wonderful that is also very real, very authentic. In a similar way, by using the word *bad* to reference something hardy, powerful, strong, and gorgeous, Black people flipped the script and changed the meaning of how we say and see what is bad. Black Americans have had so much pain that we changed language to show that we have the capacity to be as strident as the pain we face. That's what Michael Jackson meant when he sang "I'm bad." That's what we mean when we say someone is "a badass." It's a language practice that recognizes there is vigor, toughness, and life force in badness.

Okay, just one more shitty analogy and I promise we'll move on. My colleague Carrie told me that if you have a farm or stable, you have to be careful of where you pile up your shit because it can affect drainage and create a swampy mess. The same applies for the grief and pain in our inner life. If we don't take the time to grieve a loss, it sits in our psyche, leaking out now and then, just a little. But then we have other losses that compound the pungency of the previous one, and before we know it, we've got a lot of unhealed emotional manure stinking up the palace of our heart and mind so much that we cannot perceive the redolence of our greater self or that of the world that surrounds us! The good thing is that all that emotional pain is absolutely the best fertilizer to grow our wisdom and sense of interdependent joy when we practice with it.

I invite you to play with different phrases and metaphors to see how you might maintain good humor as you navigate loss of all kinds. Humor helps us prevent our body's structural and functional losses from becoming psychological losses. We do not have to lose our self-esteem. Our own estimation of our intrinsic worth need not be at the mercy of the four sufferings.

However, we will need to regularly practice cultivating the intention and resolve to awaken to our intrinsic worth, because internal and external pulls of self-doubt and oppressive social standards will persist. We must face and resist self-doubt and oppression in order to access our joy.

## From Disability to Thisability

I gave a public talk recently that was set up and recorded very much like a TED talk with sophisticated recording equipment, microphones, and lighting. As one speaker after another did their presentations before me, I realized they were all standing as they presented. I understood again at that moment that there is a social and professional expectation that anyone who is qualified to stand before us and teach is someone who can stand. Our world is so infused with ableism that it is as if being able to stand is a qualification itself—part of what makes one qualified to teach or lead. Unfortunately, I was suffering from knee and back injuries. I couldn't stand for more than five minutes; I was going to need a chair for my thirty-minute talk.

> All functioning is impermanent, so whatever ability you have now will surely fade. We all have thisability, the abilities of this moment.

I did not think of this until moments before I was to go on stage because I never thought of myself as disabled. In so many senses of the word, I am able, capable of so much. To my mind, there is no such thing as disabled. However, many of our structures, buildings, social settings, and work settings are disabled in their capacity to support people with various levels of functioning, people undergoing aspects of illness and aging that are ignored or devalued. What if bathrooms had some features for people with incontinence issues, for example? Thinking about universal design where truly everyone has access is a way that we can accommodate all humans' ever-changing and ever-declining physical conditions.

So instead of thinking about our bodies as some of us having disabilities and some of us being able-bodied, I invite you to notice that the only status any of us has is *thisability*—what you have in this moment. All functioning is impermanent, so whatever ability you have now will surely fade. So, we get to integrate impermanence into our understanding and expectations of our own abilities and those of others so that we are not defeated when our functioning changes. This will enable us to value and support ourselves and others as we navigate these inevitable changes.

My grandfather James Haynes was one of the best men I have ever known. He was a Blues, Jazz, and early R & B singer with a big, deep voice like Louis Armstrong but with more laughter in it. I used to love to hear him sing, but I also loved to hear him speak. I loved the depth of love in his voice and the way he summoned my whole being when he bellowed, "Come here, grandbaby!" He called me that well into my thirties, and he would pull me, both of us laughing, to sit on his lap or just hold me in an embrace. His call, "Come here, granddaughter," was a call to home. Grandad also worked as a plumber to care for his family—my grandmother, my mother, and her five siblings. His life was not easy. He had to bury two of his daughters after they died in childbirth and two of his sons who died from other complications due to racism—but he remained in resilient good humor until his last days.

About a year before his death, Grandad had to have surgery to remove his voice box due to cancer. When I went into his hospital room after the surgery, he began to cry. I hugged him and, of course, I started to cry myself. He picked up the writing tablet by the bed and wrote, "I am not crying because I lost my voice. I am crying because I know how much you loved my voice." That memory is only as painful as it is *because* it is so beautiful, so exquisite. Imagine loving someone so much that you could lose your own voice and the main concern for you is that you can't share your voice with your beloved anymore. Imagine someone loving you that much.

That moment, as much as many others with him, reminds me how much he loved me and how our most meaningful ability—the ability to feel and show love—is present despite all types of physical losses. And it showed me another important truth, which I immediately said to him after he wrote that: "I love you far more than your voice, Granddad!" We can use the sufferings of illness and aging, the losses of living, to guide us toward loving ourselves and one another in ways that honor our essential being, above and beyond any functions or abilities. Doing so helps us recognize all that we *still have* of ourselves and one another as we undergo all the physical changes of illness, injury, and aging.

---

Let's Practice!

## Dancing with Thisability

A few years ago I was at a retreat and the session leader invited everyone into a movement practice where you kind of dance over to different partners. Although I calmly stayed in my seat and kept smiling, I started to feel sad as I realized that with my injury, I would not be able to do the practice. Then Neil Dalal, an incredibly wise South Asian scholar, came over to me and knelt and started to do the movement practice kneeling. It was awkward for him, but he did not care. It was more important to him to include me, to be in our connection, than it was to sail around the room with everyone else. Perhaps you'll have the capacity to use your legs and dance until the last moment of your life, but just in case it doesn't work out that way, let's try a dance you could do anywhere, from a car to a chair to your deathbed.

First, put on your absolute favorite song to dance to. Next, shake it! Whatever it is—your head, your shoulders, your tongue—move it to the beat of the music, but do not stand. This simple practice reminds us that we can dance and we can *be danced with* no matter what illness or functional loss we are experiencing.

---

### Nowability: Play with the Language!

My goal is not to prescribe new language but to invite you to play with less disempowering, more conscious language. If we stop thinking of ourselves as "able-bodied" versus "disabled," if we find language that expresses and reminds us of the capriciousness of life as it impacts our bodies, then we can adjust to those changes without feeling so devastated. Knowing that the next shower, five-minute walk, or drive could change our body's functioning, practice working with thisability, the functioning that you have now. You might choose to call it your *nowability*. Play with the language. What helps keep oppressive ideas of "perfect" functioning or delusions of permanence out of your mind and mouth?

Exploring thisability is a joyous venture into appreciation, a real discernment of the almost countless bodily functions that are working for you right now! You may struggle with one of these, and that bears noticing. You can practice meeting that struggle with appreciation. Yet make sure to also notice any aspect of unimpaired functioning that you still have. For example, if you have respiratory problems, you still have respiration, right? Yes, I am a "glass half full" kind of woman!

If you have pain when you walk, as I sometimes do, notice the gift of the few steps you can take on your own. Maybe pause and take one now. If you have pain in your hands and cannot do everything you would like to do with them, pause and kiss your hands right now in gratitude for all that they can still do, including their capacity to wipe your eyes as you cry grieving other losses.

Take a few moments and offer gratitude for whatever levels of functioning you have. Try something like this:

- *Thank you, lungs, for all the countless breaths you have given me.*

- *Thank you, colon, kidneys, and liver, for bringing nutrients through my body and mind.*

- *Thank you, bladder and bowels, for cleansing me of waste.*

- *Thank you, heart, for all the blood you keep flowing through me.*

- *Thank you, bones, muscles, tendons, and fascia. You are wondrous in the ways you keep me moving.*

Notice the symphony of functions your body is conducting in this moment and say thank you. Do this for a few minutes, deepening your breathing with your gratitude and fully sensing the part of the body that you are thanking. Feel the blood; notice the bones, muscles, and tendons. Bask in the delights that are present in your current functioning, in this moment's abilities. Allow gratitude to arise for breathing . . . digestion . . . continence . . . blood circulation . . . movement, in any part of your body: Spend time noticing movement in at least eight different parts of your body. Notice your functional mind that is able to contemplate gratitude itself, and allow gratitude to arise for that. Notice the feelings, the emotions of gratitude, and thank your emotional aspect for allowing you to experience that.

## Loss of External Objects

This is the third of Bertha Simos's categories of loss. Although people often dismiss the loss of money, homes, and external objects as superficial, these too need to be mourned in order for us to move forward wisely and joyfully. Often our sense of self, our efficacy, and our self-esteem are tied up in our ability to take care of ourselves. If we lose some of the external objects that help us to take care of ourselves, we can sometimes be in danger of reduced self-esteem or other psychological losses.

It should be noted that you can miss what you have never had. Poverty and deprivation are losses, too. They represent lost educational resources, job opportunities, meals, housing, health care, and so forth. Racism institutionalizes loss for global majority people in these areas and more. Black people are subject to more evictions and more theft of property, in addition to higher rates of poverty and all the deprivations poverty entails. This is because racism impacts economics. James Baldwin said that "anyone who has ever struggled with poverty knows how extremely expensive it is to be poor."[11] Working-class and poor people are exploited for late fees, partial payment fees, and every other kind of fee. From the history of colonization and enslavement; to the KKK riding through and displacing whole towns and canceling deeds; to the current redlining, gentrification, and exploitation of global majority labor, material losses impact and cause many other categories of loss for global majority people. For example, losing a job due to racist policies and practices can result in one's children being taken away, which can subsequently result in substance abuse and the ensuing loss of health and life.

It is important to validate ourselves and our loved ones when negotiating the loss of external objects. It is never just the loss of an object, because anything we regret losing represents something to us, so usually other categories of loss are involved when we lose external objects. If you lose access to your car, even if only for a few days, that can create a loss of significant persons if you can't get to friends and family. It can create psychological loss if it starts to cause you anxiety.

That is why it is good to engage in grieving practices even when we "only" lose things. Material objects facilitate access to other resources and opportunities, so it's helpful to plan for how we manage losing them so we do not experience unnecessary distress.

We can also remember to use humor to buoy us through loss. My dear friend Bruce has been a faithful companion for me through all types of loss. He consistently helps me maintain a sense of humor about it all. Recently he mentioned a story from the Buddhist teacher Ajahn Chah about how his mug was broken by someone. Ajahn Chah told them not to feel bad about breaking it because the mug was already broken. He did not say this because the mug had been broken before but because he was unattached to it as "whole." He was so in tune with impermanence that he understood it as already gone. That "it's already gone" is a perspective that expresses awareness of impermanence. Not dismissing the loss of objects as meaningless while also not freaking out about them is an example of practicing the middle way and having a balanced view of loss.

## Developmental Loss: What Stage Are You In?

Developmental loss refers to the natural losses that accompany growth. It also refers to loss that occurs as we experience neglect or trauma throughout our lives. In 1950, twenty-nine years before Bertha Simos identified developmental loss as a fourth category of loss, the psychologist Erik Erikson proposed that we all move through eight stages of psychosocial development.

Erikson's theory posits that each stage of life has significant needs or tasks associated with overcoming psychosocial crises. If our needs are met, and we can engage these challenges successfully, we acquire what Erikson referred to as "virtues," or qualities that support our further development. However, if we experience neglect or struggle to meet these challenges, we may miss out on the benefits of attaining the virtues.

## Erikson's Stages of Development [12, 13]

| Stage | Psychosocial crisis/task | Virtue | Age |
|-------|--------------------------|--------|-----|
| 1 | Trust vs. mistrust<br>*Sense of security* | Hope | 0–1½ |
| 2 | Autonomy vs. shame/doubt<br>*Independence* | Will | 1½–3 |
| 3 | Initiative vs. guilt<br>*Self-confidence* | Purpose | 3–5 |
| 4 | Industry vs. inferiority<br>*Accomplishment, pride* | Competency | 5–13 |
| 5 | Identity vs. role confusion<br>*Strong self-identity,<br>future planning* | Fidelity | 13–21 |
| 6 | Intimacy vs. isolation<br>*Relationships, community* | Love | 21–39 |
| 7 | Generativity vs. stagnation<br>*Action, success* | Care | 40–65 |
| 8 | Integrity vs. despair<br>*Satisfaction, legacy* | Wisdom | 65+ |

Erickson's theory illustrates a commonality between the aspirations of psychological science and those of contemplative practice: the attainment of ever-more developed ways of seeing and being. Each stage of life has attending losses and, with the right supports, attending gains.

Developmental theory posits that to become empowered, confident members of society, we must successfully complete each stage. For example, in the first stage, as an infant, our primary psychosocial crisis is one of trust versus mistrust. If we have sufficiently reliable care, we are more likely to develop a sense of trust. If our caregiver is negligent or abusive, mistrust is a more likely outcome. That is a traumatic developmental loss.

> Meditative practice can alter the developmental trajectory of our lives and allow us to recover from threats to development in countless ways.

There are no absolutes, though, in terms of impact. There are many other factors that determine our development of hope (the virtue associated with the first stage), and we are influenced by other positive social or emotional support resources that may fill in the gaps left by primary caregivers. If we experience oppression, trauma, or oppression-related trauma, the loss-gain ratio can become imbalanced. Global majority people can and do experience racism-related trauma at every stage of development, and it can compromise growth in varied ways. Black wisdom practices are prime examples of how we regain balance and move toward post-traumatic growth. Reflecting on our experiences and attending to our developmental losses helps us see where we may need healing and insight.

Please bear in mind, though, that the pathologizing nature of psychological science with its overemphasis on identifying what's wrong with us is itself an expression of delusion. While many of our past and current life challenges can be understood in terms of what happened or what is happening to us at certain developmental stages, none of this is absolute, and there are more possibilities in human life than could ever be surmised by this or any theory. As a social scientist and therapist who is also a contemplative practitioner and teacher, I can attest to the fact that meditative practice can alter the developmental trajectory of our lives and allow us to recover from threats to development in countless ways.

---

Let's Practice!

## Contemplate Your Development

Now you can try applying all that theoretical stuff to your own experience. Note that reflecting on some aspects of your development might be painful, so pause now and consider how you will resource yourself. You have developed a lot of resources in your Joybox, from soothing music to the phone number of a good counselor or friend to call if you're in distress. Stay aware of your embodied responses throughout this exercise by continuing deep diaphragmatic breathing. You might even set a timer to check in with yourself every five minutes or so.

For this exercise, you will need a blank page in your Joy Journal or on your computer. Start with copying down, or cutting and pasting, just the title of each developmental stage as you reflect on each one. For example, stage 1 is "trust versus mistrust." As you contemplate that earliest stage of life, free-associate words to describe what that time of life was like for you. You may have to rely on what you've been told about these early days. To start, it's enough to find just two or three words that relate to who and what was in your world at that stage. Then find a couple of words to describe the care you had then: *What was my care like? How was I cared for?* As you progress through the stages, ask yourself, *How did I develop a sense of autonomy? How did I learn to develop relationships?* Just write whatever words come to mind without judgment. If feelings of grief arise, good! We want to face and grieve our developmental losses. That is the first step in healing and recovery.

For me, for stage 1, I would write "Grandmother, Aunt Essie, mother, laughter, separations, longing." My mother was in college when I was born, so my sense is that we had a lot of time apart those first eighteen months, but I also sense being loved by many.

Once you have done this for the first stage, keep going! What you will have at the end is an updated reflection on your development up to this point. From there you can list a few areas or virtues you would like to have as goals for your continued joyful development.

If you don't feel that you fully understand Erikson's descriptions of each stage, don't worry. It is still useful to reflect on your experiences at each stage of life. The theory offers a general overview of psychosocial development, giving us a way to consider how our needs and challenges have affected us across our lifetime. Now that you can glimpse some of your psychological and emotional origin story, you can work with what you have unearthed. You can do this work in lots of therapeutic contexts, including family therapy, bibliotherapy (reading self-care books, memoir, or therapeutic stories to support your well-being), support groups, and healing retreats to augment areas of growth that you feel need more attention.

---

## How to Grieve Well—and the Importance of Doing So

In light of the pain of grief for all people and the stark realities of disproportionate illness and death among global majority people, it is useful to practice in order to have an enlightened experience of grief. We often think of loss and impermanence as just being about death, but all our predeath losses have a real impact on how long we live. Some of the early death caused by racism is a result of mismanaged grief. As there are often fewer supports for PGM to grieve, that often leads to unhealthy ways of coping that result in more loss.

Not grieving well is not our fault when we don't have information or resources. This is often the case with global majority people. The paradox of our experience as PGM is we have much to grieve and the fewest resources to do so.

The unwritten social and cultural rules about hiding our grief—that we should always try to look composed, apologize for crying, remain active and productive, and so forth—combine with racism to compromise global majority folx' recovery from loss.

In addition to being a rallying cry to end senseless killings of Black people, the Black Lives Matter movement is mass mourning. That is why the appropriations of the rallying cry, such as "Blue Lives Matter," are so appalling. There are no "Blue" lives—police come in all ethnicities, and many police are, of course, Black. More importantly, police lives are not under threat the way Black people's lives are. Of course, the lives of police officers are important, but really, they need their own slogan. Appropriating the Black Lives Matter rallying cry is the equivalent of bursting into someone else's funeral to say, "Hey, my mom died, too!" Everyone's grief is important, but racism drives the need to subjugate Black grief, thus creating more of it because we must also grieve the loss of our articulations and expressions of mourning.

Anger is a natural part of grief. The fact that PGM, especially Black people, are even more targeted when we express anger further disrupts the grieving process.

> We are all responsible for and impacted by one another's suffering, and we can experience a profound sense of connection and freedom by engaging that reality.

In the coming pages, I will share stories about my life and family to illustrate key points and demonstrate how I make a path from suffering to joy as I walk it. I walk it with the guidance of Black wisdom traditions and Buddhist practice. I hope that my examples will support you in being able to move through your own difficulties with courage and joy. I welcome you to see and sense into the path from great suffering to great joy for yourself. It is a path *you* will create as you practice. Your own efforts to suffer joyfully will be trails that you blaze for yourself and those whom you care for.

I share my own sufferings and those of my beloveds because doing so is also how I reflect and transmit the wisdom we gain from suffering with love: from suffering with a commitment to our own enlightenment and that of all beings. In speaking about surviving trauma, Dr. Toni Morrison points out that "sometimes you don't survive whole, you survive in part, but the grandeur of life is that attempt . . . it is about being as fearless as one can and behaving as beautifully as one can under completely impossible circumstances. . . . We are already born, we are going to die, so you have to do something interesting that you respect in between."[14]

We are all responsible for and impacted by one another's suffering, and we can experience a profound sense of connection and freedom by engaging that reality. The scholar and spiritual teacher Reverend Dr. Larry Ward says, "We must understand our sorrow as divine energy."[15] Black people worldwide have consecrated the lands with our transmutation of sorrow. By sensing into that transmutation justly, all people can develop the same spiritual rigor. If we can, as Rev. Dr. Ward says, "stand up in the house of belonging" and take responsibility for the ways our oppressive patterns and exploitative privilege create pain, we can all have a more liberated existence.[16]

Joyful suffering is something I came to conceive theoretically as a therapist, educator, and scholar, but it is also something I know as a global majority woman and Buddhist practitioner, something that I practice doing myself. My goal is to help you see that it is doable. Sharing my journey of joyful suffering is most importantly an offering to my deceased loved ones—a way to say their names and shine a light on the beauty and meaning of their enduring life force.

I invite you to not just read the anecdotes and stories I offer but to watch yourself: pay attention to your mind as you do so. I share stories of suffering among my family members knowing that your view, dear reader, may be compromised when it comes to seeing, sensing, and connecting to that suffering because, as James Baldwin says in reference to how oppression-infused media distorts our perception, "Hollywood threw acid in both your eyes."[17] He says this in the context of describing our distorted notions of beauty. However, Baldwin's comment also speaks to how human suffering, especially Black suffering, is both sensationalized and dismissed as routine. I share the loss of my sister in a fire knowing that Black people were burned at picnics in this country as outdoor entertainment while white parents held white children on their shoulders to watch. I share stories of Black people in my family suffering in hospitals knowing that Black people suffer globally in hospital beds right now in the hands of indifferent, patronizing health-care providers who do not even try to really *really* see them.

So, as you listen to or read the stories of Black pain I share here, try to wake up to *how* you are perceiving them. Use your Joy Journal to make note of your thoughts and sensations. Try to notice your heart and mind to see if you feel connected to what you are reading. Do you sense it as our common human experience? Do you feel indifferent or numb? Does reading the experiences arouse your sense of responsibility to end racism as it creates Black suffering? Noticing the reactions in your heart and mind will help you chart your personal next steps onto a more joyfully just path.

### They're Playing Our Song: Dancing with Our Loved Ones Eternally in the Rhythms of Life and Death

Remembering loved ones through music can be a resource for contemplative healing. We can reflect on our good times with lost loves by playing their favorite song or a song that reminds us of them.

When I am grieving my Uncle Michael, I play "Keep Your Head to the Sky," because he loved Earth, Wind & Fire (EWF). He also called my grandad an old softie for mourning my grandmother so long. Uncle Michael was always trying to nudge my grandfather out of grief so he would not stay stuck in it, and that happens to be the theme of that EWF song.

When I mourn my magnificent Aunt Essie, I play "I Shall Not Be Moved" because it was a Gospel song she hummed to express her timeless resolve, a resolve that supported four generations of my family as she cared for her own siblings (my beautiful grandfather included), her nieces and nephews, her grandnieces and nephews, and her great-grand nieces and nephews.

When I am grieving my grandfather, I play Louis Armstrong's "What a Wonderful World," because Grandad had a beautiful baritone voice and an ever-joyful countenance.

I learned to remember my loved ones through music because of my mother, who gave me a lyrical lesson on impermanence and the eternity of life's love energy. Let me tell you how.

In November of 1976 when I was eleven, just months after Stevie Wonder released his history-making masterpiece double album *Songs in the Key of Life*, my mother sat me down next to her in our home in East Orange, New Jersey, while the song "As" was playing and she said, "Listen to the words of this song." She sang along with Stevie Wonder in her lilting soft voice this extraordinary song about enduring love.

I understood then (and understand more now as I listen to that song forty-five years later) that the lyrics have many meanings, but the main one is that love endures through the cycles of life and death. As my mother sang to me all the outrageous circumstances that love will outlast, I was struck by how much she wanted me to notice that she was singing this to me.

The point was to emphasize the breadth and enduring power of love in this song she sang to me. I am sure she sang me many songs as a baby, but this is the one I remember—her holding my hand and looking into my eyes as she sang, impressing in my memory and my very spirit the presence of her love energy so that I would remember it was there with me and that she is here with me even now when I can no longer see her physical form.

What songs remind you of the enduring energy of love from someone you know still loves you, even though they are not physically present anymore? Whose love and support can you still feel as a presence in your life? Are there any songs that remind you of them? Try playing just a short piece of one song that you either sang or danced to with a loved one or that they sang to you. What feelings can you notice? If tears come, let them. Perhaps use an aspirational affirmation such as *May these tears form a river of eternal connection between me and my beloved.* Consider what was joyful about your relationship with them and note that in your Joy Journal along with the song so that you have it in case you want to revisit it and connect with your beloved on anniversaries and other special days.

## The Story of Our Beautiful Death

I was present when the body that birthed me into consciousness slipped into unconsciousness and left the physical world. My mother's physical death was the only time I have ever been present when someone died. That's almost odd considering the yearly funerals of family members throughout my childhood and adult life up until age forty when my mother passed away.

After the doctor described to me what her body was going through, how much pain she was in, I approached my brothers with the impossible choice the doctor had put forth. He said we had to decide if we wanted to keep her in the semiconscious state she was in and let her live as long as possible in extreme pain or give her pain medicine that would allow her to subside into unconsciousness and ease her inevitable transition into death.

I asked my mother first. Her eyes were closed, and she was intubated so she could not speak. I rubbed her long, thin, beautiful fingers, saying, "Umie, I know how much pain you're in, and I don't know what to do. The doctors said if they give you something for the pain, it will help but that you will likely not regain consciousness. Umie, squeeze my hand if you want me to tell them to do that. Just squeeze my hand." As I sat there weeping and wondering if she even had enough physical strength in her fingers to respond, let alone the strength to say goodbye to this life, to her children, I began to feel her fingers moving. Her eyes fluttered open and she looked at me with a look of yearning and agony that I understood before she exerted a light pressure on my hand. She held my eyes with her gaze as long as she could, saying so much, saying goodbye to her firstborn, saying she was in pain, saying goodbye to her children and grandchildren and to this life with her big Diana Ross eyes, and then she closed them. I doubled over as much in reverence as in pain and kissed the hand that had gone still as I wept my understanding.

After a time, I went out to tell my brothers, and they concurred that we should do as she wished and let her go. The doctors gave her the palliative pain medicine and told us that we should get some rest and food and that they would call us when her vitals dropped and it looked like she was close to the end. My siblings and other family members left to do that and to care for their young children, who had been waiting during the long hours we'd been spending in the hospital.

Having no children to tend, I resolved that I was not leaving the hospital until Umie did. My brother encouraged me to take care of myself, but for me, this *was* taking care of myself, as Umie was my anchor in the world. She was the *cared-for* and the *carer* in my universe—my person.

Less than an hour later, the nurse rushed in and advised me to call my family back, saying that my mother did not, in fact, have much time left at all. Looking back, I feel like my mother knew I was there, like she did not want to prolong the agony of her dying for any of us. After I called my brothers, I took my mother's hand and said, "Let's do Gongyo together one more time." As I recited the Lotus Sutra and chanted, holding her hand, I knew she heard the weeping in my voice, and yet it's my hope that she also heard the determination in my prayer for her to have a joyful transition and new existence. I hope she felt my resolve. When I finished the prayer, the nurse came in and told me she was gone. I'll never be able to describe the desolation I felt, but I also felt profound gratitude that my mother allowed me to be with her as she left. I offered benedictions to the vessel of her body that had brought this transcendent spirit, this essential mother to me. I began a gratitude practice, saying "Thank you" aloud as I kissed her belly, the belly that had carried me into this world, her feet that had walked with the weight of me in her body and in her arms. I kissed her hands, which had guided mine, teaching me to finger-paint, and eventually, write. I kissed her head, which held her mind-nurturing mind. I kissed her chest in reverence for her heart, which had loved so many so well, the heart with which she had lifted the weight of the world to bring her children to a better life and to make the world a better place. I remember the nobility of her countenance upon death, how regal she looked. The thirteenth-century Buddhist teacher Nichiren Daishonin writes in a letter to someone who had lost a family member, "How can we possibly hold back our tears at the inexpressible joy of knowing that [at the moment of death] not just one or two, not just one hundred or two hundred, but as many as a thousand Buddhas will come to greet us with open arms!"[18]

The Daishonin is referring to the enlightened life force of all beings that embraces a Buddhist practitioner at the end of our life. All the beautiful causes my mother had made throughout her life, including decades of Buddhist practice, were reflected in her dignified demeanor in that moment, and I knew she was being embraced by the compassionate, enlightened life force of the universe itself.

---

Let's Practice!

## A Reverent Goodbye

Pause here and notice what you are feeling and thinking. Perhaps using the invocation, say Nam Myoho Renge Kyo a few times to align your life force with the universe's positive energy. Allow yourself to reflect a bit on who you loved most that you have lost, whether to death or some other circumstance. Is there anyone you would have liked to have said goodbye to differently? Chant Nam Myoho Renge Kyo and offer them a reverent goodbye now.

Due to COVID-19, many of us were separated from loved ones. Other circumstances may also have prevented us from grieving the many losses in our lives. In your Joy Journal, write about how you would like to have said goodbye to anyone you lost, almost as if you are writing a short story or poem describing how you wish it had been as you revisit their dying. If you were not able to have the kind of goodbye you want, describe that goodbye now in your Joy Journal. Wish them joy on their journey throughout all time.

The reality of our own inevitable death is often so painful or frightening to think about that we do not do anything to plan for it. It's almost as if we believe that not thinking about it or planning for it will delay our death somehow. It is the equivalent of covering our ears and screaming "No no no noo nooo," as if the certainty of death can be eliminated by avoiding it. What this means is that we don't get to do ourselves or our loved ones justice in death even if we have managed to do justice to ourselves and them in life.

I want to invite you to join me in a love-bequest practice. Of course, doing an actual will is helpful and technically easy to do. You don't need a lawyer; you can just download a free template and do it on your computer, or even record it on your phone. That is known as a *holographic* will, and it has legal power in the absence of other documents.

For the love bequest practice, though, I invite you to make a different type of offering to those who may outlive you. You are not limited to bequeathing just money and material possessions. You can pass on any positive qualities, blessings, or circumstances that you cherish! Put on some light music, get comfortable, and pass it on!

We can follow the example of the human rights educator and activist Mary Mcleod Bethune, who wrote one of the most profound bequests ever recorded. Listen to this excerpt of Dr. Bethune's bequest to Black people: "I leave you love. I leave you hope. I leave you the challenge of developing confidence in one another. I leave you a thirst for education. I leave you a respect for the use of power. I leave you faith. I leave you racial dignity. I leave you a desire to live harmoniously with your fellow men. I leave you finally, a responsibility to our young people."[19]

Now consider what you might bequeath to your loved ones and humanity as a whole. How might *your* will be an expression of your gratitude and spiritual legacy?

---

Let's Practice!

## Your Poetic Legacy

Try writing a freestyle poem bequeathing sentiments, aspirations, and affirmations to one person you love. This may be something you do for many people, but try starting with one person. What do you always want that person to know you feel for them? What are your hopes and prayers for them when you are gone? What aspects of their being do you want to affirm so they can revisit that affirmation once you are gone? Doing this type of practice now allows us to leave a beautiful enduring inheritance of wisdom and strength for our beloveds.

If you can, free associate to continue making your bequests. If you would like a poem template, try something simple that draws on what you know your beloved values in you and in life, something that describes how you will spiritually accompany them eternally. To my loved ones I write, "I envelop you in courage and laughter, freedom in confined spaces and caution in unrestrained ones, peace in storms and stillness in busy times."

Often we think of poetry as something only established artists can do, people who have some training or education about art, but that is not so. Poetry is your right as a human being. It is a nonperformative free expression of what you feel and think, so have fun with it, especially if you want to have them laughing with joy after you're gone.

------------

## Grieving with Wisdom

The natural response to extreme pain is to want to escape it or numb it. This corresponds to what Kübler-Ross described as that first stage of grief: denial. This denial is often evidenced by substance abuse after the loss of a loved one. Said substance abuse is often higher in PGM communities and among queer people and people with disabilities because it is exacerbated by lack of time, space, and resources to grieve in these communities.

When my mother died, I was both immersed in and prepared for the sorrow of grief but not the terror, the panic, the groundlessness. Many of us have heard about the sorrow that accompanies loss but we do not know its vastness and complexity until we experience it. And often no one talks about the anxiousness, about how you might not be able to sleep, that you sometimes feel as if you are falling off the earth because the person who bound you to life is no longer physically in your realm. This is why the worst losses, or fear of the worst losses, are often accompanied by panic attacks.

Immediately after my mother's transition, I called Carol, a dear friend and mentor, and asked her, "Who do you go to when your mother dies?" She said, "Someone who does not need anything from you."

Consider who might be the most helpful people to you when you lose a loved one. Creating a list of about two or three folks might help. My colleague Benita talks about having a council of women, and indeed she is part of mine. That council can be called into session anytime you need them, yet the work of forming the council is something you can do now rather than scrambling while negotiating acute grief. To add to your resources, list three people who might be your council of support in times of grief. Select people who will encourage you to cry rather than stopping you; people who will not make the moment about them by launching into long stories about when they lost something; people who are uplifting without invalidating what you are going through; people who will not need anything from you in return for their support, even the chance to vent about their own grief. If there is no one like this in your life, then now you have friendship goals! You can also begin seeking out people in contemplative circles who could augment your council of support.

Immediately after my mother died, I stepped out of the hospital into a daybreak so bright it hurt my feelings. How could the sun shine so brightly in my face as I stepped away from my mother's last breath in this world? I was viscerally shocked, mortified in the true sense of the word, but only for a moment. Because right after that thought came the truer one: "There she is, lighting the way for me through this, too—that sunlight is her shining me through!" Was that my defenses protecting me? Maybe. But it did not feel like it. It felt real, because I'd never seen a dawn like that. It also felt full circle to me, as I was born at dawn and that was the name my mother had first considered for me. "Dawn" is the meaning of my middle name. Because of the deep spiritual bond we had and because of her cultivating my capacity to look to nature for signs of interdependent life and compassion, I saw the light of her life and love in the sunshine that morning. I still see and feel the sunshine that way.

When we left the hospital, my brothers went home to their children and I went back to my mother's, alone. I knew then that home was a person, not a place, and for me home had been Umie. I'd had Umie in this world for forty years—a lifetime. I had so much to grieve and the grief was teaching me lessons I longed to share. It was from this moment that I resolved to create resources for people to grieve, and soon after I began focusing my clinical practice on grief counseling in addition to offering grief therapy at the Washington, DC, morgue.

I contemplated my mentor Dr. Daisaku Ikeda and how he said his own life had united with his deceased mentor's. I encouraged myself by reading about how he was determined to make good causes for his deceased son from the moment of his son's death. Ikeda said, "The great benefit of our Buddhist practice . . . also flows on to the deceased as well as to unborn future generations."[20]

---

## Let's Practice!

## Beloved Nature

I practiced to grieve with wisdom and courage. I am still doing that practice, and I invite you to join me by reflecting on the following questions:

- *How and when do I feel my beloved's presence in nature?*

- *In what ways do I sense them in the wind, water, trees, and soil?*

Note in your Joy Journal what elements remind you of your beloved. Journal about how you might deepen your sensing of your beloved by tapping into nature. Try this short nature meditation to tune in to the ways that nature itself is a beloved that is holding and sustaining you right now:

*Breathing in, I am aware that the sun sustains my life.*

*Breathing out, I rest in gratitude for the sun.*

Just for a moment, let your awareness take in that the sun is sustaining your life. Let gratitude flow through you for your relationship with the sun. This is the sun that sustains your life and the lives of all your beloveds.

Daisaku Ikeda says, "Become like the sun. If you do so, all darkness will be dispelled. No matter what happens, live confidently with the conviction that you yourself are the sun."[21]

*Breathing in, I allow gratitude for the sun.*

*Breathing out, I realize I am a sun warming and nourishing everyone and everything around me with ease.*

Now, allowing yourself to ascend like the sun, either sit up straight or stand. Let yourself rise like the sun as you breathe deeply. Plant your feet firmly on the earth. You are grounded in your connection to nature. Notice that your body, head to toe, is held in a perfect gravitational embrace by the earth.

---

## Engaging Impermanence and Death in Good Humor

One of the ways we describe people with good mental health is to say they are "in good humor." Good humor is reflected in the capacity to notice the pain, absurdities, and capricious aspects of life cheerfully. Our ability to experience good humor arising in ourselves as a quality of mind, heart, body, and spirit is enhanced by facing impermanence, not by turning away from it.

At first thought, decline, loss, and death may not seem to be joyful topics. However, if we can face them in good humor, we can access a more trenchant joy, one that is based on a full picture of life's ever-shifting realities. The dominant Eurocentric worldview is death-avoidant. That attitude and fear keeps us from facing the inevitable decline of our own selves, that of those we love, and the decline and death that is part of the cycle of all living things. Reconciling with death allows us to value and cherish life.

Lightly working with our own grief and anticipatory grief helps us stay engaged with the reality of constant loss in a way that connects us to joy. A couple of years ago, I asked my friend Bruce how old he was, and he said cheerily, "Oh, I'm sixty; I'm almost done." It was his lighthearted way of being in a good-humored relationship with the reality that although death could come at any time, it gets more imminent with age. We joked about how birthdays mark celebrations of life, but if we are being honest, they also highlight how we are getting closer to death. So, from then on, I began singing him a little satirical ditty I made up on aging and the march toward death, entitled "Happy Motherfu**in' Birthday." I won't torture you with the lyrics here—maybe in the next book! Bruce also had a wall hanging with an extraordinary John Brown quote. John Brown was an abolitionist who was hanged for his leadership in ending slavery in America. He reportedly said, on his way to the gallows, "It is a very beautiful world. I never noticed before."[22] This is a reminder for those of us who are activists. We can be so busy improving the world that we forget to see its beauty as it is. As Bruce says, "You might as well love the world you're trying to save."

## How You Livin'?

The popular expression coined by African Americans, "How you livin'?"—to which the telling reply is sometimes "Like a turkey at Thanksgiving"—is exemplary of the breviloquent genius of Black American idiom. Embedded in the phrase "How you livin'?" is an inquiry that is about more than the performance of life. "How are you doing?" subtly refers more to the actions one is taking in life. Rather, the query "How you livin'?" asks about the manner and quality of living. The response also reflects, lightly and in good humor, how Black people are as targeted as hunted turkeys in the service of colonialist, misrepresentative traditions like "Thanksgiving." Through laconic expressions such as this, contemplative practice manifests as play with language, and it is a means by which many Black Americans live transcendent lives while facing the brutality we meet in life with good humor.

Human aversion to the death of the earth also reflects fear of our own death. We naturally decline and decay, but often we abhor our own senescence. In some cases, we even advance our bodily decay with our denial and efforts to cling to perceived youth, beauty, and vitality. The manifestations of impermanence in our bodies are constant. We are all temporarily abled. One day we will all lose some aspect of our bodily functioning and ultimately, we lose breath itself. To grieve well, it is valuable to notice the truth that as surely as we are living, we are also dying right now.

That said, "Trouble don't last always."

This popular African American saying is a locution of Black wisdom that addresses impermanence in another way, specifically the impermanence of suffering. It is a balm to know that pain and suffering are impermanent, too. They are ever-changing aspects of existence, and no matter how brutal the suffering we are navigating now is, it too shall pass.

---

Let's Practice!

## A Contemplative Inner Dialogue

Contemplative dialogue practices allow us to put our attention and intention on noticing our interdependence with all aspects of our being and all that surrounds us. When we speak with ourselves, we are sometimes engaged in contemplative self-dialogue. I say "sometimes" because the reflexive self-criticism or self-aggrandizement that often arises in our self-talk does not always reflect intention or insight. However, when we engage in inquiry with ourselves, exploring our thoughts, words, and actions, that *is* a reflective interior conversation. Such internal dialogue is essential for mindful engagement in the world.

Practicing contemplative inner dialogue allows us to communicate with the seemingly disparate but interdependent aspects of ourselves. In contemplative dialogue with ourselves, our shame can seek counsel from our hope, our fear can listen to our courage, our doubt can encounter our faith.

In the following three-part practice, I invite you to begin a contemplative dialogue with yourself. Reflect on how you can notice that you are living and thriving.

> In contemplative dialogue with ourselves, our shame can seek counsel from our hope, our fear can listen to our courage, our doubt can encounter our faith.

## Part 1: How Am I Livin'?

Life seems to go by quickly because we rarely take time to notice being alive. In dialogue with yourself, take some time to notice the quality and sensation of life within you. Finish the sentences below using the prompts naturally, going with whatever arises. If you want to write down your responses, feel free. If not, just notice how you finish the sentences in reflective conversation with yourself.

- *I can tell I am alive physically because . . .*

- *What I feel in my body that shows me I am alive is . . .*

- *What I notice in my mind that shows me I am alive is . . .*

- *What I feel emotionally that shows me I am alive is . . .*

- *What I feel in my spirit that shows me I am alive is . . .*

First notice what that brief chat with yourself revealed about the quality of your life. What aspect of how you're livin' is going well? Did you get any information about where you might need support? Sometimes conversing with ourselves brings forth gratitude. Sometimes it guides us to concerns we need to share with people who care about us or people who can be resources to us.

Next, notice whether any of the thoughts, sensations, or feelings that emerged during that brief chat with yourself were related to nature or other beings. If what you felt in your body that shows you are alive is your breathing, that's your interdependence with the air manifesting in your awareness as how you're livin'. If what arose in your heart was love or longing for other beings, that is interdependence with other beings manifesting as how you're livin'. We cannot notice how we are living without noticing life's interdependent quality and nature.

### Part 2: How Am I Dying? Dying in Good Humor

In one of her masterclass discussions on greeting life bravely, Pema Chödrön talks about smiling at fear—specifically how smiling at fear disarms our nervous system enough to look at the fear itself as well as whatever frightens us.[23] Decline and death are frightening and not always fun to look at. But what if we adopted a wry sense of humor about the impermanence of our existence and greeted it with a smile or at least a cheeky grin?

Take a few deep diaphragmatic breaths and try this practice of being relaxed with impermanence. Take long, luxurious inhalations, counting to seven as you fill your diaphragm and then counting to seven as you exhale fully, allowing this impermanence practice to accompany your breath:

*Breathing in, I smile and greet life.*

*Breathing out, I smile and greet death.*

Now, continuing to breathe deeply, try these prompts in contemplative dialogue with yourself:

- *I notice decline and death in my body as . . .*

- *I notice decline and death in my mind as . . .*

- *I notice emotional decline and death as . . .*

- *I notice spiritual decline and death as . . .*

Did anything occur to you that you want to act on? Sometimes our reflections on death or decline in a given area of our lives remind us of how we want to take care of that aspect of our lives. We might notice bodily decline in our teeth, emotional decline from the wear and tear of unresolved grief, mental decline in our lapsing memory, or spiritual decline as our fading sense of hope or resolve. Regularly exploring our declining and dying can remind us act to revitalize aspects of our life that need our attention. Go ahead and give death and decline a cheeky little smile right now. You might even say, "I see you, death. That's why I'm living fully and taking the best possible care of myself right now."

## Part 3: The Joyful Dance with Death

As children we may have been fearless with our bodies. We may have hung upside down from porch railings or run all out, not worried about falling. We were full of adventure, flinging ourselves forward. As adults we can decide to retain that youthful courage tempered with wisdom and face decline and death bravely. As the poet Claude McKay says of resisting racial injustice, "If we must die—oh, let us nobly die, . . . pressed to the wall, dying, but fighting back!"[24] He is referring specifically to fighting racism, yet all of life's destructive tendencies can be fought with this spirit to live and die nobly.

Facing and mourning our inevitable losses as we also mourn the preventable losses we've endured helps us awaken to the losses we can prevent now. Put simply, it's also useful to think about decline and death to prevent unnecessary decline and death. Try this mourning exercise to help you notice impermanence as you examine and mourn your preventable losses. In a companionable chat with yourself, perhaps taking your own hand, ask yourself,

- *What natural losses do I mourn in my own body?*

- *What preventable losses do I mourn in my own body?*

- *What's an action I can take now to prevent unnecessary loss to my body?*

- *What am I grieving most?*

- *What am I enjoying most?*

- *What emerges in the third space between what I am grieving and what I am enjoying?*

When we practice contemplative dialogue with ourselves regularly, it can help us step off the treadmill of doing things by rote (or simply because we are expected to) and focus on *being*. Then, as we attend to being, we focus on doing what we love.

---

Often without knowing we are doing it, we drown a lot of our grief in addictive or compulsive behavior. When we are grieving well, we step out of compulsive and addictive actions and begin to be the leaders of our own healthy lives. Unhealthy addictions can include food, work, money, sex, and so forth. Facing impermanence bravely, we can decide not to poison our lives with excess, and that's how we enjoy each moment without clinging to it. That is how we grieve well.

Grieving well, grieving joyfully, is something we can get better at over time. The experience of grieving my mother's death in 2006 taught me that I had to cultivate resolve and set an intention about how I was going to grieve when my sister died.

Let me tell you about it.

On March 24, 2020, I led a webinar addressing how racism undermines human understanding of global interdependence. I led joyfully, encouraging hundreds of participants worldwide to expand their capacity to perceive and enact interdependence. About fifteen minutes after that webinar ended, one of my brothers called to tell me that our fifty-six-year-old sister, Kaweemah, had died in a fire at her home. Bewilderment, grief, and resolve swirled within me as I determined to find a way to support my nephews and brothers.

I breathed deeply and chanted Nam Myoho Renge Kyo before calling my other brothers to share this agonizing news. That brief pause to breathe and do the invocation caused enough wisdom to arise in me so that when I called my other brothers, instead of blurting out the news, I asked where each was and who he was with. I knew that they needed to be prepared, to sit down if possible, and to advise anyone they were with that there was a family tragedy.

This was one attempt of many to come in my effort to stay calm within the aftermath of a fire that was not done sweeping through our family. I had to use my meditative practices to try to prevent more damage, to extinguish embers of this experience that could ignite new disasters. Because the pandemic had just been declared, we could not jump on planes and be with one another, although we tearfully and vehemently expressed plans to do just that. We began talking in earnest about the very real hazards of trying to travel to mourn together in light of how little was known about the COVID-19 virus at that time.

That same evening, at about 5:50 pm, I looked in the mirror weeping, wondering *how* I could continue to be myself, who indeed *I* was without my only sister who had been with me all my life. She had taught me how to tie my shoes. She was the one who fought back when we were regularly attacked by white youth shouting racial epithets at us in elementary school. She was my first dance partner—from shaking our little-girl hips in our childhood bedroom to the nightclubs of our roaring twenties. In so many ways, she was such a beautiful person.

I remembered that I had to lead a women's Buddhist study meeting that night, what we in the Soka Gakkai International call a Sophia Group meeting. I resolved to discuss the timeless wisdom of Buddhism as an offering to my sister's eternal life force. I envisioned Kaweemah already beginning her next life and spiritually in attendance with me at that meeting.

As the shock wore off, every day and night was a battle against overwhelming grief and traumatic images. Looking at the flames as I turned on the stove to cook, I was painfully reminded of the awful way my only sister died. Many times, I could not cook at all, and I just sat at my altar and wept. I had never realized before how central fire is to everyday life. I realized I had to grab hold of my mind or risk being forever traumatized by the sight of fire.

My family and I continued to support one another through the painful reality that we could not gather for a memorial for my sister until the pandemic was over. I managed to make it through that summer of grieving by using the anxious energy of grief to fuel me in speaking out for justice more than ever as one murderous incident of racism after another flooded the news and sparked global protests. I realized that the whole world was burning, and I resolved to be a force for healing.

By autumn, I thought I was through the acute phase of grieving my sister's death from smoke inhalation only to be astounded by smoke and fire consuming the Monterey Bay region where I live! I was new to California, having lived on the East Coast all of my life until August of 2019. When I stepped outside my door and inhaled the smoke from the wildfires, I thought, *This can't be happening.* How could it be that just months after losing someone so precious to me in a fire, I was now immersed in one of the worst fire seasons in California history?!? The very act of breathing the smoke-filled air was a reminder of how my sister died. "I can't breathe" had multiple layers of meaning for me, as a Black woman, at that point.

One of my calming practices is listening to fictional audiobooks. Yet even as I listened to those, I realized how prominently fire is featured in my favorite books. In Toni Morrison's *Sula*, for example, fire is depicted as a way of releasing a loved one from suffering *and* as a force that is as grotesque in its consequences as it is beautiful in appearance. There was no way I was going to be able to grieve this loss out of the line of fire.

Fire has so many meanings. In our illuminating parlance, African Americans describe something really good as "fire" or "fyah." Even the word "hot" references something that ignites passion or alights us.

I decided to use every experience of fire and smoke as a meditation, a reflective prompt to remember that there can be productive, healing qualities inherent in painful or destructive forces. When I heard that the dean of the school where I teach lost her home in the wildfires, I prayed that all people suffering from fires everywhere would endure with hope, determination, and courage. I resolved to use the flames of injustice, environmental destruction, and death itself to light the path for everyone within reach of the sound of my voice.

On the one-year anniversary of my sister's death, I decided to get the COVID-19 vaccination based on my commitment to living a long, contributive life. Amazingly, as I was set to leave the vaccination site, we were told the police had issued a threat alert and that we could not leave until the parking lot and surrounding area were cleared. This was the day after the mass shooting at a supermarket that was also a vaccination site in Colorado on March 23, 2021.

I calmly sat down to wait and called my brother, too bemused by the absurdity of it all to be scared, and told him if I didn't make it, to tell everyone I died laughing—literally! The police cleared us to leave just in time for me to make it to a book talk on my chapter in *Black and Buddhist: What Buddhism Can Teach Us about Race, Resilience, Transformation, and Freedom*. Reunited at that event with Ruth King, the author who I had led the webinar with on that same date the year before, I offered encouragement to participants with my sister, Kaweemah, in my heart.

In Toni Morrison's *Beloved*, the only time the hero Sixo laughs is when enslavers set him on fire. He laughs because he knows that whatever the tortures of this life, there is always more life. He laughs, shouting "Seven-O!" in celebration of his coming child and the immortality of spiritual strength.[25]

Daisaku Ikeda said, "Life contains the capacity, like flames that reach toward heaven, to transform suffering and pain into the energy needed for value creation, into light that illuminates darkness."[26] I resolved to bravely grasp the flames of suffering savaging our world and transform the destructive energy of fire into the constructive light of wisdom.

I also resolved to use my Buddhist practice to reclaim the natural element of fire itself, as well as other things in daily life that had become laden with trauma. I offer you a model for doing that as well. I chanted Nam Myoho Renge Kyo whenever I felt a little skip in my heart or observed my mind drifting to fear or sorrow when I saw fire. I did this in order to heal the trauma response I had to the sight of fire since my sister's death. I let the awful thoughts about fire come, not pushing them away but turning toward them while also noticing fire's healing and warming qualities as I chanted at my altar with the burning candle on it.

Notice what thoughts, feelings, and sensations are arising for you now. Consider what associations you might have with some of the natural elements. Are there any natural elements that cause you to be fearful or have other painful sensations? Make a note of them now so that you can use some of the practices I have shared to work with them.

I have shared so much of my own and my family's suffering with you as an ode to the depth and timelessness of Black love, Black grief transmuted, and Black spiritual union with our ancestors throughout all time and space. I share it because Buddhism posits that we can expiate karma by words and deeds that reflect the bodhisattva vow to lead all beings to enlightenment. I dedicate the merit of this chapter and indeed this entire book to my deceased family members from whom the wisdom herein is transmitted. I also dedicate the merit to my living family members who continue to transmute the sufferings of racism, loss, and grief every day as they live joyfully. I know that this sharing, this offering, contributes something to the transformation of not only my family's karma but also the karma of Black people, PGM, and all beings.

In a famous letter to his nephew, James Baldwin brings us to the truth of our need to reconcile with impermanence:

Life is tragic simply because the earth turns and the sun inexorably rises and sets, and one day, for each of us, the sun will go down for the last, last time. Perhaps the whole root of our trouble, the human trouble, is that we will sacrifice all the beauty of our lives, will imprison ourselves in totems, taboos, crosses, blood sacrifices, steeples, mosques, races, armies, flags, nations, in order to deny the fact of death, the only fact we have. It seems to me that one ought to rejoice in the fact of death—ought to decide, indeed, to earn one's death by confronting with passion the conundrum of life. One is responsible for life: It is the small beacon in that terrifying darkness from which we come and to which we shall return.[27]

---

Let's Practice!

## Setting Our Grief Goals

This chapter has invited you to wade far into the waters of grief, so now I'd like you to return to shore and grab your Joy Journal to just note how your body, mind, heart, and soul are responding to all that we've just explored. If you want to metabolize it all a bit further and apply what you just read while it's fresh in your mind, let's try one final practice.

> With a stronghearted embrace of impermanence, we can enter into the freedom of authentic, meaningful living in each moment

I sometimes make grief goals with clients, asking them to think about where they would like to be, emotionally and cognitively, around a given loss. After all, if you don't set a destination, how can you get to it? Consider a relatively minor loss you have experienced recently. Maybe you lost something like your phone, or you had a minor car accident. Where are you in the grieving process with that loss at this moment? Where would you like to be with your grief around the loss you just brought to mind? What would acceptance and integrated learning from the loss look like? Note that grief goal in your Joy Journal. You can also use this practice with a major loss. We can guide ourselves through life's losses using contemplative practices and develop much wisdom in the process.

With a stronghearted embrace of impermanence, we can enter into the freedom of authentic, meaningful living in each moment and enjoy our existence at each moment as a celebration of eternally interdependent reality.

———————

# Conclusion

## Closing and Opening to Our Next Steps

As we come to the end of the book, notice your embodiment of our joyfully just journey. How does what you've read and practiced resonate in your being? Notice what you have learned, what you've explored. We have traversed pathways to wisdom via the traditions of Black people and Buddhism. We've noticed how these inform many valuable present-day contemplative practices. We've considered how language can shift, moving us as we embody justice and joy. We have had guidance toward joyful suffering, and we have learned that discomfort resilience and fierce compassion are the musculature that enable joyfully just living. We have excavated adultism, explored power and playfulness, and learned how to experience deep fulfillment by having power *with* rather than power *over*. We have considered how to cleanse our playful life activities of oppressive inclinations. We have begun a Joy Journal and gathered resources for our Joybox that will sustain us during challenging times. And now we get to create our own daily path of joyfully just engagement using all that we have learned.

Coming to the end of this writing brings me back to the beginning of my engagement with words and the first autobiography, filled with Black wisdom, that I read as a child. I was seven. I remember my age because in the book, *I Know Why the Caged Bird Sings*, Maya Angelou describes being raped at age seven, and I remember feeling horrified that rape could have happened to someone who was my age. Many people think the title of that book was her own poetic allegory, but she was inspired by a pioneering African American poet, Paul Laurence Dunbar, so much so that she titled her book after the theme and main verse of his poem "Sympathy." In it, Dunbar draws a parallel between life as a Black person and the life of a caged bird:

I know what the caged bird feels, alas!
When the sun is bright on the upland slopes;
When the wind stirs soft through the springing grass,
And the river flows like a stream of glass;
When the first bird sings and the first bud opes,
And the faint perfume from its chalice steals—
I know what the caged bird feels!
I know why the caged bird beats its wing
Till its blood is red on the cruel bars;
For he must fly back to his perch and cling
When he fain would be on the bough a-swing;
And a pain still throbs in the old, old scars
And they pulse again with a keener sting—
I know why he beats his wing!
I know why the caged bird sings, ah me,
When his wing is bruised and his bosom sore,—
When he beats his bars and he would be free;
It is not a carol of joy or glee,
But a prayer that he sends from his heart's deep core,
But a plea, that upward to Heaven he flings—
I know why the caged bird sings![1]

The fact that the title of Angelou's book comes from another Black author is important because we can see that her iconic artistry was inspired by the artistry of a Black poet born more than a half century before her, someone born only a few years after slavery was abolished but when it was still informally practiced. Dunbar and Angelou are part of a lineage of Black insight and creative transmutation of suffering. In Dunbar's allegory and Angelou's title, Black people are the metaphorical caged birds, singing a prayer, an intention for freedom. Since injustice anywhere is a threat to justice everywhere, as Dr. King said, we are all caged, if any of us are. However, some of us are simply oblivious to our confinement since we are in the gilded cages of privilege.

May there be abolition of all cages. May there be restorative justice and reparation. May there be joy in the process of achieving this. May your resolve, your discomfort resilience, your fierce compassion, and your own joyfully just actions make it so.

As your author, I notice how difficult it feels for me to end this book. It feels like I have so much more to say, but I know that I need not say it all here. James Baldwin says, "You write in order to change the world, knowing perfectly well that you probably can't. . . . The world changes according to the way people see it, and if you alter, even by a millimeter, the way people look at reality, then you can change it."[2] I hope that something in these pages has inspired you to create change.

One of my favorite quotes from Maya Angelou's *I Know Why the Caged Bird Sings* is when she builds on Dunbar's allegorical unity between human experience and wildlife, saying: "A bird doesn't sing because it has an answer, it sings because it has a song."[3]

I sang some of my song in this book and I hope that with you, dear reader, it resonates, that it strikes a chord for your own wisdom as so many of the teachers, authors, and musicians cited here have created melodies of wisdom and joy within me. May our chorus of joyous justice never cease, and may we find eternal community and enlightenment in a shared vow for the flourishing of all life.

In closing, I offer you one last poem: my own paean to joyfully just living.

## Meditations on Being Water and Stone

Saturated in awareness of our inherent human connection, we offer the
water of peace and friendship to one another

Awash in the water of self-compassion, we erode the stones of shame
and self-loathing in our hearts

Scouring ourselves with the wisdom of interdependence, we soften the
barriers within us and between us

When we are tempted to degrade the humanity of another, we will
shower our minds with the water of self-mastery

When stones of brutality and war are launched, we will rise up as a
torrent of peace and non-violence to sustain our humanity

When monuments to greed are erected to imprison the vulnerable,
we will flood their gates as a bottomless ocean of courage and
generosity

We will fill each other up with the water of fierce compassion to
corrode the stone walls of privilege that block our view of our
shared humanity

With the water of discomfort resilience, we will wash away the stones
of consumerism and addiction.

With the water of compassionate dialogue, we disintegrate the stones
of indifference frozen in the hearts of our friends amid the winter of
their life struggle

Swirling, rushing, rolling, ebbing, surging, sweeping, lapping,
heaving, gushing,

And finally flowing, simply flowing

over the constant unending array of rocks, boulders and mountains
in our path towards liberation

we swell,

full and undulating

with the momentum of our internal current expanding the depth of
our life force,

growing as we practice surging over one mountain of injustice
after another.

Enriched by the minerals in every rock, every stone, every boulder of
    injustice we float over, we become more brilliant
And yet, as water we know ourselves to be one with the stone
We are the water that is in harmony with the stone
As water becomes enriched by the minerals it flows over, we absorb
    nutrients from the rocks and stones and life forms we flow over and
    through
Facing licentiousness and injustice, let us use each grain of pain to
    become diamonds of dissent for decency
Our hearts pounded to gravel by the unjust gavel, we gather the dust of
    us and do what we must!
We are pillars standing against the hose of hate turned against us
We are the rock Winnie Mandela said you struck when you strike
    a woman
We are the stone of hope King hewed out of the mountain of despair
We are the stones of bones that will return to the earth as dust and we
    shall be the stones upon which our descendants will stand
Let them stand awash in a timeless current of compassion we pour
    down on them
Testing our mettle let us build discomfort resilience,
Let us become medallions of light guiding the way for one another
Let our meditative practices be the masonry that turns all stones of
    suffering into jewels of wisdom.


With you always in joy,

Kamilah

# Acknowledgments

I offer deepest gratitude to my mentor in Buddhism, Daisaku Ikeda, whose contributions to the widespread understanding of engaged Buddhism will forever enrich humanity and all life.

I am grateful for my Grandaunt Essie Williams Haynes, the matriarch of our family, who raised four generations of children and lifted us all to higher planes with her loving leadership of our family. I am grateful to my uncle John, who first guided me to feel music in my body and to my sister Kaweemah, my first singing and dance partner.

I am grateful to Keith Harewood, who ceaselessly demonstrates what it is to be an ally to women and girls, which he has done for me since I was a teenager. By speaking to me about matters of the heart and mind from an early age, he helped cultivate my intellectual freedom, my sense of hope, and my capacity to articulate despair eloquently, all while maintaining a sense of humor.

I thank Dr. Carol Valentin, my mentor and friend, teacher, and sister, who guided me in understanding the impact of racism on mental health and well-being; Bruce Margolis, my ever-cheerful companion amidst the pains of living; and Esther Jackson, the teacher of my heart, who embodies love in liberation.

Carrie Bergman has been an invaluable thought partner in the development of this book. She embodies an extraordinary assemblage of talents: master editor, visual artist, and contemplative leader in her own right. She is imbued with creativity, wisdom, humor, humility, and a natural inclination toward justice that makes her beautiful, as a person, as an artist, as an intellectual, as a spiritual fellow traveler, and as a friend. An ally par excellence, she has the integrity to ask guiding questions when the work goes off course so that I stay true to my vision, and she allies that vision with unwavering conscience and consistency. She matches my good cheer and has a surfeit of enthusiasm whenever I am running low on it.

This book would not have been possible without the guidance and support of Dr. Vaishali Mamgain, my beloved dharma sister and co-conspirator for justice.

Finally, my gratitude extends to all of you who, together with me, form a collective human tapestry of love and wisdom that we weave joyfully and endlessly with one another.

# Notes

## Introduction

1. Robin D. G. Kelley, *Thelonius Monk: The Life and Times of an American Original* (New York: Free Press, 2009).

2. Soka Gakkai SGI, "Daily Encouragement from SGI President Daisaku Ikeda," Facebook, August 28, 2021, facebook .com/SokaGakkaiSgi/photos/a.1500975466713283 /2585401318270687/.

3. Martin Luther King Jr., "Where Do We Go From Here" (speech, Southern Christian Leadership Conference, Atlanta, GA, August 16, 1967), kinginstitute.stanford.edu/where-do-we-go-here -chaos-or-community/.

4. Kahlil Gibran, *The Prophet* (New York: Knopf, 1923); "On Pain," Poets.org, accessed September 21, 2023, poets.org/poem/pain-1.

5. "Part 1: Happiness; Chapter 6: The Principle of 'Cherry, Plum, Peach, and Damson' [6.4]," sokaglobal.org, accessed September 21, 2023, sokaglobal.org/resources/study-materials /buddhist-study/the-wisdom-for-creating-happiness-and-peace /chapter-6-4.html.

6. adrienne maree brown, *Emergent Strategy: Shaping Change, Changing Worlds* (Chico, CA: AK Press, 2017).

7. Nichiren Daishonin, "The Strategy of the Lotus Sutra," *The Writings of Nichiren Daishonin*, vol. I (Tokyo: Soka Gakkai, 1999), 1001; nichirenlibrary.org/en/wnd-1/Content/139.

## Chapter One: Contemplative Practice, Joy, Justice, and Inner Transformation

1. Stephen Murphy-Shigematsu, "Heartfulness and Compassion," Dr. Stephen Murphy-Shigematsu (website), accessed June 21, 2023, murphyshigematsu.com/heartfulness-compassion-and -transformat.

2. Rhonda V. Magee, *The Inner Work of Racial Justice: Healing Ourselves and Transforming Our Communities Through Mindfulness* (New York: TarcherPerigee, 2019).

3. Jennifer L. Eberhardt, *Biased: Uncovering the Hidden Prejudice That Shapes What We See, Think, and Do* (New York: Viking, 2019).

4. Bethany Weidner, "Barbara Love Gives a Training: Building Relationships Across Race and Cultural Boundaries," Works in Progress, November 2, 2017, olywip.org/barbara-love-gives -training-building-relationships-across-race-cultural-boundaries/.

5. Daisaku Ikeda, *The Wisdom for Creating Happiness and Peace*, pt. 2, *Human Revolution* (Los Angeles: World Tribune Press, 2017), 5–9, as quoted in "What Is Human Revolution, Really?" SGI-USA, sgi-usa.org/2023/01/16/what-is-human-revolution-really/.

6. SGI (Soka Gakkai International), "Human Revolution," *SGI Quarterly*, July 2005, sokaglobal.org/resources/study-materials /buddhist-concepts/human-revolution.html.

7. Alice Walker, *Possessing the Secret of Joy* (New York: Simon and Schuster, 1992).

8. Stephen Murphy-Shigematsu, *From Mindfulness to Heartfulness: Transforming Self and Society with Compassion* (Oakland, CA: Berrett-Koehler Publishers, 2018).

9. Daisaku Ikeda, "Compassion: Solidarity of the Heart," *SGI Quarterly*, July 2010, sokaglobal.org/resources/study-materials /buddhist-concepts/compassion.html.

10. Resmaa Menakem, *My Grandmother's Hands: Racialized Trauma and the Pathway to Mending Our Hearts and Bodies* (Las Vegas: Central Recovery Press, 2017), xviii.

11. Robin DiAngelo, *What Does It Mean to Be White?* (New York: Peter Lang, 2012), as quoted in Resmaa Menakem, *My Grandmother's Hands: Racialized Trauma and the Pathway to Mending Our Hearts and Bodies* (Las Vegas: Central Recovery Press, 2017), xviii.

12. Frantz Fanon, *Black Skin, White Masks* (New York: Grove Press, 2008).

13. "Wyoma—African Healing Dance," Sounds True, YouTube video, 9:23, June 27, 2008, youtube.com/watch?v=LkLoDhSrVKc.

14. Toni Morrison, "Nobel Lecture," December 7, 1993, The Nobel Prize (website), nobelprize.org/prizes/literature/ 1993/morrison/lecture/.

15. Rachel Sylvester, "For Tory Candidates, It's All about Kerb Appeal," *The Times*, May 29, 2019, thetimes.co.uk/article/for -tory-candidates-it-s-all-about-kerb-appeal-qnxd5g3x6.

16. Smithsonian Institution, "Symbols of Black Power in Vietnam," National Museum of African American History and Culture, accessed September 21, 2023, nmaahc.si.edu/explore/stories /giving-dap.

17. Sarah Kramer. "The Forgotten History of a Prison Uprising in Vietnam," Code Switch Radio Diaries, National Public Radio, August 29, 2018, npr.org/sections/codeswitch/2018/08/29/642617106/the-forgotten-history-of-a-prison-uprising-in-vietnam.

18. Smithsonian Institution, "Symbols of Black Power in Vietnam," National Museum of African American History and Culture, accessed September 21, 2023, nmaahc.si.edu/explore/stories/giving-dap.

19. Tsione Wolde-Michael, "A Brief History of Voguing," National Museum of African American History and Culture, accessed June 26, 2023, nmaahc.si.edu/explore/stories/brief-history-voguing.

20. Raymond Lam, "Conscientious Compassion," *Tricycle: The Buddhist Review*, August 20, 2015, tricycle.org/article/conscientious-compassion/.

21. Kamilah Majied, "Buddhism and Our Ongoing Emancipation," *Tricycle: The Buddhist Review*, June 19, 2023, tricycle.org/article/buddhism-emancipation/.

22. "Black Abolitionists," Zinn Education Project, accessed September 21, 2023, zinnedproject.org/materials/black-abolitionists.

23. "Elizabeth Freeman," National Women's History Museum, accessed September 21, 2023, womenshistory.org/education-resources/biographies/elizabeth-freeman.

24. Evan Spring, "Phil Schaap Interview," WKCR, October 5, 1992, cc-seas.columbia.edu/wkcr/content/phil-schaap-interview.

25. Zora Neale Hurston, *Their Eyes Were Watching God*. 1937, pressbooks.library.torontomu.ca/theireyeswerewatchinggod/chapter/3/

## Chapter Two: Resilient Compassion

1. "Dharma and Justice Dialogues: What Is Right Justice? With Rev. angel Kyodo williams and Rev. Kosen Gregory Snyder," Union Theological Seminary, YouTube video, October 6, 2020, youtube.com/watch?v=zR8so49bKvU.

2. Daisaku Ikeda, "True, Undying Hope Is a Conscious Decision," *Times of India*, April 28, 2020, timesofindia.indiatimes.com /blogs/toi-edit-page/true-undying-hope-is-a-conscious-decision.

3. Pema Chödrön, *When Things Fall Apart: Heart Advice for Difficult Times* (Boston: Shambhala, 2000).

4. Daisaku Ikeda, "Quotations On the Theme of Interconnectedness," Soka Gakkai, accessed June 29, 2023, daisakuikeda.org/sub/quotations/theme/interconnectedness.html.

5. bell hooks and George Yancy, "Bell Hooks: Buddhism, the Beats and Loving Blackness," Opinionator, *New York Times*, December 10, 2015, archive.nytimes.com/opinionator.blogs .nytimes.com/2015/12/10/bell-hooks-buddhism-the-beats-and -loving-blackness/.

6. hooks and Yancy, "Bell Hooks: Buddhism, the Beats and Loving Blackness."

7. Kahlil Gibran, "Defeat," in *The Madman: His Parables and Poems* (North Chelmsford, MA: Courier Corporation, 2001). Public domain.

8. Daisaku Ikeda, *For Today & Tomorrow: Daily Encouragement* (Los Angeles: World Tribune Press, 1999), 50.

9. Daisaku Ikeda, *Prayer*, Buddhism for You series (Santa Monica, CA: Middleway Press, 2006).

10. Tema Okun, "What Is White Supremacy Culture?" White Supremacy Culture, accessed September 21, 2023, whitesupremacyculture.info/what-is-it.html.

11. Tema Okun, "(divorcing) White Supremacy Culture," White Supremacy Culture, last modified August 2023, whitesupremacyculture.info/.

12. Kahlil Gibran, "On Houses," *The Prophet* (Washington, DC: National Geographic Books, 1923). Public domain.

13. Jessica Caporuscio, "Everything You Need to Know about White Fragility," Medical News Today, June 12, 2020, medicalnewstoday.com/articles/white-fragility-definition.

14. Toni Morrison, *A Mercy* (New York: Vintage, 2012).

15. Bayo Akomolafe, "A Slower Urgency," Bayo Akomolafe (blog), accessed June 26, 2023, bayoakomolafe.net/post/a-slower-urgency.

16. *Toni Morrison: The Pieces I Am*, directed by Timothy Greenfield-Sanders (New York: Magnolia Pictures, 2019).

17. Kamilah Majied, "Transcending Internalized Racism with the Perfection of Resolve, Generosity, and Wisdom," *The Arrow* 9, no. 2 (September 21, 2022), arrow-journal.org/transcending -internalized-racism-with-the-perfection-of-resolve-generosity -and-wisdom/.

18. Diagram adapted from K. P. Morgan, "Describing the Emperor's New Clothes: Three Myths of Education (In-)Equity," in *The Gender Question in Education: Theory, Pedagogy & Politics*, ed. Ann Diller, Barbara Houston, Kathryn Pauly Morgan, and Maryann Ayim (New York: Routledge, 1996), 107.

19. Toni Morrison, *Paradise* (New York: Alfred A. Knopf, 1998).

20. Martin Luther King Jr., *Where Do We Go From Here: Chaos or Community?* (Boston: Beacon Press, 1967).

## Chapter Three: Power and Playfulness: Mo' Joy and Mojo

1. Online Etymology Dictionary, s.v. "mojo," accessed June 25, 2023, etymonline.com/word/mojo.

2. Lisa Friedman, "Dianne Feinstein Lectures Children Who Want Green New Deal, Portraying It as Untenable," *New York Times*, Feb. 22, 2019, nytimes.com/2019/02/22/climate/feinstein -sunrise-green-new-deal.html. Emphasis added.

3. Greta Thunberg, "How Dare You!" (speech, United Nations Climate Action Summit, New York, NY, September 23, 2019).

4. "Indicator 15: Retention, Suspension, and Expulsion," Status and Trends in the Education of Racial and Ethnic Groups, National Center for Education Statistics, February 2019, nces .ed.gov/programs/raceindicators/indicator_rda.asp; "Civil Rights Data Collection Data Snapshot (School Discipline)," U.S. Department of Education Office for Civil Rights, Issue Brief No. 1 (March 21, 2014), ocrdata.ed.gov/assets/downloads/CRDC -School-Discipline-Snapshot.pdf.

5. "Brené Brown on Power and Leadership," Dare to Lead worksheet, Brenebrown.com, 2020, brenebrown.com/resources /brene-brown-on-power-and-leadership/.

6. David Mouriquand, "Pornhub Study Reveals 2022 Trends and Which Countries Watch the Most Sex Online," Yahoo! News, December 14, 2022, uk.news.yahoo.com/pornhub-study-reveals -2022-trends-172425260.html.

7. Jo Nash, "24 Best Self-Soothing Techniques and Strategies for Adults," PositivePsychology.com, January 21, 2022, positivepsychology.com/self-soothing/#examples.

8. James Baldwin, *Just Above My Head* (New York: Dell, 1980).

9. Daisaku Ikeda, "December 17," Daily Encouragement, Soka Gakkai (global), September 9, 2020, sokaglobal.org/resources /daily-encouragement/december-17.html.

10. Toni Morrison, *Beloved* (New York: Knopf, 1987).

11. A. C. Shilton, "You Accomplished Something Great. So Now What?" *New York Times*, May 29, 2019, nytimes.com/2019/05 /28/smarter-living/you-accomplished-something-great-so-now -what.html.

12. Daisaku Ikeda, *Unlocking the Mysteries of Birth & Death . . . and Everything in Between: A Buddhist View of Life* (Santa Monica, CA: Middleway Press, 2003).

13. Frederick Douglass, *My Bondage and My Freedom* (New York: Oxford University Press, 2019).

14. Suzanne Pharr, *Homophobia: A Weapon of Sexism* (Berkeley, CA: Chardon Press, 1988).

15. "Why We Crave Comfort Food and How to Make It Healthier," City University of New York (website), December 10, 2020, www1.cuny.edu/mu/forum/2020/12/10/84906.

16. Louise Meriwether, *Daddy Was a Number Runner* (Upper Saddle River, NJ: Prentice Hall, 1970).

## Chapter Four: Joyfully Just, Conscious Cultural Engagement

1. Toni Morrison, *The Source of Self-Regard: Selected Essays, Speeches, and Meditations* (New York: Knopf, 2019).

2. "Smithsonian Returns 29 Benin Bronzes to the National Commission for Museums and Monuments in Nigeria," Smithsonian, October 11, 2022, si.edu/newsdesk/releases /smithsonian-returns-29-benin-bronzes-national-commission -museums-and-monuments.

3. Leadbelly, vocalist, "Scottsboro Boys," by Alan Lomax, recorded in New York, NY, 1938.

4. "Artist Derrick Adams on Hip-Hop and Relaxing While Black," All Arts TV, YouTube video, 13:01, April 14, 2021. youtube .com/watch?v=t-jq7jkfXYY.

5. "Quotations on the Theme of Happiness," Soka Gakkai, accessed June 28, 2023, daisakuikeda.org/sub/quotations/theme /happiness.html.

6. bell hooks, *Rock My Soul: Black People and Self-Esteem* (New York: Simon and Schuster, 2004), 101.

7. Jill Louise Busby, *Unfollow Me: Essays on Complicity* (New York: Bloomsbury Publishing, 2021).

8. Gholdy Muhammad, *Cultivating Genius: An Equity Framework for Culturally and Historically Responsive Literacy* (New York: Scholastic, 2020).

9. Nichiren Daishonin, "On Attaining Buddhahood in This Lifetime," *The Writings of Nichiren Daishonen*, vol. I (Tokyo: Soka Gakkai, 1999), nichirenlibrary.org/en/wnd-1/Content/1.

10. Richard Lapchick, "Racist Acts in Sports Were on the Rise in 2017," ESPN.com, January 11, 2018, espn.com/espn/story/_/id/22041345/racism-continued-rear-ugly-head-sports-2017; Lee Escobedo, "Boston Has a Race and Sports Problem. But It's Hardly Alone among 'Liberal' Cities," *The Guardian*, April 25, 2023, theguardian.com/sport/2023/apr/25/boston-racism-sports-denver-portland-salt-lake-city.

11. Diana Evans, "Viola Davis on Hollywood: 'You Either Have to Be a Black Version of a White Ideal, or You Have to Be White,'" *The Guardian*, April 18, 2022, theguardian.com/film/2022/apr/18/viola-davis-interview-michelle-obama-the-first-lady.

## Chapter Five: Joyful Suffering

1. Toni Morrison, *Beloved* (New York: Knopf, 1987).

2. "Working Together to Reduce Black Maternal Mortality," Center for Disease Control and Prevention, April 3, 2023, cdc.gov/healthequity/features/maternal-mortality/index.html.

3. Daisaku Ikeda, "Mahayana Buddhism and Twenty-First-Century Civilization" (lecture, Harvard University, Boston, MA, September 24, 1993), sokaglobal.org/resources/study-materials/buddhist-study/the-wisdom-for-creating-happiness-and-peace/chapter-10-5.html.

4. Latoya Hill and Samantha Artiga, "What Is Driving Widening Racial Disparities in Life Expectancy?" KFF, May 23, 2023, kff.org/racial-equity-and-health-policy/issue-brief/what-is-driving-widening-racial-disparities-in-life-expectancy/.

5. Elisabeth Kübler-Ross, *On Death and Dying: What the Dying Have to Teach Doctors, Nurses, Clergy & Their Own Families*, 50th ann. ed. (New York: Scribner, 2014).

6. Seneca the Younger, *The Epistles of Seneca*, Loeb Classical Library, LCL 75: 74–75, loebclassics.com/view/seneca_younger-epistles/1917/pb_LCL075.75.xml.

7. Daisaku Ikeda, "Life & Death," Daisaku Ikeda: Buddhist Philosopher, Peacebuilder, and Educator, n.d., daisakuikeda.org/sub/quotations/theme/life-death.html.

8. Bertha G. Simos, *A Time to Grieve: Loss as a Universal Human Experience* (New York: Families International, 1979).

9. Benjamin N. Breyer, Stacey A. Kenfield, Sarah D. Blaschko, and Bradley A. Erickson, "The Association of Lower Urinary Tract Symptoms, Depression and Suicidal Ideation: Data from the 2005–2006 and 2007–2008 National Health and Nutrition Examination Survey," *Journal of Urology* 191, no. 5 (2014): 1333–39, doi:10.1016/j.juro.2013.12.012.

10. Pengfei Wang, Yan Wang, and Xiaoqiang Jia, "Association between Fecal Incontinence and Suicidal Ideation in Adult Americans: Evidence from NHANES 2005–2010," *Journal of Psychosomatic Research* 170 (2023), doi.org/10.1016/j.jpsychores.2023.111377.

11. James Baldwin, "Fifth Avenue, Uptown: A Letter from Harlem," in *Nobody Knows My Name* (New York: Vintage, 1993).

12. Christina Fenske, "Stages of Psychosocial Development," Orchard Valley Counselling Services, September 9, 2020, orchardvalleycounselling.ca/stages-of-psychosocial-development/.

13. Rhonda Lewis, "Erikson's 8 Stages of Psychosocial Development, Explained for Parents," Healthline, February 8, 2023, healthline.com/health/parenting/erikson-stages#summary-chart.

14. "Toni Morrison on Trauma, Survival, and Finding Meaning," CTFORUM, YouTube video, 2:23, November 13, 2020, youtube.com/watch?v=5xvJYrSsXPA.

15. "The Fires of Grief Are Burning: A Message from Dr. Larry Ward," Lotus Institute, YouTube video, 13:07, May 31, 2020, youtube.com/watch?v=tCi4vM-NvGw.

16. Larry Ward, "Race, Reclamation, and the Resilience Revolution," Lion's Roar, June 1, 2020, lionsroar.com/race-reclamation-and -the-resilience-revolution/.

17. James Baldwin, *Just Above My Head* (New York: Dell Publishing, 1978), 529.

18. Quoted in Daisaku Ikeda, "Joy in Life and Death—the Boundless Life State Attained by Dedicating Ourselves to Our Eternal Mission," World Tribune, August 3, 2020, worldtribune .org/2020/toward-a-century-of-health-4/.

19. "Dr. Bethune's Last Will & Testament," Bethune-Cookman University, cookman.edu/history/last-will-testament.html.

20. Daisaku Ikeda, "From a Speech at a Spring Memorial Service," Soka Global, March 21, 2006, sokaglobal.org/resources/study -materials/buddhist-study/the-wisdom-for-creating-happiness -and-peace/chapter-10-8.html.

21. Daisaku Ikeda, "December 22," Soka Gakkai, September 9, 2020, sokaglobal.org/resources/daily-encouragement/december-22.html.

22. "The Hanging," John Brown's Holy War, American Experience, PBS, 2000, pbs.org/wgbh/americanexperience /features/brown-hanging/.

23. Pema Chödrön and Carolyn Rose Gimian, *Smile at Fear*, Shambhala Publications, audiobook, November 1, 2011, shambhala.com/smile-at-fear-15086.html.

24. Claude McKay, "If We Must Die," Academy of American Poets, Poets.org, poets.org/poem/if-we-must-die.

25. Morrison, *Beloved* (New York: Knopf, 1987).

26. Daisaku Ikeda, *For Today and Tomorrow: Daily Encouragement* (Los Angeles: World Tribune Press,1999).

27. James Baldwin, *The Fire Next Time* (New York: Modern Library, 1995).

## Conclusion: Closing and Opening to Our Next Steps

1. Paul Laurence Dunbar, "Sympathy," *Lyrics of the Hearthside* (New York: Dodd, Mead, 1899).

2. John Romano, "James Baldwin Talking and Writing," *New York Times*, September 23, 1979, nytimes.com/1979/09/23/archives/james-baldwin-writing-and-talking-baldwin-baldwin-authors-query.html.

3. Maya Angelou, *I Know Why the Caged Bird Sings* (New York: Random House, 1969).

# About the Author

D r. Kamilah Majied is a mental health clinician, clinical educator, researcher, and internationally engaged consultant on building inclusivity and equity using meditative practices.

She received her MSW and PhD in clinical social work from the University at Albany School of Social Welfare and was a tenured professor at Howard University prior to being appointed as professor of social work at California State University, Monterey Bay. She has taught clinical social work for the past twenty-five years, emphasizing mindfulness-based interventions as a resource to improve mental health and social functioning in historically exploited populations suffering from trauma. She also teaches research methods, social and organizational policy analysis, and community organizing through a social justice lens.

As founder and CEO of Majied Contemplative Consulting, she uses meditative practices in diversity, equity, and inclusion leadership development. Dr. Majied is also a research consultant with the UC Davis Center for Mind and Brain and various medical schools around the country, as well as the founding development consultant for the Mind & Life Institute Global Majority Leadership and Mentorship Program.

An author and editor of multiple articles, podcasts, and webinars on contemplative practice, Dr. Majied is a contributing author to *Black and Buddhist: What Buddhism Can Teach Us About Race, Resilience, Transformation and Freedom*, the first anthology of African American Buddhists' wisdom. She authored a chapter in the second edition of

*Advances in Contemplative Psychotherapy*, titled "Contemplative Practices for Assessing and Eliminating Racism in Psychotherapy."

Born in New York City and raised in northern New Jersey, Dr. Majied currently lives in northern California, where she enjoys practicing with her local SGI sangha and dancing in the ocean at sunset.

# About Sounds True

Sounds True was founded in 1985 by Tami Simon with a clear mission: to disseminate spiritual wisdom. Since starting out as a project with one woman and her tape recorder, we have grown into a multimedia publishing company with a catalog of more than 3,000 titles by some of the leading teachers and visionaries of our time, and an ever-expanding family of beloved customers from across the world.

In more than three decades of evolution, Sounds True has maintained our focus on our overriding purpose and mission: to wake up the world. We offer books, audio programs, online learning experiences, and in-person events to support your personal growth and awakening, and to unlock our greatest human capacities to love and serve.

At SoundsTrue.com you'll find a wealth of resources to enrich your journey, including our weekly *Insights at the Edge* podcast, free downloads, and information about our nonprofit Sounds True Foundation, where we strive to remove financial barriers to the materials we publish through scholarships and donations worldwide.

To learn more, please visit SoundsTrue.com/freegifts or call us toll-free at 800.333.9185.

Together, we can wake up the world.

**sounds true**
WAKING UP THE WORLD